Personal. Training. Business.

Personal.
Training.
Business.

Three pillars of creating a relationship-focused, scientifically-based, successful and sustainable personal training business.

Written by Andrew Seymour
Edited by Julie Seymour and Brandyn Ambrosy

ISBN: 978-8-218-26718-6

The events in the book are products of the author's perspective. Certain names may have been changed to protect those involved.

Front cover image by Christina Ney Photography
(https://christinaney.com/)

Book design by Elite Authors (https://eliteauthors.com/)

First printing edition 2024.

www.seymourhealthandfitness.com

TABLE OF CONTENTS

Training

PREFACE

Maybe you are reading this as an undergraduate interested in diving into the personal training world. Maybe you are currently a personal trainer at a corporate gym trying to improve your craft. Maybe you are contemplating building your own business and branching off on your own. Maybe you are already a successful trainer who simply wants to regroup and refocus on the important basics of our business. Maybe you are trying to grow your team by hiring additional trainers and you want them to adhere to your philosophies and values, as well as bring their own perspectives to benefit the entire business. Maybe you are in a completely different career field and simply have interest in growing as a professional, whether you have interest in health and fitness or not.

Whatever your situation, I hope this helps you in one way or another because this field is ever growing and there is so much more to personal training than simply creating workouts and counting repetitions. Regardless of who you are, I want to help you grow and build your business into something you had never imagined. I've had the amazing opportunity to branch off on my own and build a company that I absolutely love waking up for at 4 am, and I want you to experience that same feeling of accomplishment. Do I know everything about personal training, strength and conditioning, programming, the psychology of the trainer-client relationship, or business? Absolutely not. I've had some incredible mentors and coaches to look up to, but I still have plenty of room to grow and improve. Hopefully this book can act as a bridge to the next step in your career.

Finding success in the personal training field requires you to do so much more than have a certain certification, take a weekend course, or know how to workout. If only it were that easy. Sure, we program and create workouts for our people, but we have to address nutrition, stress, sleep, mental health, working through prior injuries or hesitations that people may have, and we do our best to provide a service that is all-inclusive with those offerings with reassuring smiles on our faces. Not every day is easy. Some days are long. Some days we're tired (thank God for coffee). Some days that alarm seems like it buzzed way too early. And yet, we get up, we provide the same high-quality service for our 5 am client as we would our 10 am or our 7:30 pm. It might be our tenth hour in the gym but it is their first. It is our job to be 'on' and make each experience the best possible for our people. It is our job to be there for them in more ways than just giving them workouts and counting to twelve. When you sign up to be in the fitness world, these may be things that you're not ready for. It isn't for everyone, and not everyone lasts. I get it. If you want to make a career out of this amazing job, I hope you take the time to read this book. I do my best to relay and break down some areas that I believe will be useful for you to be the most successful at your job and provide the best service to those in your life. However, regardless of what is thrown your way, you can either let it take you down or you can figure out a way to solve the problem, learn from it, and be better because of it. Growth mindset is a real thing and by applying that to your life through your actions, it can be contagious and people love to be around someone who lifts others up.

To all of you in the health, fitness, wellness, or personal train-ing business, you were most likely taught about science, anatomy, physiology, exercise prescription/programming, progressive over-load, and maybe even sport psychology in school or one of your certifications. Those are all essential to know, understand, and use as the basis of your business. As important as those are to becoming a successful personal trainer and to run a reputable business, I would argue there are more important details. Learning how to connect with others, creating lasting relationships, showing up to work early and with a good attitude, and genuinely caring about the people you work with are areas that may not have been taught in the classroom but are the backbone of a successful, sustainable personal training business. I hope this book helps provide you with a better toolbox to use to improve upon these areas that may have been overlooked in the textbooks. From one personal trainer to another, let's improve the quality of service we provide others in this industry through bettering ourselves with the willingness to learn, change, and adapt the way we were taught to help others.

The text is split up into three pillars: *Personal, Training,* and *Business.* The first and most important portion of a personal trainer should be the relationship and the connection with others. If you create connections and take care of your people, good things will happen. It is fine to be money motivated but if that's the only motivation, you will be exposed quickly. Secondly, people come to you for a service. Training clients is no easy task. Progressing individuals out of their comfort zones; providing honest feedback when changes are not immediately seen; and identifying each individual's goals and limitations are all factors we must take into account when preparing to train each day. Lastly, it is a business. I give some insight into what has helped us build a successful small business (before, during, and after a global pandemic) and how to continue to grow your name, brand, and product so you can flip this job into a career. All three pillars play a crucial role in creating and sustaining a successful personal training business. It is important that you address all three areas. In doing so, you not only uphold your recognition as being a well-educated and intelligent coach, but you become known for treating people with respect and maintaining a reputable business. Check all three boxes and you will notice similar success.

Thank you for your support and for setting aside time in your busy schedule to read what I have to say. I look forward to continuing to help others and wish you the best in your personal training career!

-Andrew

PERSONAL

The mission of Seymour Health & Fitness (SHF) is to teach our clients that the gym can be more than a place to work out and reap physical benefits. Providing them with an environment where they can be themselves, find comfort and confidence, and help enable their belief in themselves can create a culture of positivity and consistency. Consistency leads to sustained results and through helping others find joy in the gym by making it a place of comfort, Seymour Health & Fitness aims to be a place that can elicit physical benefits while addressing and improving the overall well-being of those invested in us. We pride ourselves in making each and every person feel at home. Feeling comfortable, confident, and having fun in our gym is one of our philosophies.

When I first stepped into the personal training world, I assumed I'd be writing, prescribing, and assisting in running people through workout programs. Wrong. At the base level, that may be what the job is described as but it's so much more. When meeting prospective clients, most people will come to you with some generic reason for them reaching out, such as "I want to lose weight for X occasion," "I want to tone my arms and lose belly fat" or something similar. Dig deeper. That's not really why they sent a feeler your way. There's usually more to why they sought you out. Whether it be a fear of family genes catching up with them, insecurity in their own skin, rehabbing from an injury, wanting to improve athletic performance, or simply having someone hold their hand and walk them through how to reprioritize their health and themselves. There is always a gold nugget that may not come out right away but it is your job to find that true meaning for them contacting you. When you figure that out, you two not only connect on a profound level but you can understand them for who they really are, not just to help someone lose body fat around their midsection. When people feel connected enough to open up with you, everything becomes easier. You get along better. You get to learn more and more about them, how they grew up, their thoughts/feelings on just about every subject, and how you can best help them. Everyone needs to be coached differently and every session should have a different flow and feel to it. That is subjective and is based on your ability to find that gold nugget, connect with that person, and relay the information you owe them with your service through that session to maximize their experience with you.

That ability to personalize each session and to cater it to what that person needs and is looking for is what will help you with client retention, which in a business-sense is huge for continuous income. When we prioritize our people and do our best to help them help themselves, it's known as servant leadership. We lead them by educating and guiding them to understand what we're doing, feel confident in themselves, and serve them, rather than playing the part of a dictator that abuses their power, which you will unfortunately see out of some individuals in this profession. Just because we are experts in the field of health, fitness, and kinesiology and we're providing a service to others doesn't mean we're any better or above our clients. They're experts in their field, as well and we have so much to learn from them. I have learned so much from so many of my clients but it's because I am curious, ask about them, invest in them and their interests. Connecting with your people and continually choosing to further invest in them will allow you to create an unbreakable bond that will provide so much for both parties for years to come. In order to find sustained success in this industry, establishing and maintaining those relationships is the best way to create and uphold a reputation of being known in a positive light. Learning how to do this but then applying the ideas to your everyday interactions with your clients, their family and friends, and others in your community can help you pave the way to creating an increased demand for the services you provide.

CHAPTER 1

Why I Do What I Do

"If you're looking for a superior personal trainer, look no further. Andrew identifies your personal goals and works with you to accomplish them. He appreciates and understands the various aspects of health and how they relate to fitness. He offers individualized workout plans and nutritional consultations that allow you to transcend prior goals. If you're looking for a cerebral trainer whose dedication, results and client testimonials speak for themselves, you're looking for Seymour Health & Fitness."

We all choose different careers for different reasons. Some people prefer working a 9-5 job that allows them to mentally and physically get away from work beginning on Friday at 5 pm until Monday morning. Other people enjoy working jobs, such as sales, where they get to travel the country (or world) and speak to potential customers about why they should purchase a certain product. Others just have a job to pay the bills and don't really mind working demanding positions, as long as they have enough money to put food on the table and get to enjoy their life. To each their own. One is not necessarily better than the other; it just depends on what you want your individual life to look like.

I chose to become a personal trainer. From the outside looking in, this seems like a pretty straightforward gig: sell clients on buying your services, provide them with a workout template, correct their form, and count their repetitions. Trainers tend to get scoffed at because this seems like such a simplistic job and "anyone could do that." Unfortunately, some personal trainers do take the easy way out and only provide those select services. Collectively, fitness professionals seem to have a negative connotation surrounding them, and this can be very frustrating to those of us who are different from those certain types of trainers.

I would consider myself an introvert. My job consists of conversing with other people all day, but outside of that, I live a very 'under the radar' lifestyle. I enjoy spending time with clients, family, and friends most days, but I've become very comfortable secluding myself outside of the gym. When away from work, I like spending time to myself. I would rather stay at home, eat a good meal, and have a night in than go out, any day of the week. Some may consider that style of life to be boring but this, along with spending precious time with my family, is how I fill up my cup. I haven't always been that way. In fact, I used to love going out, being around people and attending social events but over the past few years, I've really figured out and accepted what truly makes me happy and allows me to feel my best self. In recent years, I've figured out that I'm content missing some of those nights out, and I'm thoroughly satisfied with spending time away from all of the hustle and bustle. This is my way of resetting and relaxing. Everybody has his or her vice to recuperate and this just happens to be mine.

I was first exposed to the art of strength and conditioning in high school. This initial experience was not the ideal scenario. Our strength coach was given that title simply because he played collegiate football. This was the only qualification needed in order to be deemed the strength coach at that time. Looking back at it, all of the athletes on our high school teams would have benefited much more had we had proper instruction and were taught exercises the right way. Luckily, most high schools are now adopting strength-and-conditioning coaches with proper qualifications to correctly instruct their athletes in the weight room.

Due to the lack of qualified instruction in the weight room, I didn't benefit from lifting weights or eating proper nutrition until later in my life. I grew up playing sports all year round. I stayed very active in sports and showed my face in the gym on a regular basis toward the end of high school. Unfortunately, this did not result in getting significantly stronger or more knowledgeable about proper health and nutrition. Although I worked out, my technique was probably abysmal and I focused on all the wrong things. I wanted to be able to bench press a certain amount. I was spending a lot of time doing dips and curls; I dedicated numerous workouts doing countless crunches and sit-ups. I spent no time learning the basics of multi-joint, power, and core exercises. I worked out for so long with no real benefit other than finding comfort in the weight room.

Come college, I was introduced to my first organized strength-and-conditioning program. It was a shock to my system. I was not ready. The coaches showed me how to properly perform squats, cleans, pressing, hinging, and pulling exercises. These complex movements were a new discovery to me. Because of this, my lanky, thin frame took some time to put on some muscle, but I adjusted quickly. Playing football in college was great for a few reasons. First and foremost, I met some incredible friends. Along with that, I learned humility and discipline like I had never before. Lastly, I created a solid foundation in the weight room and it became the basis in which my career was built upon. For these reasons I'm so thankful that I was given that opportunity.

Once I received my final concussion and decided to hang up the cleats following my sophomore season, exercise was my reliant release. The majority of my friends were all still playing collegiate sports, so it was difficult to find something to fill all of the time that football took up. Feeling comfortable in the gym, changing my major from Biology to doubling up in Exercise Science and

Human Performance & Fitness, and then obtaining an internship as a strength and conditioning coach at a local high school were all large attributes in deciding to make a career out of spending time in the gym. I felt comfort in the gym. I've had first-hand experience of the physical and mental benefits of a regimented health plan. A combination of regular exercise, high-quality nutrition, and sufficient amounts of sleep have been part of the routine that I've used to find happiness in my own life. Understanding this and being able to provide others with this knowledge is why I decided to take my first step into the health and fitness field. This is where my story begins as a personal trainer at a corporate gym in Des Moines in 2016.

This initial opportunity provided me with a great platform for my first personal training job. I was able to network with a wide variety of people. I had an opportunity to make a name for myself and build up my credibility, while building a brand for myself. After nearly two years in the same position, I was drawn to provide an even better service to my clients and give myself a chance to more genuinely enjoy what I set out to do in my career. This was when I used that brand to create Seymour Health & Fitness. My father used to tell me that whatever job I had, do whatever it takes to be the absolute best at that position, "even if that is flipping burgers." Beginning SHF has allowed me to become the best version of myself, and in turn, provide the highest quality product to those that work with me.

Another piece of advice I was given when I was growing up was "find a job doing something you love and you'll never work a day in your life" similar to a quote by Mark Twain. This may sound cheesy and not everyone has the chance to carve this out of his or her career path. Luckily, I have found that gratification. Not every day is easy, but I can honestly say I enjoy waking up in the morning, knowing that I get to spend my days helping others reach their health and fitness goals and building strong relationships. I know the power that a valuable health plan can have, so

I take pride in providing a quality product for my clients. Being whatever role my clients need me to be, which can look like a teacher, coach, therapist, and someone that my clients feel they can talk openly to brings me enjoyment. Like any field, my job has difficult parts to it, but the good vastly outweighs the bad. Directly out of school, I saw personal training as a stepping stone to strength-and-conditioning coaching or other health and fitness career paths. Now I recognize this is something I want to do and continue to grow for my career. It is no longer a stepping stone to another field, but rather a stepping stone in the quest to be the best personal trainer for my clients.

With the health craze in America, personal training careers are becoming more and more valued. All trainers have the platform to help endless numbers of people immensely improve their lives. It is our job to educate, provide quality resources, and guide people in a direction that allows them to accomplish their health and wellness goals. This field is on the rise, so up-and-coming trainers need to learn there are difficulties in this workforce. You will have to wake up at unimaginable hours. You will go to sleep very late some nights. You will work holidays and weekends. You will work when other people are off work. Your schedule and paycheck rely 100% on those who invest in your products. Provide them with the best product possible, and they will return the favors. As a trainer, it is our job to have flexible schedules, be selfless, take care of others, listen to people's problems, and provide them with a well-thought-out exercise and nutrition program. It isn't as easy as it may sound. It takes a toll on your body and your mind, but the eventual reward is well worth it and it is what I foresee doing for a very long time.

After creating a bit of a name for myself, and gaining the self-confidence to venture out on my own, the trigger was pulled on creating Seymour Health & Fitness. This was terrifying to do. It wasn't a guarantee that any of my clients would continue training with me. I didn't know how to run a business all by myself, never having taken any classes in business or marketing or finances. This experience was entirely new, and extremely exciting.

By deciding to go the entrepreneur route, throwing myself in the fire, and learning as I went, I figured out how to run a successful business. It was a lot of hard work and to this day still is. Individual, partner, and group-training sessions take up a good portion of my hours. It is very nice to be out of the gym by 9, 10, or 11 am some days, but that doesn't mean the day is done. Some days may require you to work a split shift, because one thing that comes with this profession is the fact that some of our clients can only workout before or after work, so our schedule often reflects that. When you're not training, online programming, meeting with local businesses, marketing, ordering apparel, writing newsletters, staying up-to-date on my own education, advertising, business planning, and taking care of the finances are some of the behind-the-scenes scenarios completed during my "off hours" away from the gym. An additional 3-5 hours are usually spent each day at home, tying together loose ends and programming for future sessions.

My number one goal for my business is to help others create the best versions of themselves. We are all a work in progress, myself included, but the passion and drive to improve is what is most important. The relationships I have formed through this business are why I do what I do. Even though it is my job to help others, my clients help me more than they can ever imagine. Gratefully, they have accepted and treated me with the utmost respect. They help me out and listen when I have things to get off of my chest. For those of you to whom I'm referring, you know who you are, thank you. Thank you for everything. If you, as a trainer, take care of your clients, they will take care of you. I am so grateful that I have been able to experience that first-hand.

Part of the reason for gaining the respect that I have in the fitness community in my mid-20s is because I practice what I preach. What I sell is exercise routines, nutrition advice, sleep recommendations, and lifestyle changes. Adversely, if I'm not following my own advice and believing in what I'm selling, why would anybody else buy that product from me? Living the lifestyle is something every trainer should do, while also proving to your clients that a balanced life includes rest, time away from the gym, and a healthy relationship with your workouts and nutrition.

Another reason I believe I am successful in this field is my admission of not knowing everything. I am very confident in my abilities as a trainer. While there are certain topics I know better than most, acknowledging that others know more than me in this field, opens up the constant opportunity to learn and further my education. If there is something that I don't know, I will research and find an answer. If I know someone is a better resource on some specific subject, I will refer people in that direction. Humbly, I am able to admit that other people may be able to help with certain things better than me. I think this philosophical strategy has allowed me to acquire another level of respect amongst my peers and others within our community.

Coming out of college, I never imagined all of the miniscule details which go into personal training. Because of how I was raised, who I surround myself with, and my vision for this business, I intend to continue growing at a rapid pace while continuing to provide the best service to those who have conveyed their loyalty and belief in me. In 2019, I was voted City View's Des Moines' Best Local Personal Trainer and find much pride in this award. I have a difficult time accepting compliments, but this accolade is recognition for extreme hard work on a daily basis. One needs to allow credit for accomplishments. Would I like to be given that award again year after year? Absolutely. If I'm not, that doesn't mean things are trending in the wrong direction. I know what my worth is and how valuable of a product that I have to offer. I've become a very optimistic individual. I am confident in saying that I will help you get in the best shape of your life if you are up for the challenge. I am proud of where SHF is, but there is always room to grow and more to work on. I can't wait. Thanks for being part of it with me.

CHAPTER 2

Be You

Be yourself. Each trainer/coach finds success in this field because they provide a service for which people are looking and also manifest genuine care for those working with them. These qualities, and what sets us apart, should be embraced and celebrated. Doing things one way doesn't mean it is the only way to do it. Please don't walk away from this book thinking every section is the only way to become successful and to take care of your people. In the world today, it's often too easy to become overwhelmed with all of the information thrown our way. You need to decide what works for you. It's a process of figuring out how to best sift through material you discover to determine what is most useful; what should be left behind; and how to apply your findings toward situations that make sense for you. The goal of this book is for you to find additional tools to utilize when facing unfamiliar or challenging situations throughout your business ventures. Take in my opinions and my perspectives. Decide what to do with the information you absorb. Use what works best for you, your environment, and your patrons.

All trainers can benefit from being around other trainers and coaches. That's the beauty of this field. We can learn from each other's differences in personality, coaching styles and cues, and the way we interact with our clients. When we truly are open to bettering ourselves, we can pick up on the way coaches lead. By observing a variety of styles, we have the choice to use those tactics or not. Stay true to your roots because at the end of the day, being yourself is much easier than trying to be someone you're not. Use your strengths to your benefit. Be open to learning from others and accepting feedback to work on areas you may want to improve to be an even better person, coach, and trainer. Learning from others is important in improving and sharpening our craft. Being yourself and creating your own spin on the job will bode well to create a sustainable and reliable business reputation.

When you are able to be your authentic self, people will trust you more and understand you aren't putting on a facade to just draw in business. While it's important to be your true self, it can also be helpful for trainers to learn to be somewhat of a chameleon. We play different roles for people who need different things from us but that doesn't need to take away from us being an authentic version of who we really are. It's important to impart a variety of versions of ourselves to people because you will have different relationships with your clients. You must acquire the ability to remain yourself while varying the type of coach you are for certain clients. The coach I am at five o'clock in the morning with a bank executive isn't exactly the same coach I am with the group of high schoolers early in the afternoon. I am not any worse of a coach in the morning or afternoon, nor am I creating this false version of who I am. Instead, I am adjusting to better connect and to make sure those individuals are more comfortable being in the gym while training with me. The level of mutual respect remains high, and we all enjoy the workouts equally. Be the person you believe you are deep down at your core; work on improving different areas you feel will bring out the best version of yourself, and don't be afraid to adapt based on the situation.

CHAPTER 3

You Cannot Pour from an Empty Cup

Every job puts high demands on people, the training business is no exception. Work on staying mentally, emotionally, physically, and financially stable, and find a support system that has your back. You will often question certain career moves as you calculate risks and decide which paths to take throughout your tenure. Finding and sticking by people who believe in you; challenge you; are there for you; and who support the vision you have can be crucial to sustaining a successful business and a work-life balance. You will miss parties, outings, happy hours, and even some family events. You aren't going to miss those because you don't want to see those people, but because you'll have clients, need to program for the next week, or have had a long day and your bed looks pretty appealing. Your support system will not judge you for not choosing to pick your bed over going out and socializing. They may give you a hard time for it, but hopefully that's all in good fun. This job requires you to converse with others for a majority of your day, coach, program, market, and take care of your finances. Outside of work, we have other obligations to take care of at home. This can create a full schedule and may become overwhelming or seem like it's too much to handle, at times. When the job requires you to talk with people for 8, 10, or

12+ hours a day, in addition to coaching; programming; spending time with family and friends; and addressing accounting, marketing, or personal business, you're truly packed full to the brim. Deciding to take time for yourself when you have the opportunity can be the choice you make to ensure you don't burn out. Having a strong support system can help remind you to stay on track and maintain focus. They are there to push, support, and encourage you. Those who invest in you, help you realize your worth, cheer you on when you need encouragement, and keep you focused on the important aspects in life. Unfortunately, as in any circle of friends and family, there are plenty of skeptics, who may question your occupational decisions and judge you one way or another. Try to avoid surrounding yourself with such negativity. True friends and supporters will back you no matter what and will even challenge you when you're in need of a reality check. Having the extra push from those who are on your side can elevate your mindset, motivation, and entire business plan. Allowing negative energy to infiltrate your mind and your environment will only bring you and your clientele down. Turn any adverse energy into a means of extra motivation to get to where you want or simply choose to ignore it and move on. When I began SHF, I had people questioning why I would leave a safe, secure company. Five years later, with better relationships with all of my clients, more success for everyone involved, more money in my pocket, and big plans for the future of our business, it's clear my path in this career overrides any naysayers' words. Starting my own business was a risk, but a calculated risk and one I dove into 100% headfirst. By giving it my all and surrounding myself with a strong support team, my choice to become a businessman and personal trainer has worked out wonderfully.

Who that support system is made up of may differ from person to person. For me, my wife Vernesa has done so much behind the scenes to hold down the fort at home. She takes care of the dogs when I can't make time. She cleans, cooks, takes care of the lawn and plants, and is quick to jump into my arms when I get home after a long day. She's had my back from the beginning and although there are days and times where I know my job consuming my time at home is frustrating for her because it may take away from time for her and me, she supports me in every hard decision this job has sent my way. She sees how the sausage is made, and it isn't always pretty. She sees the hours of planning and programming behind the scenes away from the gym. She is there for my 3:45 am wake up calls. She knows how drained I can be at times. She is always there in ways that I couldn't ever imagine a partner being: the one who upholds our world when I am busy with work. She does it with such grace, as she works full time and has her plate full with other parts of her life but I truly couldn't do this without her. I can't thank her enough and I hope you find someone who is as supportive as she is for me, for you. We all need that person to be our rock on the home front to make it easier for us to enjoy our work-life balance.

My brother, Collin, is a huge supporter. He entered into this business and has followed in my footsteps in some ways. Yet, he has etched out new avenues for our company. He started out observing me and various other trainers, taking what he liked, analyzing the best ways to set up programs for a realm of individuals, and began developing his own style of training. Working with a sibling who I connect with outside of business and whose values and vision align with mine at our workplace is a constant reminder of the support I have in all areas of my life. He's got my back, and I have his.

My family provides me with a much-valued sense of support. My parents, siblings, and extended relatives have all been consistent in supporting what Collin and I have going on at SHF. My parents were the first people I spoke to about opening up Seymour Health & Fitness. They have always had my back, believed in me, and thankfully provided two fresh sets of eyes to bring up realistic questions regarding my decision. Out of sincere concern, they have questioned me, brought up hypothetical situations, told me how proud of me they were, and have backed me. They have always been my siblings' and my biggest supporters and it's been no different with business. They've aided us financially and instilled values in us that are priceless. The integrity, morals, and ethics they've impressed upon us growing up have been ingrained into our business. Two main lessons to share include: Control what is within your control and never quit once you start something.

My friends, clients, fellow trainers, and others in the health and fitness world who have helped me out and pushed me to be a better trainer are also such a big part of my support system, whether they know that or not. Without being able to grow as a friend, trainer, coach, and person, I wouldn't be able to provide the same product to those who I get to work with. My friends and others in this field push me and have allowed me to sharpen my tools to become better at my craft.

Regardless of who your support system is, find that crew and keep them close. Make sure you thank them for all they do. We probably don't say it enough, so to my entire support system, THANK YOU. I know that being engulfed in trying to run your own business can lead to you neglecting relationships and other parts of your life, so if you catch yourself realizing that you may be guilty of that, take a moment to reach out to those people. They have your back and are there for you when and if you need them. Be sure to return the favor and prioritize those relationships because missing out on time with special people is something you don't want to look back on and regret.

CHAPTER 4

People First, Clients Second

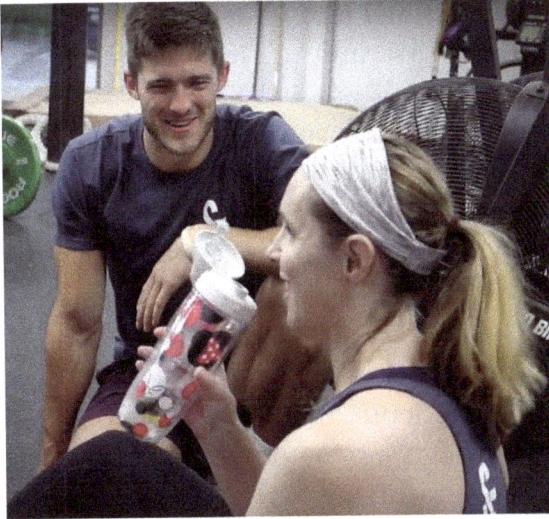

As a personal trainer, it easily could be believed that the most important portion of our job is to know the most information about the body, how we move, the science behind exercise, and how we go about applying those scientific principles towards the betterment of our client's health. In reality, the most important portion of our job is taking care of our people and finding ways to help them feel better about themselves. There are so many talented and intelligent personal trainers out there and, although it would be nice to be known as the greatest amongst that entire community, it is much more important to me to be the best fit for my clients. I want to make them happy and help them reach their goals. My personal training method may not always align with what other prospective clients are looking for, and that is okay. If I work at a sporting department store and a customer asks me for a size 11 shoe, but I only have sizes 10 and 12 available, that doesn't mean I've failed them. I just didn't have the product for which they were searching, and it is my job to either order them their right size or direct them to another store that can accommodate the customer. Using your resources is much more important than simply giving up, regardless of whether or not you are compensated by a potential consumer. Take care of people. Help them first, and you'll have opportunities for sales down the road.

Yes, personal training is a business in which you need to make money, but if you prioritize the person in front of you and truly take care of them despite the money, the money will come. Servant Leadership is a term I was unfamiliar with until being introduced to it through my advisor and professor at the University of Missouri, Dr. Greg Sullivan. He actually wrote the book, Servant Leadership in Sport: Theory and Practice (2019), which covers this subject in great depth and really opened my eyes to what it means to lead through serving others. Dr. Sullivan's ideology on the matter is that by satisfying the three main psychological needs (autonomy, belongingness, and competence), coaches and leaders can positively influence performance, well-being, satisfaction, and self-confidence. When we use this approach to help guide others, we do so by placing their needs at the forefront of our priority list. This is not to say we neglect ourselves because we can't pour from an empty glass, but by serving others and providing others with the tools necessary to succeed, we can help make waves in people's lives.

In a world that revolves around helping others, there has to be at least a small background in interpersonal relations, reading people and situations, and having the ability to build trust with those you're working with. You need to trust them and they need to be able to trust you. This isn't something that just comes when you first meet. It takes time, communication, vulnerability, honesty, and patience. In order for someone to open up to you, you must also give a little bit and demonstrate those same traits so they can relate to you and they understand you are both on an even playing field, not that you are any better than them. When this connection is made, it can evolve over time and some clients will open up more, while others will keep things a bit more surface level. Either way, as long as they feel comfortable around you and believe in the service you are providing them with, this can lead to a great partnership and will only benefit them in pursuit of their fitness goals.

Learning how to read others and interact with people of all different walks of life is something that will help all trainers and people in this profession. This may take time for some, while it comes naturally for others. Just like we continually work to improve our health and fitness knowledge, stay up to date with science, and work to provide better programs for our clients, we must also continually work on our people skills. This can come from a mixture of experiences, role playing with others wanting to improve in a similar area in their field, and researching resources that can help with that. From my experiences, what I've found to be most helpful as a trainer is to be open minded, a good listener, and create an environment where clients can be themselves and not feel out of place whatsoever. When people know the gym and being with you is like their second home, it allows individuals to open up further and really show you their true selves. As their trainer, this provides you with the chance to experience who they are when they are at their most comfortable. Learning how to listen with the intent to hear, rather than listening to simply respond; being open minded; and reserving judgment are all crucial aspects in developing interpersonal skills in the gym. The desire to connect with and help improve the lives of 'your people' makes you grow and improve as a trainer, too. Getting to know amazing people, ultimately leading to the creation of some of the best relationships and friendships you'll ever have in your life, as well as experiencing immense pride in watching your clients flourish, are reasons why one must put people first, and clients second.

CHAPTER 5

Take Care of Your People

Taking care of my clients goes far beyond the hour of working out together in the gym. Taking care of them includes educating each one to create better, healthier choices in all aspects of their lives. The ultimate goal is for each person I work with to become a happy and healthy individual. This means that we have to work together as a team. Teams don't always see eye to eye on everything and sometimes that leads to difficult conversations, but successful teams use those moments of discrepancy as an opportunity to grow and create an even sturdier base. What clients want and what they need, don't always add up. When we are hired as personal trainers, we take on the role of recognizing when to draw the line and go in a different direction. These contemplations and conversations can make us out to be the bad guy in certain situations. Yet as long as we address these discussions in a respectful manner and with good intentions, our clients will eventually understand why specific routes have been chosen for them.

Teams that win have a common goal. They approach that goal with minute steps that pile upon one another to inch closer and closer. When we sit down with clients for the first time, we get to know them, figure out why they came to see us, and what they want to get out of working together. This usually consists of creating goals. Understanding why someone wants to accomplish something is arguably more important than the end goal. This "why" may initially come off as "to look better" or "get in shape for summer" or "because my doctor said so." These are valid reasons, but more often than not, there is something deeper. We all have reasons for doing what we do, but completely adopting an entirely new lifestyle or drastically changing your habits by incorporating healthy food; thought-out workout routines; getting adequate amounts of water and sleep; and living other healthy habits tends to have more of a backstory than what you may be given initially. Dig deeper. Ask open-ended questions. Listen to hear (don't listen to respond), and allow your client to open up to you by creating a comfortable space for both parties. This will invite you both to get to know each other better; begin to grow a connection; and will give you both a better understanding of who is seated in front of you. The more people open up, the better chance you will get to the true reason as to why they are meeting with you. Coming into a gym can be intimidating, and being a friendly face right off the bat will help a new gym-goer feel more at ease. This comfortability is huge in creating a relationship because if one feels like the new person or even an outcast, there is a pretty good chance they won't stick around long. Make them feel welcome. Make them feel at home. Make sure you give them an environment where they can be themselves and truly show you who they are. Just like any other relationship, if we aren't our true selves, we don't really know who we are dealing with and we can be caught off guard down the road. Lead by example by being your true self and creating a safe space where they can be them. This is a great way to kickstart what could be an amazing change in their life.

Once you and your client get to know each other and you have some ammunition to start creating a plan for the two of you moving forward, it is important to be transparent and lay out your plan. Once they understand how you will go about things, you can start putting one foot in front of the other. The importance of you two being on the same page is huge in the sense you can keep each other accountable and hold up your two ends of the bargain. You have been sought out to help provide a service, and you have the choice on how to go about providing that service. Just like workout programs, there is not one size that fits all. The way that I train may differ completely from the way that you train and that doesn't mean that one way is right and one is wrong, just that there are different routes. Figuring out your style of training will come with time, but in order to find that, you have to start somewhere. You will train different clients in different ways, but always be yourself and be honest with your people. Your clients trusting you has a direct correlation on whether or not they will stick with you as their choice of trainer.

Just like in the real world, plans change. What you and your client had originally planned for your programming may be thrown a curveball and you need to adapt. Don't fret, but rather figure out where you need to go and how you need to get there. The beautiful part of working in this field is everyone has room to improve. I truly believe this logic is the fun part of what I do. Regardless of who you are; how in shape you may be; how much weight you can lift; or what your genetics look like, there is always room for improvement. As personal trainers, we have the unique power to help others recognize how much control they have in their life. When others realize that, they can begin working towards taking their lives in whatever direction they so choose. We will be faced with adversity and unknowns in all aspects of our lives, but working out, eating well, sleeping enough, and drinking plenty of fluids can do so much good for all of us. These actions are so simple but so mighty in not only our physical wellness, but our mental and emotional being as well. The benefits of exercising and living healthy lifestyles are endless. Because of this amazing fact, we can always improve in one way or another. This chase allows for us to pat ourselves on the back and celebrate when we accomplish different tasks. Ideally this puts us right back on the path to our next goal. The endless pursuit of improvement is why I love this job. It is important to recognize when we surpass milestones and accomplish goals, but it is fun to always have something new to work toward. Many of us are ex-athletes. Whether we played team or individual sports, we had that competitive drive (some more than others). Harnessing that drive to continue improving yourself and your well-being is within all of us and it can be a great tool or a huge distraction, whether you are a former athlete or just an individual looking to better yourself. Unfortunately, when we observe that constant quest for improvement in a negative light, we can become fixated on how we may not quite be where we should. Depending on if you have a positive or negative outlook on your journey and achievements, this could boost you up or bring you down. When plans change and we are challenged, we have the choice to be affected or to use that as fuel to our fire to continue moving forward. This goes for trainers and clients alike. When faced with road bumps and surprises, it is up to us to decide what to do when we encounter those. As a leader and fitness professional, we have the platform to help determine which route our clients decide to take. It is up to us to remind our clients that there will be ups and downs. The most important thing is to continue moving forward, regardless. There will be good and bad days. Our professional attitude can influence our clients to flip their mindsets into a more steady, optimistic outlook on life in and out of the gym.

CHAPTER 6

Jimmys and Joes > Xs and Os

When you look at championship caliber sports teams, there is always a common denominator: chemistry plus an environment which propels all members of a team toward one ultimate goal. The Xs and Os, commonly used symbols in sport that are shorthand for play designs and strategy, are very important to the ultimate outcome of success measured in a single play, throughout a game, or over an entire season. The Xs and Os in a playbook may be important and should not be overlooked. If a team builds chemistry, gets along, and can push one another to new heights, you will have a squad capable of attaining any goal imaginable. The play designs themselves are not as important as the players and camaraderie within the locker room or on the playing surface. You rarely see a successful team at the top of the mountain that doesn't get along. Unique teamwork and harmony take time and trust. Each individual has to do their part to help the team as a whole become immune to internal destruction. Regardless of individual opinions, selfishness needs to be set aside and everyone should have the understanding that partnership and team come first. Once everyone is on the same page, remarkable outcomes lay ahead. This same concept pertains to the partnership amongst trainers and clients. Creating this culture may take time, but once synchrony and understanding between both sides is accepted, your partnership and success will grow by leaps and bounds.

Sports teams are a melting pot of people from differing backgrounds with every type of personality. Successful teams utilize differences to help their groups grow together. Prospering organizations recognize varied capabilities, and use these variations to build a more well-rounded group of individuals. When people set aside differences and come together to learn as one, the possibilities of success dramatically improve. It would be incredible if everybody in the world could experience the culture created in locker rooms. Being put into a team with people from all walks of life, and having to set aside previous perceptions to come together to reach a united goal, can be an invaluable learning experience. As it relates to our specific scope of practice, personal training allows us to experience this same unity between clients and trainers. Not every client will have the same background or opinion as us. As we navigate that connection between ourselves and our clients, we must compromise and create a cohesive environment that works for both parties. This will allow us to learn from one another, set aside touchy differences, and ultimately come together to produce the results we both want to reach.

Because of this connection created between trainer and client, it is common to stumble upon intimate or personal topics of conversation during training sessions. Be cognizant and careful regarding certain subjects. Whether we know it or not, some topics may have a direct impact on our clients, so tread lightly. Remaining open to discussion, while avoiding judgment, is crucial in establishing a respectful, trusting relationship with your clientele.

In this business, we should always be our most genuine selves. However, at times, we may wear a variety of hats. A personal trainer is much more than simply creating a program and walking clients through it. Because the individuals we end up training all differ in a variety of ways, we must pride ourselves on being inclusive to ensure each and every person who walks through our doors feels part of the community. We celebrate those differences and view the things that make each of us unique as opportunities to learn about others and see the world from another perspective. With clients stemming from unique family dynamics, different genders, sexual preferences, races, religions, political parties, and all other variables, going into this field with an open mind is the only way to truly market yourself to, and be respected by, others. You do not have to agree with the political takes of each of your clients. You do not have to compare backgrounds or justify your differences. Nevertheless, we should all respect one another and genuinely listen when others voice their opinions and stances on certain subjects. At times it can be difficult to always find common ground, to make our sessions entertaining, and to uphold relationships. Nevertheless, it is your job to adapt so your clients feel comfortable and stay interested in a long-term relationship in order to accomplish their health and fitness goals. We will agree on certain things and disagree on others. When disagreements do arise, we can express those differences in a manner that doesn't anger them or elevate tension between the two sides. Just because your opinions differ doesn't mean that you can't get along. That's something that needs to be understood on a much larger scale but it applies to us as trainers, especially when we so frequently have such a variety of conversations with a variety of people on a regular basis. With balancing differing clients, not everybody will have values and opinions that parallel yours. Be open minded, adapt when we need to, and use that as an opportunity to learn. Creating the type of relationship where you can ask those hard questions and have those potentially difficult conversations, when done in a respectful manner, can bring both sides closer, even if the views are bi-polar. It is also important to have self-awareness to know when to bite your lip in order to not initiate an argument when you notice a client of yours is passionately expressing support for one side of a controversial subject. Remember your professional environment and reputation are at stake when you interact with clients. Respond with respect. Differences don't need to create a wedge between us. Instead, use them as a chance to better understand someone.

Having difficult conversations, especially when two participants have differing viewpoints can be extremely hard to navigate without tripping up. The best way to manage these situations is to be honest with your clients. When a touchy topic is brought up, listen first, think about your response, and then respond or even ask questions if you're unfamiliar. Some very common subjects that may fall under this umbrella in our field are body image, body dysmorphia, and eating disorders. Outside of those, occupation, politics, religion, or other subjects may come up in more regular conversation. These topics need to be taken seriously, but you also need to tread very lightly. Emotions and feelings can run high, depending on who you are speaking with and the experience that they may have with said subject. Be mindful and listen attentively, but be careful advising on subjects in which you may not be qualified to explore. This could be a very vulnerable time for them and even though they are opening up to you about whatever the topic may be, it doesn't give you free reign to fire away question after question. Be conscientious and take context into account. If they want to elaborate or tell you more details about the subject, they will. Don't pry too much. Simply be there for them when they need you. If you do have questions, ask them if they are comfortable elaborating. Some people will be fine with telling you more while others may not be ready and you need to respect that decision and not push them to a point where they feel uncomfortable. When clients really open up to you about sensitive subjects, especially ones that have had a profound impact on their lives, it can be very fragile and you must treat it as such. It is part of your job to be kind and listen. When a client opens up to you, this demonstrates a trusting relationship has been built.

For less delicate topics, showing interest by asking more detailed questions can create more of an understanding amongst you and your client. Regardless of the topic, always be respectful of others' opinions, especially if you have a differing perspective. We will not, and should not have to, always agree on all things. Often, during discussions of differing ideas, we can learn more about how others think and approach topics. Don't get defensive about your beliefs. We will agree on certain things and disagree on others. It is okay to bite your lip in order to not initiate an argument when you notice a client of yours is passionately expressing support for one side of a controversial subject. If you do end up debating on a subject, make sure it does not become a heated argument. In today's society, people encounter the issue of automatically wanting to dissociate from one another when there is a difference of opinion. This reality causes separation and creates a larger gap in understanding. Oftentimes, we disagree and quickly jump to the assumption that because we deviate on a specific subject, we can no longer see eye to eye. That is one conclusion. A more productive response would be to discuss, learn, and grow individually and together by helping the other see your side of things. In order to sustain a relationship and even grow it into something sturdier, differences can be a learning opportunity to see certain situations from an opposing point of view to get a better understanding of the world from which someone else comes. Get to know your clients. Dig in deep and learn who they are, where they came from, and why they are the incredible people that they are today. These pillars will allow you to better align your goals and build an amazing affiliation with all of your clientele.

CHAPTER 7

Your Service is Your Product

Most people don't know the difference between an average exercise program and a great program. They will recognize the difference between average service and great service, though. We are in a unique situation where we can use exercise as our tool to help people improve so many aspects of their lives. Exercise can improve confidence, build resiliency, help with accountability and responsibility, relieve stress (so life outside of the gym is easier and more stress-free). It is up to us to provide that service in a way which allows our clients to carry those values out into their lives. They may not comprehend that this is part of our goal as trainers, but eventually they will recognize the lessons learned in the gym, can positively impact their everyday lives. We've all been there. Maybe life threw a wrench in things, or we just felt off for some reason, but then came into the gym and had an awesome workout. When we walked out of the gym, we had a fresh mindset and faced the rest of the day with a different perspective. As personal trainers, when we assist others with that shift in mindset, our clients will notice. Their coworkers will notice. Their bosses will notice. Their families and friends will notice. The aura people walk around with after leaving the gyms can do wonders for self-confidence, work productivity, relationships, and other parts of their lives. It's something that not many other professions have the chance to alter, and we are fortunate enough to get to do that for people on a regular basis.

In order to provide this type of experience for our clients, we need to pride ourselves on the service we offer. Again, there's a recurring theme here that has absolutely nothing to do with exercise, kinesiology, or science. Take care of your people. Get them moving, and treat them as best as you can. We are fitness professionals, but we play so many different roles for each of our clients. First and foremost, be a good person. Make that your top priority, not perfecting your programming. Training improvement will come with experience, education, and trial and error, but being respectful, caring, and putting others' health and safety first is something people will remember. It will open the door for people to want to work with you so you can prove your abilities within the exercise science world. Your first impression and the way you continue to treat your people will stick with them forever. We will not get remembered for our training program so much as we will for the way we have treated others, boosted them up when they needed us, and for giving them the necessary tools to find and love the healthiest version of themselves, in and out of the gym. Cater your service to what it is your clients are looking for and what they need. Yet, at your deepest core, always pride yourself in the service you provide and care for others as people first, clients later. We learned the Golden Rule to 'treat others the way you want to be treated' as children. When in reality this is such a simple act, it can really set you apart from others in this profession. Be consistently good to others and you will notice your clients will be happier and more excited to continue working with you. This leads to improved client retention and solidifying the reputation your brand of business holds. The profession of personal training revolves so much more around the personal side than it actually does around the act of training.

CHAPTER 8

Create a Relationship, but Keep It Appropriate

The relationships created and maintained through working in this field are what reeled me in, have kept me around, and hopefully, have established some lifelong friendships. I am so thankful for each person who has come into my life from when I began training, through those who believed and stuck by my side when I opened Seymour Health & Fitness, and for those who have taken a chance on Collin and me since. We literally would not have a business without you and we owe you so many more thanks than just for your business. The personal side of this career path was unexpected, and it completely altered how I viewed where to go in my career. The benefits of connecting with people who bring out the best in you, challenge you, and believe in you are endless. When there is that strong of a connection though, there can be a blurred line between appropriate and inappropriate relationships with your clients. As a personal trainer, it is your job to be there for your people, helping them grow stronger in both mind and body. During training sessions, you may enter into conversations that could possibly be shared only with you. When you and a client have established that level of honesty and openness, anyone can be vulnerable. If somebody is having a difficult time in a relationship, they may vent to you. They tell you things they may not even tell their significant other. Sometimes, clients may be in an emotional state because of whatever is going on at home. You're there for them. You listen. You give advice when asked for it. Establishing a strong connection with each person makes them comfortable enough to trust you with very sensitive information. The challenge that arises when bonding with your clients is the misperception that can be created in the eyes of some. The vulnerability of a situation while you are there for someone can easily be misconstrued into a level of attraction. Remain professional. Create appropriate boundaries with your clients. You've already established trust with one another and with trust comes great responsibility. If ever a questionable or unprofessional situation arises, you must firmly retain your professional, friendly manner. Never let your trainer/client relationship get to the point of becoming physical or sexual. Since you work very closely with your people, it's possible for one-sided, deeper feelings to develop. It's up to you, as the ultimate professional, to maintain a respectful relationship with the people who trust you day in and day out. There may be feelings coming from one direction and I'd be willing to bet that if you've been in this field for a while, you have seen this type of occurrence take place, whether it was first or second handed.

Forming relationships and creating a connection with clients is needed to build trust and fully understand them in order to get them progressing forward, but too often that line is crossed. At the end of the day, it is your responsibility to never cross that line. Trainers, unfortunately, have this horrible stigma they frequently sleep with their clients. It does happen. As a matter of fact, it happens often. Be careful. Word spreads quickly, especially in close-knit gym communities, which in turn may give you an unwanted "branding," thus tainting your decent name. If a line is ever crossed, not only do you put yourself in a problematic dilemma as you attempt to balance your business and personal life, but you also may create complications with that client and their decisions moving forward. You're asking for trouble if that is the choice you make. As a professional, it is wrong. It tarnishes the reputation of the entire profession, and you're abusing your position of leadership by crossing that line. Don't be known as the trainer who gets a little too cozy with their clients. Spending time with people you trust and open up to is perfectly fine, as long as both you and your clients know a level of dignity should be maintained in and out of the gym. Avoid putting yourself in too intimate of a situation and it won't be an issue. End of story.

Are there instances where it is acceptable to spend time with your clients outside of the gym? Absolutely. We invited some clients to our wedding. I've gone out for dinner and drinks with clients. Watering plants; taking care of pets; moving furniture; going to art shows and musicals; supporting at sporting competitions; and attending funerals for clients and loved ones of clients are just a few ways I interact with the people with whom I have a personal training relationship in and out of the gym. It can be a bit tricky trying to navigate how to act when you're hanging out with people as friends, knowing they are also paying clients. Honestly, I love hanging out with my people, and have figured out how to maintain a level of professionalism and be fully self-aware of situations. Be respectful of others. Understanding who you are in public has a direct correlation to the reputation of your business, and don't put yourself in any situations that could be mistaken or taken out of context by other people. What it comes down to is being a decent person and continuing to exemplify the values you prioritize in your place of work when out in social settings.

CHAPTER 9

How to Get Clients to Buy-in

"Andrew is an excellent trainer who is knowledgeable about nutrition, health, and exercises. He helps his clients feel comfortable in trying a new exercise and takes time to explain anything you may not understand. He is very approachable with any questions you may have also. I highly recommend Andrew Seymour for his growing business of Seymour Health & Fitness!"

Confidence is good. Arrogance is not. There is a big difference between these two descriptors. Being confident in your profession is a positive characteristic which allows you to continue along your path without second guessing your abilities. Arrogance is an expression of superiority, at times cockiness, that has potential to get in your way and trip you up. Avoid bragging about your ability, your status, or even your personal successes to everyone in sight. You know your stuff. Show others how you can use your talent, knowledge, and experience to benefit your clients.

Personally, confidence is something I have always struggled with. I feel comfortable with my acquired intelligence, as well as knowing how to provide my clients with the most beneficial and progressive products needed to keep their health and fitness on track. The battle I face is questioning myself. I create fake scenarios in my head which snowball into even bigger, fabricated problems in my mind. This causes me, oftentimes, to question my decisions and my discourse. Fortunately, since finding my niche and creating my own fitness business, the conviction in my choices has improved. Believing in and surrounding myself with people and clients who display happiness, positive habit changes, and lifestyle alterations as a result of my influence has boosted my confidence levels tremendously.

As a personal trainer, it is important you create a culture where your clients believe in you. When others genuinely believe in who you are, what you do, and the role you play in relation to them, it helps them buy into you. The concept of "buying into *you*" elicits a more treasured field than simply buying into your *business*. We are fortunate to have the opportunity to connect with our clients on a deep level. When people decide to train with you, they are not only buying a workout program. They are purchasing you and all of the services you provide, if you decide to go that route. One important aspect of being a successful personal trainer is leading by example. You can live a very different lifestyle after you leave your gym for the day, but you will find it more productive, successful, and enjoyable to be a walking role model of the product you are pitching to clients and prospective clients.

Believing in your product and helping your clients buy into the services you provide should be a key factor in your personal training business model. Getting your clients to buy into the product and services you are offering to them is elaborated on further in *Lead Clients Through an All-Inclusive Training Experience which goes Beyond Expectations*. In summation, that section suggests that through offering and following through in providing an assortment of services that check multiple boxes off of what clients are seeking for in coming to your business, you can set yourself apart from others and retain clients through that unmatched service.

Are we all built the same as our clients? No. Are our personal goals parallel to our clients' goals? No. Do we workout the same amount or eat similar types and/or amounts of food? No. Even though there are differences, sustainable results can be attained with guidance, patience, and persistence.

Be the guinea pig in your own training and show your clients you are working alongside them. This ensures them that they are not on this journey alone. Help your clients find balance. Attempting to sustain an overly strict lifestyle of working out 365 days a year, avoiding desserts and foods that bring you pleasure, and not enjoying what you're doing does not equate to a balanced or even reasonable undertaking. When asked for advice on this topic, I share what works for me. My daily life includes a mixture of everything. At the gym, I enjoy doing squats, hip thrusters, chin ups, bench, rows, core, steady state cardio and HIIT workouts. Outside of my professional life, I enjoy walks with my wife and our dogs, eating a balanced diet, getting an adequate amount of sleep, drinking plenty of water, and listening to my body when it is telling me certain things. I also enjoy ice cream, pizza, and taking a day off where we don't leave the house or leave the couch while watching something on the television. Helping your clients find the balance of accomplishing what we need to do, along with relishing what we want to do, can lead to sustained success. It is our job as trainers to adjust the details within those parameters to figure out how each of our clients can attain this feat.

Selling a product is easy and any good conversationalist can sell personal training. Making a sale and getting your clients to buy into your long-term plan to get them where they want for the rest of their lives is much more complex. Because of how closely we get to work with our clients, we are capable of bonding with them and influencing them on a much deeper level. Being able to create a close affiliation with each individual client is one of my favorite parts of this job. With this familiarity though, things can get tricky. When you click and find that link with your clients, it can be easy for it to turn into more of a friendship than a transactional relationship. Maintain a professional standard of conduct. When things become more laxed, we tend to ease up a bit. Although feeling comfortable around your people is a good thing, they are still paying us to deliver an exceptional training experience so we cannot let that level of comfort intrude on the quality of service we provide.

Finding that balance of friendship and continually elevating your training will prove to your clients that you care for them on a different level. When you reach that point, not only will it boost your confidence in the services that you are selling but you will raise the bar for what people are expecting. The biggest positive to come from this is the openness that your clients will feel. This may initially come off as a sense of vulnerability, but we must not take advantage of our clients when they show this side to us. They are putting their trust in us and our product, buying into what we are selling, and are finally committed to the long-term goal.

This point of emphasis can make or break us. When clients open up to us because of the massive amount of trust amongst both sides, we can lead them down one of two paths. When people trust you and will do as you say, it can cause them to blindly follow. We must keep educating ourselves and proactively working to be the best version of ourselves for the sake of our clients. When we have people blindly following us, it could be easy to simply give up and lose that drive but when people buy in, that is really just the beginning. It is such a huge milestone that oftentimes it can be mistaken for a peak, when in reality it is the first step towards much larger accomplishments. Once people buy in, we have to turn our services up a notch and keep pushing them along towards their goals. When clients buy in, they are finally all in and ready to allow those daily habits to become their new normal behaviors. Those behaviors will begin to illustrate the changes that we've been working so hard to see. All of that hard work begins to pay off and the real fun begins when people buy in.

See that victory as a huge accomplishment, acknowledge it, and run with that newfound sense of ambition. Whether you are the client or trainer, once you realize that both sides are bought in, there will be refreshment and determination to continue moving forward. Use that to jumpstart your next goals. Learn how powerful it can be to create that relationship where both sides are all in and ready to do whatever it takes to help the other. As a trainer, this can be one of the most accomplishing positions to be in. It is always fun and satisfying to see clients check off little goals here and there and to recognize when they are improving. Seeing that sense of achievement when people realize what they've accomplished and where their potential is, it is an irreplaceable feeling.

This new phase also comes with a new set of challenges. Although clients may now be more understanding of the concept that things will take time, patience, and hard work, they still want to look forward to each training session. In reality, there will be days when they don't feel motivated or want to workout but teaching them how it is important to be disciplined during those thoughts of uninterest. What you want in the end should outweigh your cravings right now. This is a concept that can be difficult to keep at the forefront of our mind but it is our job as trainers to remind them that each workout has a place in the program to get them to their end goal.

When clients buy in and do as you say, you really have to dial in on what you are trying to accomplish. Each and every repetition, set, and exercise choice should have a reason for being chosen. It comes down to a science. The formula for a successful program is providing your client with a little bit of what they want and a lot of what they need. We must prescribe them with movements that progress them as much as we can, all while allowing them to enjoy what they are doing. There should be a purpose behind each exercise selection. We must prepare ahead of time and provide rationale as to why we chose the exercises that we did. It should be welcomed by your clients to vocalize this reasoning to them. If you simply tell them to do a movement but never explain why it is important or what place it has in bettering them, the disinterest could lead them to not believing in your product. Part of the buying into the process is showing them why we created their program the way that we did. Explaining the muscle groups being activated, the joints being targeted, and showing them why this exercise benefits them on an individual level. Connecting each movement back to their personalized goals helps them realize that you really are individualizing your programs to each client. You aren't just creating one cookie cutter program and feeding it to every single client. You have done your homework, pieced together a periodized plan that will lead them to their end goal, and you should be able to explain each portion of that. Not everybody will show interest in the background of why and how you created your program but it is important either way to tie your selections back into their wants and needs. Being open about your process and explaining so through terminology that they will understand will help them buy in even more so.

Proving you know the scientific background of kinesiology is important but through my experiences, the majority of your clients just want to ensure you created this program for them, it is helping them work towards their goals, and that you're going to keep them accountable. More importantly, people want to be pushed, both physically and mentally, and they may want to converse with you during their exercises. This doesn't apply to all of your clients, as some will show much more interest in the science and the process behind your programming. When clients ask about the science behind your programming application, take this opportunity to explain why you chose the exercises and choices you did specifically for them. Elaborate on certain subjects. Do they understand why it is important to eat carbohydrates, as it applies to exercising? What is ATP (Adenosine triphosphate) and why is it important to sustain and elevate your workout productivity? Is there an interest in learning why you mix up their cardiovascular workouts from aerobic to anaerobic levels? Are they interested in the benefits of resistance training as it applies to bone density and aging? Why should you try to improve the range of motion at each joint from all different angles? These are just a few "fun" topics you may have the pleasure of sharing with your clients. Being able to bring back the course knowledge and the practicality you've acquired through your years of education, helps others learn what works best for their own personal fitness path.

People learn in a variety of ways. Recognizing what allows each individual client to comprehend what exercise selections you have chosen will help you understand how to better connect them to your programming, and will help them buy in even further. Catering your teaching style to how your client learns will help make each client feel more at home and will help enhance their ability to absorb the material you are providing them with. Because there are several different learning styles, we must learn and improve upon each of them in order to teach our clients in the most efficient way possible. Some clients are visual learners and understand what they need to do through watching you demonstrate exercises, while others are more verbal learners and will pick up on things through you explaining the movements in a detailed fashion. Some have good kinesthetic awareness and are able to move their body well while connecting their senses to their musculature, while others are very logical and see the reasoning behind exercises, which allows them to understand it more. Some clients will work better in groups and will have more fun with that, while bettering themselves whereas others will be more productive and driven when working with you one on one. Being able to capitalize on all of the different abilities, interests, and traits of our clients will help expand our toolbox, but will also make each and every client feel at home with us. The ability to show up, be comfortable, and workout knowing that you have everything catered to your individual wants and needs is something that not every trainer provides. Do your part to allow your clients to feel at home with you so that they can improve their chances of buying into what we are providing. This not only helps them achieve results quicker and more efficiently, but allows for us to have more stability in our business.

When we know that people are dedicated to the long-term plan that we've created together, we can stop stressing so much about where our next paycheck will come from. We are at a disadvantage in the sense that every one of our clients has the ability to drop us at any given moment. You hope that you have created enough of a sturdy foundation that this won't happen without a heads up, but attrition will happen. Expect attrition amongst your clients. More often than not, when a client stops training with you, it won't be because of a personal issue. People stop training due to all sorts of reasons, ranging from financial to family matters to changing jobs or homes. Just because someone ends their client-trainer relationship with you doesn't mean that you did anything wrong. Rather than getting offended, ask them for feedback as to what they enjoyed and what they would've done differently during your tenure. Use that review to fine tune your craft and create an even better experience with your current and future clients. Do not burn bridges. End things on as good of terms as you possibly can and understand that sometimes when people stop training with you, you've served your purpose in educating them so well that they're ready to go off on their own. Regardless of the reason, attrition happens and not everybody trains with you forever.

Due to this unfortunate fact, client retention is the key to long term success. If I had one thing to pass on to other trainers who wanted to be successful in this field, it would be to do what you need to do to maximize client retention. Focus on your current clients and give them the best possible experience while they're with you. Spending time attempting to get new people in your doors is important because as much as we don't like it, we do lose clients at some point in time but our main focus should be appreciating the people we have and giving them the absolute best that we have to offer. When we capitalize on the people and tasks in front of us, we improve the chances of creating longer relationships with those people. If we are constantly distracted by the chances of losing a client or not knowing where the next paycheck will be coming from, we become distracted. Be aware and dialed in to the task at hand. When we become distracted, we become distant. When we become distant and occupied with thoughts in our head, clients recognize that and will feel as if they are secondary to whatever is occupying your brain. At the end of the day, it is important to our business and to the relationship with our clients to believe in them, believe in ourselves, keep all of us accountable, and provide the best customer service possible to continue to boost the reputation of your business while taking care of your clients and yourself on a daily basis.

Through putting forth the time and effort to get to know and believe in your clients, your relationship with them, as well as the trust between the two of you, will become stronger. This won't suddenly happen in your first session. Some people are more open than others but in order to find out the depths of your clients, it will take time. As with results in the gym, you must be patient. Things may be forced towards the beginning of working with a new client so it is important to find those connections between you two as quickly as possible. Once that is formed, they will enjoy returning to your sessions and it becomes a little less intimidating and more enjoyable for both. Continue showing your skillset, helping them one day, one workout, one repetition at a time, and as you go, make a conscious effort to know and learn more and more about them. As you learn more, you may get a glimpse into why they want to achieve certain goals, why they may think a certain way, or why they have the opinions they may have. These are great little nuggets to reach because it shows the strength of the bond that you have created and that is difficult to break. Never stop learning from your clients. Never stop respecting them. Never be afraid to have difficult conversations, as they have the potential to elevate your connection to a whole other level. Be a chameleon and blend in when you need to but always be conscious of the conversation at hand and be sure to tread lightly when you know the discussion is heading in an undesirable direction. This way of thinking will allow for you to adapt so your clients can feel more at home. When you adjust to make them more comfortable, it can help them be themselves and when that happens, it makes it a much more conducive environment for growth and success. This is what it takes to have all parties buy into the mission of the team.

CHAPTER 10

Use SDT to Create and Lead Clients Through an All-Inclusive Training Experience

"Andrew makes himself available 24/7 (vs. just the hours we train) ...
he answers my questions and researches work-arounds for injuries
I have."

When first entering into the personal training world, I didn't recognize the importance relationships would play in finding success in this field. Fortunately, I've come to the realization that the Self-Determination Theory sums up why relationships are important in creating lasting connections with the people in this industry. Self Determination Theory (SDT) is a framework that motivates others through satisfying their basic psychological needs. The three pillars of SDI include *autonomy,* which helps people feel control over their own life and the path that they are on; *a sense of belonging,* that allows people to realize they fit in with the group they spend time with; and *competency,* which is another way of stating people feel like they can progress and continue to grow. By utilizing this theory in your coaching, or really any position of leadership, you can help your clients realize how important they are, they have power to make their own choices, and they can continue to progress and grow within a certain/specific/determined environment. Each of these convey powerful feelings. When we use the SDT to structure the way we coach and lead, it provides others with the tools they need to take control of their own life. It may sound cheesy but similar to how food, water, and sleep are physiological needs for humans; autonomy, belonging, and competency are the psychological needs for autonomous motivation and psychological wellness.

Because trainers tend to work with a variety of people, we may need to adjust how to help satisfy each individual's needs. At the end of the day, accomplishments can be attained by keeping things relatively simple. *Autonomy* can help improve intrinsic motivation and this can be elevated through empowerment. As trainers, we can program certain parts of our workouts to be decided by the individual for whom we are programming. For example, offering a structured choice at the end of a workout by doing close-grip bench presses paired with supinated bent over rows or skull crushers supersetted with single-arm dumbbell rows is a very simple, yet effective way of allowing the client to choose the final route of the workout. Assuming they don't have any glaring limitations and are capable of performing all of those exercises equally, opening up the choice of the workout route helps them feel empowered and part of the decision-making process. It can be more complex than that, but simply inviting clients to pick certain parts of the workouts can be a fun way to include them and help them understand their voice matters.

Belonging best comes from you genuinely caring for others and making sure they realize this. Belonging to a group is a bit more subjective because we may not realize we are excluding someone. What it comes down to is perception versus reality. Clients, especially those who feel uncomfortable at the beginning of their journey in the gym with you, may believe they stand out as the newbie, and they perceive that they don't fit in. This is justified and real in their eyes, but as the trainer it is our job to reassure them they are part of the group. This attempt at inclusion can be more successful through our conversations and actions. We can easily help a client feel more part of the family at the gym by introducing them to others who you know are welcoming and inclusive. Other ways to help new clients build a sense of rapport in the gym include paying attention to their facial and physical expressions, as well as catering our tone of voice, choice of words, and exercise selection to make them feel better about themselves. In doing so, they will hopefully become more and more at home, which then allows progression in exercise choices, better connections with them, and possibly even building new friendships with others. It's important for you, as the trainer, to be both the leader and middle-man in creating a bridge from the newness and discomfort of being in an unfamiliar environment to a feeling of inclusivity. If we take it upon ourselves to be sure other people feel a sense of belonging, their comfort level will improve, allowing them to refocus on what they initially intended to accomplish, thus increasing the probability of finding more sustainable results.

The final pillar of the Self-Determination Theory is *Competency*. This is the focal point of motivation. It is much easier to improve motivation when people feel they are capable of doing the work necessary to continually improve. Admittedly, many of us have hard times staying motivated when we are in a rut, feel like we've hit our ceiling, or we cannot progress further. Having room to grow without feeling overwhelmed with what lies ahead is an important part of people being their best selves. One very effective way I have found to help improve competency in the gym setting is having clients teach exercises back to me. This is especially helpful for novice lifters and children, but even the most advanced in the gym should be reminded of the basics time and again. The most successful way to do this process is for the trainer to explain an exercise while demonstrating it to the new learner. This way it helps the client understand the cues to use, and if they are visual learners, they can see proper form being executed. There is a lot of information to take in, especially for complex movements, so don't expect clients to retain and repeat each and every minor detail right away. Once the client performs the exercise and is ready for the second set, it's time for them to be the teacher. Have them teach it back to you. This is a meaningful strategy to analyze what parts of the exercise stuck with them, as well as a great way for them to retain information. Thinking about the correct form before doing an exercise reinforces knowledge and helps build confidence. Learning something new, being able to teach this new concept to another individual, and receiving feedback are strategic ways for one to feel capable and competent to keep working and growing.

Because of the diversity of people you come in contact with through your business, be patient in working to understand others. Through the process of getting to know someone, opening up to one another can take time. It definitely can be a scary and uncomfortable situation for some people, especially in the world we work in because the gym can be intimidating for some people. Think about it. Remind yourself of a situation in which you felt out of place and uncomfortable. People new to a gym may experience similar feelings of anxiety and exclusion. A good number of people we train initially decided to work with us because of some sort of desire to feel more comfortable. Being more confident in their own skin throughout their everyday lives, gaining knowledge and an improved level of comfortability in the gym, or having some insecurities mended by incorporating a regimented exercise program with a trainer are a few examples of why clients come to us. Those are all common reasons to hire a trainer and as their coach, which we must keep at the forefront of our mind when working with each client. You may not truly find out why a client begins working with you in the first few sessions but until and even when you finally discover this, be sure you are self-aware with the verbiage you use or the topics you cover. In order for clients to become more comfortable in the gym and with you, they need to be able to be themselves. For some people, they show their true selves the first moment you meet them, while others take some time to open up. It may take time for us to truly understand who someone is, but when the opportunity is given to us it is important to be patient with them and remain open-minded. You'll notice better connections with some people, while others take more time and adjustment to create a strong bond. For both situations, and everyone in between, we must remain respectful, supportive, and do our best to help others feel like they belong.

Coming from different backgrounds, different experiences, unique perspectives shaped by a combination of influential people in our lives and the way situations affecting us have been handled, we may be hesitant to show our true colors. In a vulnerable situation where we do not feel as comfortable, we may act differently or put on some sort of hypothetical mask to fit in and make other people believe we feel a certain way. I have done this method countless times. I am one who likes a regular routine. Getting out of my comfort zone can be stressful, creates anxiety, and really throws me off from being my usual self. Therefore, I empathize with the difficulty one may experience entering a gym, especially working with a trainer who may be a complete stranger to you. What allows us to open up and be more ourselves in those types of circumstances? Time and the ability to better connect with the people and environment in which we find ourselves. As trainers, we have the unique chance to help expedite the process of creating a more welcoming and inclusive atmosphere.

At the end of the day, by combining the Self-Determination Theory, your own unique coaching strategies, and being kind and open-hearted to your clients, you will create a more comfortable environment for them. This may potentially attract others who seek your type of motivational and growth-minded atmosphere. People new to the gym may experience similar feelings of anxiousness and exclusion. Being a coach who takes pride in creating a safe space for each and every person can help your clients open up, be themselves, and view your gym as their home. This is one of our personal business goals, and we hope each person who walks through the doors of Seymour Health and Fitness feels this hospitality and acceptance.

It's one thing to talk about it but it's another to apply those ideas and allow them to come to fruition. You can implement those ideas in your business by simply going above and beyond to set yourself and your business apart from others by implementing all-inclusive training programs. Check off all your clients' boxes by providing them with every resource needed to successfully attain their goals. To better explain this concept, compare it to an ideal getaway. All-inclusive vacations are hard to beat. Why? Because they take all the legwork out of decision making. They provide you with the ease of not worrying while you're trying to relax on your much-deserved escape. The same goes for training. Improving health and fitness for long durations of time to make lifestyle changes is not easy. It can oftentimes be very overwhelming for our clients. It is up to us to make this difficult, and sometimes intimidating task, as simple as possible. Help with exercise. Help with rest. Help with food recommendations. Help with habit changes. Help with stress. These are all part of an all-inclusive training program. Creating and providing clients with such a plan involves laying things out in a manner where they won't have to worry about many outside factors. This plan signifies a step-by-step route that will lead them to their goals. People like simplicity and when it comes to training, some prefer to use that hour as a portion of their day where they don't have to make any decisions. Get to know them on a deeper level so you can give them what they want. It will make your clients happy. Aside from their health and safety, your clients' happiness is one of the most important things. We all know the phrase "happy wife, happy life." The same goes for clients. Happy client, happy trainer.

Providing clients with an all-inclusive training program will justify your initial price. From that point forward, it will be your job to live up to the standard presented and preached as a selling piece. In order to remain a client's paid asset, we need to not only provide them with services above and beyond their expectations, but also have to buy in. Once you establish the standard of the high-quality, all-inclusive service clients will receive, and you continue to provide this to them day in and day out, the money conversation will be eliminated. The price of your services will be an afterthought because of how much bang for your buck you are providing. This complete buy-in does not simply come from your client writing a check time and time again. There is more than a mere monetary investment in what we provide. When we guide our clients through providing exceptional service, help them obtain the results they are looking for, and aid them in understanding the benefit of repeated habits allowing for more sustained growth, their buy-in will ensue.

Buying into something, or investing yourself completely, may evoke cheesy connotations. Yet, it is evident when individuals buy into the greater good of an organization, both parties benefit. Buying in can impact culture. Buying in can reflect the attitude of yourself or your clients. Buying in comes with the understanding that not every day or workout will be your best. The important thing is to continue controlling what you can control and use that to fuel the fire the next time you have an opportunity in front of you. Buying in means trusting one another and being able to be transparent with one another. When something becomes difficult; when we need to be pushed further; when we need someone to vent to, we each deserve an environment where we can obtain these pursuits. That is buying in. Buying in means allowing guidance and education to take place. Buying in means we remain humble and have the ability to step back from what may not have worked to revisit and revamp a training program to start anew. Buying in puts your stubbornness aside for the greater good of the bigger goal. Buying in means you are there for one another, through the good and the bad.

Regardless of what you want to call it, getting people to buy-in or dive into the service you provide will allow you to build a business empire. In order to grow to this point, not only do clients need to buy in, but as a trainer and as their coach, you must reciprocate that. What this means is you need to show up day in and day out, prepared and ready to help each and every client of yours continue in the right direction of their goals. You need to do work, including progressive programming, behind the scenes to get yourself ready for those sessions. You have to do your homework, which goes back to concepts presented in *Show What You Know, but Admit When You Don't*. You must lead by example. It is so incredibly important for you, as a trainer, to lead by example! If your clients see you partying until bar close, neglecting your physical and mental health, and regularly participating in unhealthy behaviors, yet you preach to them the importance of living a healthy-balanced lifestyle, they may lose faith and trust in you. Does every trainer have to have bulging muscles and a shredded six-pack? No, but each trainer should follow certain rules they preach day in and day out. Your clients should have every opportunity to look up to you. When they see you living your recommended lifestyle, while allowing yourself the healthy balance between what you enjoy and what you need, and those behaviors are eliciting noticeable results for you, they find the added motivation to continue believing in the services you provide. Leading by example, and having your clients follow along, will boost the entire culture of your business. Everyone around you will better understand the importance of consistency, hard work, and patience because you are leading by example while properly educating them on how to obtain similar results.

With any successful professional sports team, what are some common underlying themes? Culture. Buying in. Winning environment. Leadership. Rarely do you find a team that ends up winning a championship in its respective sport that doesn't get along and doesn't play for one another. Although personal training may not seem like a team sport, it is. It is a much smaller team but as a coach you need to do your best to create a winning environment for your clients. A culture where your clients understand what tasks they have to take care of on a regular basis in order to accomplish a much larger goal. In football for example, each lineman wants to win his individual battle against the man lined up across from him. He also wants to help his teammate next to him. They want to block for their team to score touchdowns, win games, and ultimately hold a trophy up at the end of the season. Each drill, each practice, each repetition in each game is important to build up to the end goal of winning the championship. In our world, each repetition; each food choice; each workout; each positive thought will lead to a healthier life. Your decisions and leadership will have a snowball effect. Healthy habits will be recognized. Others will feed off of this; surrounding themselves with similar-thinking individuals, which in turn evolves into numerous people putting forth effort in the same direction, helping everyone.

We need to understand the importance of consistency and devoting time and effort to our own goals. As a person and personal trainer, you owe it to yourself to be happy and healthy. We often sacrifice so much for others. Remember to grant yourself permission to be attentive when it comes to your own health and wellness. Insert time each day to get in your own workouts. Experiment with recipes to assure your healthy food choices bring you satisfaction and joy. Make it a priority to find time to yourself doing what makes you happy. Surround yourself in and out of the gym with people who inspire and ignite your passion for this job. You deserve to live your best life. You deserve to be part of a winning team. With your training business, you have the opportunity to change the lives of so many people in such different ways. To be a successful leader in this business, you must remember to take care of yourself.

Creating a winning culture comes from a variety of factors. If there is shared leadership amongst those in a group, it improves accountability, pushes others to grow, and builds community. The Power of Positive Leadership has an excerpt which simplifies what a leader does. This book, by Jon Gordon (2017), breaks down some areas we can all work to improve ourselves and others. Gordon notes:

> "No matter what anyone says, just show up and do the work.
>
> If they praise you, show up and do the work.
> If they criticize you, show up and do the work.
> If no one even notices you, just show up and do the work.
> Just keep showing up, doing the work, and leading the way.
>
> Lead with passion.
> Fuel up with optimism.
> Have faith.
> Power up with love.
> Maintain hope.
> Be stubborn.
> Fight the good fight.
> Refuse to give up.
> Ignore the critics.
> Believe in the impossible.
> Show up.
> Do the work.
>
> You'll be glad you did.
> True grit leads to true success."

When we exemplify some or all of these leadership traits, it demonstrates we are determined to accomplish a greater goal for ourselves. Because of the nature of our career in the service industry, that goal involves helping the people who dedicate themselves to us. Being a leader means providing others with the tools necessary to find success in their own world. Being a leader is giving outward credit to others when they succeed, yet, looking inward at one's self when things do not go according to plan. Being a leader is taking care of your own health and wellness, as well as others. When you do so, you are filling your cup (*You Cannot Pour from an Empty Cup*). Leadership is putting all of the chips on what you do and what you believe in, while understanding that by learning along the way you may be able to become a better leader. Be open to change and improvement. Exemplifying the characteristics of what a leader does for others and themselves, creates and establishes a business built on a supportive culture, a positive reputation, and an unmatched, all-inclusive service specifically tailored to helping others be happier, healthier, and enjoying their lives to the fullest.

CHAPTER 11

Show Your Support Outside of the Gym

Y our hour of paid in-person training doesn't stop once the client leaves. As easy as it would be to put that hour of training and the person you trained in the past, when your client is done for the day with you in the gym, you are still on the clock.

Check in on your clients. Send a quick text asking how they feel after a hard workout. Inquire as to how their day turned out, knowing they expressed they were struggling emotionally during your session together. Keep them accountable. If they chose to forgo a session, reach out and see if they took a different plan of exercise for the day. Send them suggestions for healthy meals or recipes you enjoyed. Learn about them outside of the gym. Ask how their kid's ball game went. Show up to concerts, sporting events, and graduation parties you're invited to. Don't just play the part. Go out of your way to show how much you genuinely care about them as people as well as clients. The gym is our home base, our safe zone. Seeing others in their own element, doing things they love, and being there to support them can make their day. When you're in a field that allows you to create relationships and friendships with the people you work alongside, you want to see them doing what they love. My friend and fellow trainer, LG, introduced me to the concept of returning the favor clients so frequently do for us, by showing up to their events. I have attended clients' numerous youth and high school activities throughout the years, gone to art shows, and tried to show up to support them when I can. Witnessing how successful your clients are in their respective sports and activities, and how well they perform, is a cool way to bridge the gap between their interests and what we do in the gym. It's also fun!

Soccer, volleyball, basketball, and football games; tennis matches; track meets; road races; triathlons. You name it. Being an audience member watching a client brilliantly perform the lead role in Des Moines Christian's rendition of <u>Mary Poppins</u> was truly a highlight. I have been lucky enough to be there for my people. You are there for the people who are there for you. Showing up to events others are passionate about, can make a world of difference. This simple action proves you care. It shows families you are in this job for the right reasons. When you continue to go out of your way to make others feel included, cared for, and loved, regardless of the situation or profession, it will strengthen your relationship and allow you to establish yourself as a person who genuinely is there for others. That says a lot. This is also a great way to set your standard above others in your field of business. In our world, establishing relationships and retaining people is the best way to build a sustainable business model. Your attention to clients outside of the gym is an affirmation of your investment in them.

CHAPTER 12

60-Minute Sessions Do Not Always have to be 60 minutes

On our Seymour Health and Fitness website (https://www.sey-mourhealthandfitness.com), we offer the service of 60-minute individualized personal training sessions. By the book, those sessions should begin and end exactly on the hour. In a perfect world, that would allow us to schedule multiple sessions consecutively to maximize the efficiency of our work day and to allow our clients to schedule their day accordingly around our workouts. In reality, the number of times I've stuck around the gym at the end of my shift for the day to continue a great conversation with a client for an additional 15, 20, 30, 45-minutes is more times than my wife probably would like. However, when people feel comfortable enough to spend so much additional time speaking with you, learn to appreciate and acknowledge those relationships by granting extra attention, even after your paid hour ends. A handful of people come to mind when I think about spending time after workouts sitting around and chatting for a bit extra. Those conversations may revolve around exercise, health, fitness, or other related subjects, but often our conversations are about other topics. There may be times you want to get home and eat or spend time with loved ones, but it's important to invest in and make those deeper connections. Those in front of you, sticking around and sacrificing their time doing the same exact thing as you are there because of how they feel about you and the relationship you have with one another. Having clients stick around after a session is a testament of how comfortable someone feels around you as a professional and a person, which is incredibly special.

So many of my clients have become close friends, and they are people I trust implicitly. Your clients can become people you can count on to be there for an assortment of ways that not everyone can say about their friends. It is a pretty special bond when you find that type of connection with people, which is another perk of getting to do what we do on a daily basis. There will be connections you make with some of your clients that lead you into friendships, time spent with one another outside of the gym, and very memorable and in-depth conversations in and out of workout times. It is important, though, to find the balance between wrapping up your conversations and training sessions on time, whether that be book ended with another session or at the end of your day. Be cognizant of your time as well as your clients' time, as all of you are busy people. You will discover sometimes, even when a session may have technically wrapped up, interactions with certain individuals may not organically be finished. Know that those few minutes spent talking after a session with those individuals matter to them. They'll matter to you, too, because you recognize your clients are more than just purchasing a service from you. They understand you care about them as people first, customers second.

CHAPTER 13

Close Your Mouth and Open Your Ears

Listen. Stop talking and open your ears. Listening allows us, as individuals, to become more engaged and interactive in conversations. You can learn so much by taking in what others are trying to tell you with their words. If we, as a society, put more time into digesting what is being articulated to us, many reckless reactions could be avoided. When in conversation with others, listen to the words people are speaking but also recognize the tone, the way they phrase certain sentences, and the emotion they put into their words. When we listen to understand, versus listening to respond, we can learn a lot from people. In doing so, we better relate to our clients, thus strengthening connections. Not every part of a conversation needs to be a back-and-forth dialogue. Sometimes active listening is more imperative than jumping in and giving our two cents.

From a personal trainer's point of view, the simple act of listening is an imperative part of your business. Your clients will have incredible stories, amazing past experiences, and knowledge beyond your scope of expertise. Pay attention. Ask questions. By showing curiosity in what your clients know, do for a career, or are interested in, they will better connect with you as a person and a trainer. Most people enjoy talking about themselves. Your clients' livelihoods make up their reality. Becoming familiar with, and better educated on, subjects your clients value opens up opportunities for further discussions and opportunities to build a level of comfort between you and your client.

You will train people from a wide variety of professions. Company executives, self-employed entrepreneurs, actuaries, teachers, realtors, accountants, stay-at-home parents, students, and grandparents exemplify some of your potential clients. As a trainer, you should be aware, however, that the roles each individual plays in their professional lives may not always define who they are. Each person has had unique experiences and may have lived a completely different life than you. They have learned different things and have seen life from a different set of eyes. Getting other people's perspectives on certain things can be so fascinating. Our perception is our reality. Even though two people may be watching the exact same situation unfold, it may be perceived in two completely separate ways. Picking the brains of your clients and listening to what they have to say will allow you to better understand them; show more interest in their lives outside of your sessions; and make an even greater connection, which is unbeatable.

Along with listening to the stories and interests of clients, be sure to acknowledge when they tell you things hurt, are uncomfortable, or even feel good while training. Listening isn't always done with the ears. Learn to notice and pick up on body language cues, which may differ from client to client. Pay attention to little things from session to session. If a client shares they didn't sleep well the night before and you can tell they're dragging, tone down the workout. Don't put them through the ringer if they are only going to be even more exhausted and put their central nervous system at risk of fatigue. Learning to listen to those cues should serve as a benefit to our coaching. Clients may not outright say how they are feeling each workout but it is your job to sift through what they say, their body language, and other nonverbal cues to recognize if the original workout still fits what they need in that session.

Sometimes we may second-guess ourselves or question our exercise prescription or different tactics of our training. Listen to that little voice in your head. Go with your intuition, and trust your education and the program you originally set up. Not every program is perfect, so feel free to adjust as needed. We need to be constantly tweaking and refining our programming for each client as we learn from every training session. Adjustment is a good thing, as it means we are truly learning from the little cues we may notice on a day-to-day, session-to-session, or person-to-person basis. Trust yourself. Be confident in your abilities and allow your judgment to keep your clients safe and constantly progressing.

Creating an open line of conversation between you and your clients will allow you to gel much better. You will not only form a stronger connection, but you'll also be able to learn from each other and risk downfalls, such as injuries due to lack of communication. These are all goals we should strive for as trainers. Communicating through actively listening, being transparent with one another, and providing honest feedback will do wonders for your client's training experience and the success of your training career.

Listening is an overlooked quality as there is so much noise in today's world. Some noise can benefit us, while some can be additional stimuli that do not serve us well. The ability to listen to what is important can help you decipher useful information from information that will just add more unnecessary filling to your plate.

In this field, having the ability to listen to others can have a positive impact. This position primarily requires us to help people workout. That being said, when we are able to create relationships, people will open up to us and share what's going on in their lives, whether it's good or bad things. This shows a strong connection when your clients are comfortable sharing feelings and thoughts with you. Once you get to this stage with your clients, identify how they best need you. If they are emotionally spilling deep information about their home life that may be very difficult to open up about, note they don't always want your opinions or your advice. Sometimes people simply want to get things off their chest, and they may view you as a person upon whom they can dump those internal thoughts. Again, this can be a good sign they are comfortable around you. With that, we need to read the scenario to see if we should advise, smile and nod along, give them a hug, ask questions, or simply remain an active listener. Use your best judgment, be aware of the situation, and continue to actively listen to better understand others. This is another great way to create a very unique connection with the people in your business.

Be observant, ask questions, and don't be afraid to do your homework to better relate to others. Another very underrated duty of our job is that we need to research things outside of the health and fitness world. Does your client rave about a certain show? Watch that show instead of rewatching The Office for the 57th time. Did your client mention how he really wants to read a specific book but hasn't gotten around to buying it yet? Spend that $15 and go buy it as a gift to him. Those little tiny acts will mean the world to people and will give you so much more to converse over down the road. These extra deeds don't put much of a burden on our lives and will demonstrate we are hearing what our clients are saying. So many people listen, but not everyone hears. Who knows? You may enjoy that show or read that book once your client finishes it. Go above and beyond to make training the most enjoyable for your client. If they enjoy it, more than likely you will too.

When you combine the ability to listen well to others, connect with people, and create an environment where they feel confident opening up to you on a deeper level, you may notice individuals may rely on you as a way to relieve the thoughts and feelings that weigh heavy on their minds. In some ways, personal training sessions can transform into an outlet for clients, where it may even imitate therapy in their eyes. Admittedly, many of us in this field are not educated counselors or therapists. However, active listening is a healthy way for trainers to be sounding boards for our clientele. If you dedicate yourself to this field, you will put on all sorts of different hats for your clients, including a version of being their therapist, counselor, teacher, coach, accountability partner, and a steady rock who they know will be there for them regardless of what craziness life throws at them.

A therapist is educated on how to assess individuals, provide treatment, counsel, and diagnose certain disorders or diseases. Compared to therapists, we, as personal trainers, may differ in our educational backgrounds and some of the roles of our jobs, but we do check a few similar boxes. Most clients who seek our assistance are looking for more than just a workout program. Many want someone they can talk with, open up to, trust, and hash out whatever is going on in their minds. Clients will speak to you about their daily lives, relationship troubles, as well as friends and family. When you become a consistently reliable part of their lives, who they know they can go to in times of need, your client-trainer relationship strengthens. Studying up on psychology, counseling, and mental health will equip you for the additional roles you may be undertaking as a trainer. Finding tools people can utilize when they are dealing with certain issues may also be another one of your endeavors. Because we don't have the certifications or licensures therapists have, we cannot actually prescribe official plans of action to our clients. That being said, when we take the time to diligently do additional research to find tools to help and assure our clients, suggesting certain ways to work through issues is appropriate and may even better equip them for similar issues in the future. This ability comes from a sense of social awareness, but also from caring for the people who are comfortable enough to be transparent with you.

There may be times your clients will tell you things they have told no one else. As much as you may be honored by this honesty, be cognizant of their vulnerability. When these instances arise, first and foremost, be attentive. Take in what they are saying, and really focus to hear what is being shared. Provide feedback when necessary, but oftentimes, being a figurative shoulder to lean on and an ear to listen is what your clients may need most. Developing this type of relationship with your clients can be mutually beneficial, as it provides us the chance to work through something together as one and come out better on the other side.

CHAPTER 14

Show What You Know, but Admit When You Don't

In this business, as in life, it's okay to admit when you are wrong or do not know an answer to a question. Being honest is extensive in helping your clients. It is perfectly acceptable and normal to not know every answer. For the answers you do know, educate your clients, help them understand, and give them ideas and tools to take that new-found understanding forward so they can apply it to future situations. For questions you may not know the answers to, admit that, use your resources, and research or utilize the guidance of other professionals in our field to pinpoint answers. With the combination of new information, scientific revelations, and ever-advancing technology continually presenting itself, it's normal that we don't know each and every minor detail of every subject related to health, fitness, and training. I know that I don't know A LOT of things. Because of this, I continue to learn and expand my knowledge in these areas. Whenever there's a new area we dive into with clients or other professionals in this field, I have found it is most helpful to either ask the inquisitor more about it or if we both are unfamiliar, I'll research on my own afterward to touch up on that subject. Interestingly enough, the conversations we cover in training sessions extend far beyond exercise. It may sound strange, but you'll delve into technology, activities of family members, menstrual cycles, sports, complaints about coworkers, dogs having reconstructive ACL (TPLO) surgery, and so many other subjects, just to name a few that my clients and I have covered. Knowing very little about so many of those things prompts me to ask more about them, do additional research during down time, and become more educated to help my clients, as well as contribute to future conversations. These extra touches of showing additional effort to become more knowledgeable on subjects your clients are interested in can be important in building stronger relationships with your clientele.

When it comes to areas in our realm of the fitness industry we may not know, we have a few options. One can either reach back into past murmurs of possibilities we think we heard from someone years ago that may or may not be true, or we can be honest that we don't know but we'll look more into it. There's enough misinformation out there, especially in the world of health and fitness, so please choose not to add to that. In admitting we don't know something; I've noticed this simple action helps reassure clients you aren't letting your ego get in the way of improving their lives. They can feel more comfortable around you knowing that you don't know it all. Admission that you may not know something can show that you are not self-conceited. For some reason, many people have difficulty admitting they don't know something. In reality, understanding and admitting you don't know everything about a certain matter allows for improvement of knowledge, curiosity, and can open doors for exploring. Not knowing something does not show a lack of intelligence. In fact, those who understand there is room to grow in their field of expertise will better relate to and satisfy their clients. Becoming more knowledgeable for the sake of your clients shows you are willing to go above and beyond to try to better assist your people.

Subsequently, if you find you answered something wrong and you stumble upon a correct or more efficient response at a later date, admit to it. Are you required to do so? No, but as an ethical individual that is a way to show your honesty, demonstrate transparency, and build more trust and belief from your clients. One big miss I had when I began training was the big Ketogenic Diet craze. At the time I was training a handful of people who had shown interest in trying it out. Looking back now, I recognize that by following a diet craze, it really set my clients up for difficulties. Even after much research and being my own guinea pig before having my clients try this diet out, I look back now and see the mistakes I made by allowing my clients to partake in this fad. Nevertheless, some followed through with it, and it is something I should not have approved for them. Thankfully, we didn't have anyone stick with it for very long because like any fad diet, it wasn't sustainable and only really worked as an unhealthy version of caloric restriction. To those who asked, and I assisted with helping guide along this diet for the time being, I apologize. I now know better and wish I could go back and redo that situation. Learn from situations, admit your wrongdoing, and move forward.

Sometimes we may second-guess ourselves and question our exercise prescription or different tactics of training. Listen to that little voice in your head. Go with your intuition, and trust your education and the program you originally set up. Adjust as needed. Not every program is perfect. We need to, and should be, constantly tweaking and refining our programming for each client as we learn from every training session. Adjustment is a good thing, as it means we are truly learning from the little cues we may notice on a day-to-day, session-to-session, or person-to-person basis. Trust yourself. Be confident in your abilities and allow your judgment to keep your clients safe and constantly progressing.

CHAPTER 15

Use Your Manners and Show Your Gratitude

'Please' and 'thank you' are some of the earliest phrases children learn. As these two phrases are a natural part of our everyday lives, it's important to make them a component of your business practice. One technique I have more fully evolved over time with my clients relates to the language used in our gym. More specifically noting gratitude. Use of simple "please" and "thank you" phrases throughout sessions and around the gym establish an environment of gratitude and respect. These words show others you prioritize manners and etiquette, and most importantly appreciate them, thus creating an environment of mutual regard for each other. Those small habits of telling someone you appreciate them, thanking them for going out of their way to help or support you, or simply adding a 'please' at the end of a favor request can shape your reputation. Using manners throughout your entire life seems like a given, yet we all are guilty of getting so caught up in hectic schedules and everything going on in our lives that we may forget the simple, yet so important act of thanking people. Thank them for working out with you. Thank them for supporting you. Thank them for remaining faithful and for all of the hard work they put in. Say please when you ask them for a favor. Use sir and ma'am. Do the little things that show others you respect them. The more you consciously do those things on a more regular basis, the more that becomes second-nature.

I try to do this on a regular basis in person, through email and text, and the way that I post on social media. When people notice you vocalizing your appreciation for others, it may even attract new clients who like the way you treat and respect your clients and coworkers. Gratitude is a very attractive, yet under-rated trait, that can bring people your way and shape the way they think about you. On the other hand, keeping that appreciation and gratitude between you and other individuals can be special, also. One thing that Collin and I do each and every year is purchasing Christmas gifts for our clients. As a small thank you for them supporting and believing in us, we have done apparel orders every year since we opened in 2017, designing clothes that are exclusive to our clients. On the other hand, when we receive gifts from our clients, which are greatly appreciated but completely unnecessary, we try to return the favor with a handwritten thank you note, which may be seen as a lost art. Everything in today's world is done on a computer, phone, tablet, or some sort of electronic device. There's something that really makes others feel good about receiving a note that has been handwritten and personalized to thank them for what they've done for you up to that point. These notes don't have to be a novel, but including specific actions they've done and the different ways they've been there for you really tugs at the heartstrings. It's the least we can do for all that others do for us. We are in a service industry, and serving others is what we signed up for in our job. Setting aside five minutes and writing a thank you note once a year is really nothing compared to the reward we feel when clients trust in us every day. Writing thank you notes at a certain point each year or on a more regular basis has always been well received. I've found small acts of appreciation and gratitude toward clients go a long way in maintaining strong relationships.

No matter how you decide to do it for the people in your life, show gratitude. We can all think of a handful of individuals who have positively impacted our lives, whether they know it or not. Randomly contacting someone and expressing appreciation can make someone's day and make this world a better place. In fact, before the section of this book is over, why don't you fire off a text, email, or call to at least five people. Take a few minutes out of your day to get a hold of those people and start working on showing gratitude on a more regular basis. Without people's gracious support in our business ventures, we would not be able to travel down this path. Thank people, put smiles on their faces, and you may be surprised how much that makes your day better as well.

CHAPTER 16

Don't Only Be Money Motivated

"If your only goal is to become rich, you will never achieve it."
-John D. Rockefeller Sr.

Personal training can be a financially lucrative business. However, while money can be a goal of yours, in this business the main focus should be creating personal connections and providing an unmatched service that appeals to others. When you do so, your rewards, both tangible and intangible, will follow. A business's success is 100% reliant upon revenue coming in and expenses going out, profit and loss, and ultimately whether or not it can stay afloat and make a profit for a sustained amount of time. As personal trainers, we run a business. When done the right way, there is very good money in training people professionally. When we put money and profit as our top priority, that means we put clients and their needs as secondary priorities. This is a recipe for future failure. Just like a healthy lifestyle, this business is built for longevity, and it is important we recognize it as such. Client retention is your key. Take care of your people, build trust, create relationships, provide the best service you can deliver, and you will see those retention rates grow. This will be discussed further in the Business portion.

When I first decided to train out of college, I told my dad what a friend of mine made his first year in this profession. Making $60,000 personal training his first year out of school seemed unbelievable! The sound of this salary as a starting job had me a little skeptical, but I had faith I could follow in his footsteps. I was excited to make money, but knew my motivation wasn't solely reliant upon paychecks. I wanted to help others. That inspired me to apply at a large health facility as a personal trainer to become more educated in the field. This position was paid partially on commission, which forced me to work even harder. How did I get there? I got out of my comfort zone and met a whole bunch of people around the gym. I gave away time and free sessions with hopes that dedicating time to others may pay itself back down the road. I created relationships by getting to know people and learning more about them. Those relationships drove me to be a better person, trainer, and to provide the best service to those who invested in me, which in turn strengthened my desire for my job. Money came as a by-product, but taking care of my people stayed my main priority. By being there for my clients in and out of the gym, I eventually started to see both the personal and financial benefits of our affiliation.

So many people enter fields to chase dollar signs. It is part of the American way to make money so we can live the life we want for ourselves and those around us. Being loyal, caring for those who take care of you, and giving your best effort to the people who trust you provides fulfillment in a way money cannot. This job is one that can fill numerous buckets in your life. You can create amazing friendships. You get to work in a gym in shorts and a t-shirt. Another bonus includes having the ability to ultimately decide your schedule! You also have the chance to make a very respectable amount of money. There are so many benefits to this career, but if you solely focus on the money, you are not going to check the boxes of the other important portions of the field and you may not find full success or satisfaction. Making six-figures one year by hustling, selling, and overpromising to people who want to make drastic changes in their lives isn't a sustainable business model. Instead, be patient. Take your time getting to know people. Put in the extra effort to help accomplish your clients' goals, and place your client's health and well-being at the top of your priority list. It may take you a bit longer to reach that first $100,000 revenue year, but by building a strong clientele bond you will be able to sustain that year after year without much problem. Prioritize the way you take care of and serve others, and you'll financially benefit. Trust me.

CHAPTER 17

Be Open to Learning from Your Clients

Learn from your clients. Just because they are there for a service you provide them does not mean you're the expert in every subject. Each person we interact with has something unique about them. Listen and learn from others. Allow your clients to be mentors in other aspects of life. Understand that, although you may be guiding them with their health and fitness, you can be the student to their expertise in whatever field they may have dedicated their lives. Personally, upon reflection, there are many of my clients who have expanded my knowledge and outlook on various topics. Off the top of my head, one training session I always look forward to is with two specific clients who share with me the commonality of enjoying education. She is an ESL (English as a Second Language) teacher. He works in the IT field and is like a walking encyclopedia. Whenever I meet with these two, I thoroughly look forward to what I will learn next. They have such a broad spectrum of knowledge ranging from the latest in technology to the chemistry behind making homemade wine to delicious and unique food dishes to their love of dogs. I truly feel like I walk out of each of our training sessions knowing more than I did when we began. Those two are well versed in such a wide variety of subjects that it inspires me to learn more outside of my kinesiology niche.

Another prime example of clients teaching me certain things revolves around an entire family. Mom, dad, their daughter, and dad's brother are all part of our gym. First and foremost, this whole clan epitomizes what it means to be a family. Before I branched off to begin Seymour Health & Fitness, I started training the mom of the family. She then introduced me to her husband and his brother, and soon after their daughter joined our program. Growing up, my entire family was close, which makes me value the bond of family togetherness. The family we train have shown through their words and actions that they are there for each other through the ups and downs and exemplify unconditional love. The relationship the male siblings have parallels my own brother's relationship with me. The parents are a model couple who are strong independently, but even stronger together. Their daughter is extremely talented, with a bright future ahead of her. In being able to work with this impressive unit, there is a constant reminder of the importance of family. Observing and interacting with entire families, in our line of work, can be such a blessing.

One more example of lessons learned from clients, is from the very first person I was contracted to train. In working with this client, she has made me a better person and trainer. This client taught me the importance of hard work, determination, never giving up, and learning to trudge through in order to thrive in uncomfortable situations. She wanted to shift her lifestyle and begin working out, so she did. She wanted to lose a certain amount of weight, so she did. She wanted to begin running half marathons, so she did. She wanted to do triathlons, so she did. She wanted to do an Ironman 70.3, and guess what? She did. This lady continues to exceed every expectation in the gym, but those aren't even all of her amazing accomplishments. She prioritizes her family, never losing sight of the importance of her husband and four incredible children, while continuing to progress in her profession. She puts others first and is humble about all she does for herself and others…so I'll brag for her. She has taught me what it means to provide for others. She has taught me that if you want something bad enough, even if you're faced with the most trying circumstances, you step up, face those, and figure it out. She's shown that again and again, in and out of the gym. She loves a good lung-burner on the assault bike, which proves both her drive and determination. Ultimately, having clients like this one can help mold your regimen and perspective as a professional and a person.

In addition, make it a point to remember little details about your clients. Find out more about their background, spouses, kids, interests, hobbies, and job. Recognize them on their birthdays. When getting to know your clients, invest in the things that are important to them and what makes them happy. Remembering little details will mean the world to them, because it proves they are interesting and valuable. This is one of the best customer service actions you can take. When you find yourself surrounded by great people, do what you can to keep them around.

When training each of your clients, you may have to put on different hats to fulfill what it is they are expecting out of you as their trainer. That role may vary from person to person but I've found that through the acts of listening and having the genuine desire to learn from your clients, you will connect on such deeper levels. When you ask about them, their interests, hobbies, and subjects they may know more about than you, it allows them to be themselves. They don't feel judged and are much more prone to open up about subjects and topics that they are passionate about or relate to them directly, so being open to learning from them is the first step. The second is to notice when an appropriate opportunity presents itself to ask about certain areas they may have more interest in, and then it is up to you to carry on that conversation and take in the information they're giving you. Learning from your clients will provide you the chance to learn about areas you were never taught in school. The experiences, stories, knowledge, and creativity you may learn from your clients all stem from whether or not you are curious enough to learn from them, even when they are coming to you for professional services.

CHAPTER 18

Learn from Others in the Field

Help others and be kind. While this statement is an overall ideal philosophy on being a good person, it should apply to your clients and competitors, as well. As personal trainers, we are all in the same field and although we may be vying for the same clientele, that doesn't mean we can't help one another. Become the one who other trainers admire and want to emulate. As stated previously, respecting others is part of this occupation. Should you become aware or notice someone simulating you or your training style, don't be offended. See that as a form of respect and possible flattery of your ability.

As a novice trainer in my first professional job out of college, I was on staff with roughly 30 other personal trainers. Some knew what they were doing; some were there as a stepping stone to another profession; and others had a difficult time maintaining a steady client base. As with any job, some trainers were more successful than others. When you first get into this field, those successful trainers are the ones from whom you should instinctively want to learn. Pay attention to the little things that set them apart. We all learn roughly the same material in school and through obtaining certifications, but textbook knowledge is not the key to a successful training career. Interpersonal skills, creating and sustaining relationships, proving to be reliable and responsible, and money management skills will help elevate you to the next level. Becoming stronger in each of these abilities can be acquired through experience and by observing, studying, and interacting with reputable fellow trainers. Picking up on little things you notice other professionals doing well can be the big difference in having an abbreviated career or making a living in this field.

Notably, experienced trainers are ones who are always willing and open to learn new and better ways to assist their clients. This field is ever changing and although we may have established a routine that has allowed us to have success to this point, we must not become complacent. When we get stuck in a routine, we can oftentimes neglect our growth and become too cemented in our ways. Watching other trainers and picking up on their energy, skillset, knowledge, and coaching cues can bring us a fresh perspective, in turn helping move our clients forward. It is completely normal to compare your coaching styles to other trainers. Remember, different styles aren't a bad thing. Be open to observing and possibly using approaches of other trainers.. Our job is to help people lead healthier lives through the daily choices that we make. Allow learning from other professionals to be an acceptable choice you frequently make.

Have a sense of humor. Laugh. Smile. It makes everything easier and it may come off as cheesy but when you laugh and smile, it can sometimes set the tone for that workout for your clients (which can even carry out to the rest of their day). This one is short and sweet. There really isn't much to elaborate on. Oftentimes you will get to know your clients enough where you can read body language and the tone of their voice to sense that something may be wrong, but you really never know. When in doubt, lead with compassion and pride yourself in being understanding and empathetic. Kindness and putting a smile on another's face can help them in more ways than you may think.

CHAPTER 19

Be Around Those Who Make You the Best You

S urround yourself with like-minded individuals. That doesn't mean that you have to agree on every little subject, but you should align yourself with others that have similar drive and aspirations, as you will pick up tendencies of those with whom you surround yourself. If you always hang around people that are content with where they are in their personal and professional lives, you may have hit your ceiling. If that's what you're looking for in your life, great. There's nothing wrong with that. That ability to be content with what you have is a great quality. If you want to create something bigger and take the risks necessary to set yourself apart, find others that support that dream and begin working with them to work towards those aspirations. A rising tide lifts all boats. If you spend time around goal-oriented and motivated individuals, chances are that both sides will be elevated through that relationship.

Who makes you a better version of yourself? Who has repeatedly shown that they have your back, in good times and bad? Who has shown their true colors and opened up to you through trust and vulnerability? Who has pushed you to do better, especially when you have grown complacent? Who helps you by going out of their way to grab your hand? Those are the people you want to make part of your circle. Take 3-5 minutes to jot down who these people are in your life. Who checks those boxes?

Now, contact those people. Tell those individuals how blessed you are to have them in your lives. Write them a letter, thanking them for whatever it is they have done to help you grow. Call them and express your gratitude. Text them and say how thankful you are for their friendship. Nothing compares to hearing from someone and having them express how you have impacted their lives in a positive manner. They've done so much for you and maybe today is the day to return the favor by thanking them. Such a simple act could turn their whole day around.

The people who help us grow don't have to be in our field or even any related career. You may have an old professor, a parent, a sibling, or a friend who has always supported you, but you haven't touched base in a while. Just because you haven't talked in forever doesn't mean you aren't close. I am fortunate to live in the same city as my brother, Collin, so I get to see him on a regular basis as we are partners and work together daily at our business. My sister, Erin, lives much further away. Although we don't communicate as frequently as we probably both would like, we are closer than ever. Even though we are both crazy busy with our careers and personal lives and don't talk as much as we should, when we are with each other we don't skip a beat. As most siblings do, she and I used to butt heads growing up, but now we support each other and have grown closer as adults. Relationships evolve and change over time. Remember to treasure the ones which make you a better person and help you through life's ups and downs. Find your people, support them, and express how grateful you are for them helping you in your life.

CHAPTER 20

Consistency, Not Perfection, Will Take You Where You Want to Go

One big flaw which causes a misconception about living a healthy lifestyle is the belief that people need to be 100% perfect with every choice they make. As it relates to health and wellness, consistency overrides perfection in every single situation. Perfection is wrongly thought to be what is necessary to accomplish the certain health and fitness goals your clients may have. When in reality, all we need to do is instill minor changes to most people's current situation to live a healthier life and not become overly obsessed about eating super strict or working out every single day. Consuming less junk; integrating more real food (vegetables, fruit, meat, healthy carbohydrates and fats) into your diet; drinking more water; getting better quality of sleep; and moving a bit more frequently will get people on the right path. If we push our clients to be perfect on every single thing they attempt to do with exercise, nutrition, stress relief, sleep, and other slices of the health and wellness pie, we set them up for failure.

Through this overwhelming amount of pressure, we create this fictitious polarizing idea that if they don't adhere to the rules of thumb we provide, they are in the wrong. It's not always black and white, one side or the other. There is a lot of gray area where you can fall in the middle. Life isn't supposed to be only worrying about what you eat or how often you workout. These habits should be done on a consistent basis so you feel better, live healthier, are able to participate in the activities you enjoy, and not feel guilty for straying from that path.

Whether you are speaking of the client or the trainer, consistency is more meaningful than perfection. From the trainer's perspective, consistency is important in providing a dependable service aligned with what your clients need and want. Proving day in and day out you can be a steady, reliable staple in the lives of those around you, helps individuals take one stressor or question mark off of their plate. As a professional, you should never be late to sessions. You should rarely cancel out of the blue (life happens and there are going to be moments where you have to make a choice, but if this ever becomes a regular habit, clients won't stick around). You need to be reliable and show up prepared for each and every session. One of the main duties of our job is to help others with accountability. Some people will pay for us as trainers simply to have a steadfast source to help them stay on track and remain accountable. If we aren't reliable and responsible for the service we provide, it will be very difficult to create and maintain a clientele following that remains at your side.

From the client perspective, consistency is important. Clients need to notice improvements and continually progress at a healthy rate, without burning out by overdoing it or becoming frustrated because they are not doing enough. It is important we preach to them how consistency over time is more important than intensity of any given workout. A metaphor, used in *Chapter 68: Market Your Product as an Investment, Rather Than an Expense,* relates daily behaviors of someone working to improve their health and fitness to the stock market. This comparison elaborates on how, if you zoom in too close you may notice the market fluctuates daily, but if you zoom out, there are trends over time. The behaviors we create relate to this analogy because not every day will be perfect, but consistently doing little things in the right direction of which we want to be headed, will get our clients closer and closer to their goals. It may take a bit more time doing this, and may not be the alluring, quick fix response people want, but these behaviors create a healthier, more flexible path toward achieving goals. This consistent route allows for desserts to be enjoyed, drinks to be had, and days off from the gym because similarly to the stock market, there will be days that are 'red.' A red day or two will not negate all of the little steps done to get to this point. The importance of finding a consistent pattern that works for you and your lifestyle will help your clients actually accomplish sustainable results that will change their lives. This takes time, patience, and a lot of hard work. When people begin to understand they cannot immediately reverse the lasting effects of their previous habits and behaviors, but recognize they need to slowly start working in a different direction with guidance from you, their commitment to you will be long term. These clients will appreciate you helping them realize the importance of consistency. Everybody will be in a better, healthier place once they ascertain how to achieve a healthy lifestyle the right way, instead of crash dieting and doing a 60-day challenge every few months.

Regardless of your job, role, or position in relation to where you would like to see yourself, long and short-term goals are both important to work towards, although it can be difficult to stay on track for one while pursuing the other. We've all faced this dilemma in relationships, at work, and with our personal life. We have a grand goal we want to accomplish, but it seems so hefty and the path to accomplish that goal can be intimidating and overwhelming.

This is where the principle of SMART goals can play a role. SMART is an acronym that stands for **S**pecific, **M**easurable, **A**ttainable, **R**elevant, and **T**ime-Based and allows us to decide whether or not a goal makes sense by checking each of those boxes. To expand on each of the components of what a SMART goal looks like, we can further break down each letter of the acronym. Specific refers to using who, what, when, where, and why to show the direction in which you want to move this goal. Measurable gives some sort of metric that can determine whether or not that goal has been successfully accomplished or not. Attainable should act as a motivational detail to show that you have the tools and path to accomplish and achieve this goal. Relevant would refer to that goal making sense for what it is your large picture looks like. Time-based is setting some sort of deadline to work towards achieving that goal by.

Some people like that tool, while others prefer to go a different route. Personally, I have a generic goal of helping as many people as possible. It sounds cheesy and broad but through my daily regimen, with interactions outside of my business life, and through writing this book, my desire is to help provide others with a few simple tools to help make their life easier or their wants and desires much more possible. This book, for example, has such a wide range of sections with such different takes on a variety of areas so not every area may resonate with each reader but if I can provide a handful (or even one) piece of advice that helps provide a new perspective for others to take with them and apply to their job, personal life, or to pass along to others, I'll consider it a success.

When figuring out how to brainstorm, plan, and accomplish goals, consistency will be your best friend. Although there are countless ways to go about remaining consistent, one simple way that I've leaned on over the years, and specifically for the creation of this book, is through working backwards. We all have these grand ideas and goals that we hope to achieve. Rather than setting that and blindly shooting in hopes of attaining that end goal, I've found that through setting that goal but then detailing how to go about working from that end goal back to where you currently stand, you then have these checkpoints that allow you to pursue more achievable tasks while knowing that through following that thought-out plan, it will guide you to the ultimate goal at the end. Through setting that goal, strategically setting those minor stepping stones to check off on your way, and remaining consistent with the behaviors necessary to stay on your path, those once scary goals become much more within reach. That's how I went about writing this book. I knew what I wanted and what the end product would roughly look like. Working backwards from that, I then knew I had to have it published, edited, categorized, organized, free written, and had to come up with the different avenues in which I wanted to write. Having those tasks laid out ahead of me allowed me to work through the book with the end in sight but without becoming overwhelmed with how far that may have been out. In the process of writing this, I also knew that writing had to be done outside of training hours. My clients have always and will always come first. They are my top priority in this business. Writing was important but it was secondary to making sure my day-to-day business stayed at the top of its game. Because of that, I wanted to still make sure I responsibly stayed on top of progressing with this book so I would schedule out time slots within my schedule when I wasn't training others to be sure I created time to write. It made for a busy schedule but I'm so thankful I set aside that time to consistently work towards finalizing this project I wanted to accomplish so badly.

The same type of strategies can be used with your clients. Once they share their ultimate goals with you, it is your job to help them realize the process necessary to work toward that goal. The way you go about relaying these messages may differ from person to person. It isn't always about glorious, trendy catch-phrase goals that float around social media. Creating new habits to be more achievable is a simple way to start the ball rolling in the right direction. When we help our clients establish new habits and teach them how to sustain those, the habits will transform into newfound behaviors. For example, if a client is drinking four sodas a day, maybe start by helping them figure out ways to cut those numbers down. One suggestion would be to still have them drink one soda, while incorporating sparkling water or another alternative when they feel the need to drink something other than water. This won't be easy for them at first, but by slowly and consistently changing their daily regimen by providing healthier options, they will notice physical and mental changes faster. In return, there is almost a reward-mechanism that associates healthier habits with feeling better. When this habit is established and the client understands the benefits, those practices become new behaviors. Once those small behavior changes become second-nature through repetition and reaping the benefits from those decisions, they eventually evolve into full-time lifestyle changes. Once noticeable progress is seen, people recognize they are getting stronger and feeling better about themselves, and sleeping better. Other people in their lives may be noticing the by-products of these alterations, as well. Small, yet sustainable habit adjustments can transform into lifestyle changes with consistency and patience.

When we begin to work toward helping others change their habits in a sustainable way, it is important to not work toward too many goals at once. If we approach a client and tell them they need to go from working out once a week to four lifting days, two to three cardiovascular days, cutting out all junk food, only drinking water, and completely flipping life on its side, there is no way they are going to stick with that for a length of time. Success is about slowly incorporating changes to help people take little steps in the right direction toward pursuing larger goals. By repeatedly taking one step at a time, large, overwhelming goals suddenly become more attainable.

One visualization to use when getting caught up in the difficulties of day-to-day grind that can apply to your career or to the journey your clients find themselves on is to imagine climbing a mountain. To get to the summit of the hill, you take step after step after step. Each and every step you take gets you that much closer to the top. If you slip up a little bit, it doesn't automatically drop you directly to the bottom of the entire mountain. One step backwards does not negate all of your previous progress. One step backwards is normal. It happens. You know how hard you've worked to get where you are at this point in time and it is important to recognize that that one step backwards doesn't place you back at zero. One step "backwards" may even be part of the plan. The goal is to continue forward after your reversal. Figure out how to maintain balance. I eat ice cream. I eat pizza. I will have the occasional mixed drink or glass of wine. If you find yourself in a similar situation, don't feel guilty. Don't get frustrated. Stay consistent and keep your eye on the prize. Keep moving forward with one foot in front of the other, and you'll slowly, but consistently, continue advancing toward your goal.

CHAPTER 21

Regeneration

When discussed in a scientific context, regeneration is understood as the process of renewal and restoration of damaged or missing parts of the body (White et al., 2017). In plants or animals, this transformation can pertain to cells, tissue, organs, and even entire body parts of plants or animals. Some animals even have the abilities to regenerate or even regrow limbs or tails. As humans, we physically see our bodies regenerate through the form of hair and skin regrowth; healing bones; and scar tissue build up, aiding injured portions of the body. The body is truly an amazing thing and, when given the opportunity, it frequently delivers an incredibly adaptive response. People experience this adaptivity on a daily basis. When creating a well-rounded lifestyle by maintaining a full-time job, spending time with family and friends, taking care of tasks around the house, working out, and dealing with unexpected circumstances, individuals tend to constantly have their feet on the gas.

Being in the health and fitness field and trying to accommodate daily needs of our clients can have us trainers working from dawn to dark. We talk to people all day, prepare for sessions in advance, adjust on the fly, and provide our early morning clients with the same exact quality of product as we do those during regular work hours or late into the evening. It might be your tenth hour in the gym but it may be their first and you need to provide them with the same quality of service as you would anybody else. This can take a toll on us, mentally and physically, so finding a way to take a load off and focus on yourself is huge in long term success. To avoid burnout, it's crucial to admit when you need to regenerate your emotional, physical, and mental self.

Although it may seem counterproductive at the time, finding balance and allowing yourself to take your foot off the pedal to slow down will actually provide you with the regeneration and reboot you may need to continue living a high-performance life-style. Stressors are all around us. Nearly everything we surround ourselves with on a daily basis causes some type of stress on the body. Work, family, friends, school, working out, creating a healthy relationship with nutrition, planning for the future, and count-less other parts of our daily lives are actually stressors on us. Not all stress is bad, but when good and bad stressors pile up on one another, it can become overwhelming and create a setback for us. This is where regeneration comes into play. You shouldn't wait for that build-up to take place, but rather begin incorporating regeneration tactics into your regular routine to help even out stress levels and allow yourself to take a step back before becom-ing overwhelmed.

Regeneration allows your body to heal, regroup, and recover in order to continue in a productive manner for a longer period of time. Regeneration can be done and shown in such a variety of ways that are ultimately decided by the individual. As long as the activity is benefitting your mental, physical, and/or emotional recovery, you could consider it to be a type of regeneration. Some ways to incorporate regeneration tactics into your routine could include self-reflection, getting outside to walk and enjoy the fresh air, prayer and/or meditation, exercising, planning a trip away to physically remove yourself from work, and consciously putting forth effort to be present in the moment, instead of consuming yourself with work-related thoughts.

When it comes to health and fitness, it's easy to get wrapped up in the aesthetics of who looks the best, who lifts the most, or who is the skinniest or most muscular. In reality, longevity should be the centralized goal for all of us. Setting personal bests should be just that: PERSONAL bests. It should be you against yourself. Did you get better today? That may involve pushing yourself a little further than the last workout, taking some load off so you can improve your form, or simply feeling strong and confident in yourself to get through a workout without allowing a negative thought running through your mind. So many little decisions come our way on a daily basis. If we can get 1% better every single day and take action to consciously do even the smallest of things to better ourselves, over time those miniscule improvements will add up. In the future, that will allow us to look back and notice how much we've grown, all while simply focusing on little changes on a daily basis. It can be overwhelming to look at goals, which may seem unattainable or even scary, but instead of being turned off, take small, manageable steps to inch your way toward that goal. Keep that ultimate goal in the back of your mind, and focus on slowly progressing forward with one foot in front of the other. Before you know it, that big goal comes into view and is more obtainable.

In the fitness industry, especially with our clients, there is a common misconception that if we don't work out hard enough or sweat to the point of complete fatigue, we aren't being productive, which is not necessarily true. Although it is very common and normal to crave and chase the endorphins and exhaustion of a sweaty, physically difficult workout, that is not the most effective nor the only way to improve your health and wellness. Society has created a fictitious idea in our brains that if we aren't gasping for air and drenched in sweat, we have not had a productive workout. As fitness professionals, it is part of our job to rewire the thought process of our clients and teach them new ways to view their fitness routines. Productivity, when dealing with exercise and fitness, is so much more than highly-intense workouts.

When programming a client's workout regimen, an ideal goal is not to always have them lying on the ground trying to catch their breath. Sure, we do different versions of cardiovascular exercise to improve heart function and blood pressure and to strategically burn fat, but the goal is not to completely wipe them out. Align your goals with each of your clients' personal goals. Create a program that gets them to their goals in an efficient, enjoyable way. Will they accomplish their goals by next week? Probably not, but there are certain steps you can help them take to create a safe and comfortable environment so your clients continue to improve and enjoy themselves. This concept can help them establish a routine that ultimately guides them closer to their goals in a manner where they don't associate working hard and consistently with any negative connotations. This allows them to relish the process of working out. When you enjoy something, you tend to stick with it for a longer period. If working out doesn't become a burden, healthy behaviors continue and progress toward goals may be reached quicker. The extra bonus with this philosophy leads to adopting healthy lifestyle choices that can stick with you forever. A solid exercise program should be one that includes exercises, volumes, and intensities which reflect what you are trying to accomplish. The main key is to make working out fun. Put that on a t-shirt and help spread that simple message. Once you lose that enjoyment and pleasure, it becomes a difficult hobby to upkeep. The same goes for us as coaches. If we lose that enjoyment and passion in helping people through the realm of fitness, we will burn out and begin to dread waking up to train on a daily basis.

Another way to sustain longevity in fitness is to find time to self-reflect and regroup outside of the gym. Exercise and health are much more than just spending time in the gym. Improving your physical and mental health comes from what is happening on the inside as well as the outside. We all have different methods of slowing down and it is important to find what works best for you. Once you figure out your method, ensure you incorporate that on a daily or weekly basis so you find some balance in your world. Different forms of therapy, yoga, Pilates, or meditation are common types of regeneration activities, as well as reading, writing, setting time aside specifically for conscious reflection or prayer, and even allowing yourself to obtain proper amounts and quality sleep. The list goes on and on. You'll notice the majority of these exercises are focused on breathing and internal conversations with yourself. Your mental and physical well-being plant their roots between your own two ears. Creating a healthy space in your mind that provides you with a positive outlook on different situations tossed your way will allow you to thrive when it comes to your physical fitness. You will build confidence, focus on self-improvement, become an even better version of yourself, and create well-rounded relationships with those around you.

This ability to slow down, reset, and regenerate can be difficult to fit into our busy lives because we may not see it as the most important thing at that specific time. However, it is crucial in making sure we are spending time on ourselves, as it will help us accomplish more down the road. Before finishing this section, take a minute to sit back and think; really think about what it is you can do to allow yourself to press pause in your hectic life and provide yourself with a few minutes to an hour every single day to regroup. It doesn't have to be time consuming every single day, but consciously scheduling time into your routine to take care of yourself is essential. In this sense, it is okay to be selfish. We deserve to be the best version of ourselves. In order to do that and thrive in the long haul, we need to respect ourselves through giving ourselves the same time and effort we would for a relationship with a loved one.

Everything is now so fast and rushed that we sometimes forget about taking care of ourselves. We live busy lives and have become reliant on instant gratification. Because of such reliance on instant gratification, when we are faced with a challenge that takes time, patience, and effort to reap any type of benefit, it can be difficult to wrap our heads around why we would even waste our time. We must constantly preach to our clients they won't see changes overnight. They must be patient, work hard, and the changes will be seen after those behaviors are repeated for an extended period of time. Patience and trusting the process of a well-thought-out plan will provide us, as well as our clientele, with more long-term rewards. Find ways to regroup, reset, and allow your body and mind to become rejuvenated. We can only achieve as much as we allow ourselves. If we don't take time to take care of ourselves, we are setting a ceiling on what that limit is. Allowing time for regeneration will be a very temporary pause to your busy life so you have a chance to reset and keep moving.

*Take 3-5 min here to really think about what allows YOU to regenerate. Write those down and begin brainstorming how to actionably implement those into your routine. Why? Because you deserve the time you'll be giving yourself. We all do.

CHAPTER 22

Communicate and Create a Toolbox of Coaching Cues

L earn and utilize different coaching cues. Whether you are in the field of personal training, coaching a sport, or teaching a classroom full of students, it can be helpful to have a variety of ways to explain the content you are trying to get across to your audience. In this specific field, cues can be known as the explaining of words, physical adjustments, or verbal suggestions made by the trainer when a client is performing a movement. Communication between trainer and client is crucial to ensure there is a mutual understanding during exercise prescription, pricing, scheduling, and what the expectations are for both parties to cohesively work toward the goals upon which you agree. Communicating with one client may be completely different than that with another. In response to these situations, the way we coach and describe certain exercises may need to vary based on the client. What clicks for one client may not register for another. Just because a coaching cue resonates with one client does not mean the next person will be able to comprehend what you are trying to say. We may have been taught how to do exercises with verbal and nonverbal cues from our coaches, through research, and from educational resources such as textbooks, but we can always expand our toolbox of cues to adapt and adjust the way we speak, so everybody can equally comprehend what we are trying to get across.

Learn from other successful coaches in the field and get creative in describing and teaching movement patterns. We all learn differently and if we, as coaches, only know how to teach things one way we may have a difficult time connecting with all of our clients. Just like in the classroom, not all students grasp information the same. Some are more visual learners. Some have the ability to comprehend the textbook verbatim. Some simply memorize and can't apply it when it comes time to the exam. Each of us are unique learners and because of that, it is part of our job to be able to converse in such a manner where we can help each of our clients understand our exercise methodology. Because of how important it is to help people progress and remain healthy, we should pride ourselves in thinking outside the box, learning from other professionals, and coming up with creative ways to help other people learn in a way that best suits them.

Similarly to how we should individualize each client's program, we should individualize the way that we speak with each of our clients. We get to know our clients well and in such depth, therefore it is our job to utilize that knowledge to our advantage, verbalize with them in a way that makes sense to them, and create a mutually understood line of communication between parties. Using our prior knowledge of how our clients comprehend information and what they are able to easily connect to will help us formulate cues they are able to realize so they can properly execute any exercises we are trying to explain. This may require some trial and error and it may even fluctuate on a day-to-day or client-to-client basis, but when we find cues that work, make either a mental or written record of successful signals. Since most of our days are spent talking, it may be most valuable to jot down notes, especially observations that will benefit future clients and yourself down the road. It is incredibly useful to note certain cues as a reminder when you find yourself describing the same exercise down the road to someone else. Try to become regimented when it comes to writing down tidbits you may want to revisit in the future, by using the Notes App on your phone, or any other quick-access tool which may be at your fingertips while working with a client. Later on, when you have more time, you can go back and elaborate more fully on specific subjects or observations you may have noticed during your sessions. It's also good practice to write down things you need to do on a daily basis or even a checklist of tasks you want to accomplish. I not only write down cues I have personally used, but also cues I have heard other coaches use with their clients. This all comes back to recognizing that there is more than one way to get to a destination, and sometimes our way isn't the only or even the most efficient way. Learning from your peers and keeping an open ear to the way other quality trainers break down exercises can be a great asset to your growth as a professional.

So much of this job comes down to being humble, willing, and wanting to grow and improve your craft. When we think about the way we teach exercises and speak to clients, remember this may all be foreign to them. We may know our information and be extremely well-informed on a subject, but sometimes we must explain it as if someone has absolutely zero previous experience. Having the ability to understand or perform a concept or exercise is one thing. Being able to teach others how to do that or in a way they can wrap their heads around is the true test of comprehending that material. Some clients may have interest in learning about kinesiology, biomechanics, and anatomy in more depth, but the majority of your clients may simply want to be given direction and the occasional explanation of why we have chosen to do a specific movement. When they want to know why you chose a certain exercise, volume, or intensity, feel free to elaborate with more of a scientific explanation but put it in terminology to which they can relate. Obviously, if they have a background in a similar field, they may be able to speak your language, and in that instance, dive into things a little deeper and speak freely with a dialect you both recognize. Read the room. Understand how you should go about speaking to people based on the information given to you and with the prior experience you have with your clientele. This ability to connect with clients on a level they understand will give you more credibility, but most importantly, will continue to build and strengthen your relationship.

For novice lifters, cues can be the key to whether or not they understand how to correctly perform exercises. Technique needs to be stressed. Verbalizing how to perform a certain movement in a simple manner will allow clients to better understand how and why they are doing the movements you have chosen. Our bodies are all different. Our genetics are all different. Our mechanics are all different. Our knowledge and level of expertise are all different. Our goals are all different. There is not a one-size-fits-all, nor should there be, when it comes to programming or cueing. It would be ignorant to think everyone should understand and comprehend your cues, or that there is only one way to reach a certain goal. Become versatile in your coaching techniques to cater toward a much larger audience by proving you can connect and educate people from different walks of life.

To branch off of learning and refining different cues, we need to remind ourselves people learn in such unique ways. Along with the words coming out of our mouths, we must also pay attention to the volume, tone, and pitch at which we speak. So many conversations can be misconstrued, not because of what is being said, but rather how it is being said. Although verbal cues may be the most common form of explaining movements, we must also adapt and adjust all aspects of communication with our clients. Verbal cueing tends to help clients understand movements, when done in depth and with efficiency but non-verbal communication, such as your body language, facial expressions, and even posture or distance from your client can impact the effectiveness of your communication through your cueing. When we figure out a way to explain a movement, we must also understand the way we accentuate those cues. Showing how interested and invested we are with our actions can have an impact on the level of investment of our clients.

Even though you may believe your cues are concise and purposeful, your clients may view things differently. This is why keeping a clear line of communication open is vitally important in our profession. When you do argue or have different opinions, talk about it. Be empathetic about the other person but open your ears to hear, not always to respond. Learn why they feel a certain way. Acknowledge we all come from different walks of life and we all have gone through different experiences that have shaped our thoughts and emotions. Just because someone has a different opinion does not mean you can't connect with them or be their friend. In fact, it should be the opposite. You should use those differences as a unique opportunity to see that situation from a different perspective. Rather than blowing up at someone because they have a different outlook than you, respect their viewpoint and figure out a way to see things in their shoes. We all are guilty of reacting and judging others too quickly, when in reality, those who are different from us are by no means any less than us. They allow us to grow individually by seeing things from outside of our normal realm. When we learn to understand why others act and think the way they do, we can relate to them more. Don't be too quick to judge because more often than not, you and your clients are going to have more differences than similarities. Use those differences to grow and to learn more about them. Go out of your way to inquire about those differences. Learning the ins and outs of what has shaped each of your clients will not only allow you to get to know them to their fullest, but it will help you cultivate the type of environment they will require to get the most out of your sessions.

Communication takes work. Communication may not come easy with some clients. First and foremost, your job is to provide people with the tools necessary to improve their health and fitness. Along with that, the thing that will set you apart from other personal trainers is unmatched communication. Communication stems from trust and building a relationship. Similarly to the work your clients will put in to reach their health and fitness goals, we must put in that same amount of work, if not more, to communicate with each of our clients, despite our differences and do our best to put them in a better position to reach their goals. Through working to actively improve our communication, building up a toolbox of coaching cues, and applying those communication tactics and cues, we can really excel in our ability to connect with our clients, family, friends, and anyone else in our lives.

CHAPTER 23

Make Your Gym Feel Like Home

Personalizing the area you train in, as well as each training session, will help promote inclusion and provide a more comfortable environment for your clients. The most important point, obviously, is you should personalize your programming with each individual client, but we'll dive more into that in *Personalize Your Coaching for Each Client.* When attempting to establish an atmosphere of inclusion in your gym, think of the little things that can make each client feel at home. Providing the music each client enjoys at the volume they prefer, during sessions, are simple ways to set a welcoming/inviting/supportive/reassuring tone. Catering conversations toward each client's interests, while genuinely paying attention to their words invites an interactive, respectful climate. When Collin and I opened our own facility, we brainstormed ways to make sure we provided an environment where every single person who walked through our doors was more comfortable, less intimidated, and didn't have to worry about trying to fit in or prove themselves. We buy hair ties, so those were readily available if anyone ever forgets their own. We have feminine products in the restroom, for any unexpected needs. We stock the office with snacks, in case someone has not had a chance to eat before a workout or needs some sort of fuel. We supply cups for people who forget their water bottles. We put a goal board on the wall so people can keep track of their goals, and celebrate when those goals are met and increased. We hang all types of jerseys belonging to our clients and friends along the entire perimeter of our gym. These do not solely include elite, professional, or collegiate athletes. We want all of our people to know they have a special spot on our wall, to show our pride in their abilities. The invite to fill our wall brought in baseball, football, basketball, soccer, volleyball, and tennis jerseys and uniforms. We also have swim caps, dance team sweatshirts, and recreational league uniforms. Bring one, bring all.

One more detail that can elevate your gym, in the eyes of others, is by keeping it clean. It sounds so simple, but many gyms actually neglect their space, don't regularly clean their equipment, and have dust bunnies in every corner. This can be a turn off for clients. It may take 30 minutes to vacuum your gym space and mop the rubber floor every few days. There is more to cleaning a gym, but doing this simple task frequently makes a difference in the cleanliness of your space. In addition to cleaning the gym, equipment, and having cleaning supplies readily available to disinfect between usage, clean the bathroom. People do not want to use a dirty toilet with stains all over it. Restock the toilet paper and paper towels. Stay on top of this. Your clients will take notice, and you will prove to them that little details matter. These particulars speak volumes about you as their coach. It shows them that you pay attention to even minor details when it comes to their health and fitness. Nobody has ever complained about being in a gym that was too clean.

Are there things you can do better to continue providing a personalized service that exceeds the expectations of your clients? Absolutely. Taking detailed precautions and hearing their voices and opinions shows you really do care about them. Think of the things you have noticed that make other gyms, offices, or even homes feel more comfortable. Utilize those ideas to create a more inclusive environment at your gym. Continue to go above and beyond to personalize your area to make your clients understand your gym is their gym and their home away from home.

TRAINING

Depending on the trainer, client, their combined goals, and the type of facility they meet in, the experience for all parties can be so different, yet still yield such positive results. Every trainer brings a unique set of skills, education, experiences, and perspective to the fitness industry. All clients have individual goals, aspirations, prior experiences, and learning tactics. The space we train them in will determine how much or how little we have access to and how creative we must get in order to align the exercise selections with the goals we have set together.

Ultimately, the focal point of why clients work with trainers begins with them wanting to accomplish some sort of physical or health-related goal. As described in the *Personal* section, it is so important to connect with those who want to work with you in order to create a lasting relationship but unless you are also providing them with the physical results they are looking for, they could realistically seek out and find those relationships elsewhere at a lower price point. While dedicating ourselves to creating relationships, we must make sure we are eliciting the results people want. If we can combine an enjoyable experience with a strong relationship while progressively improving the way people feel and look, we've figured out the magic formula.

Our knowledge on the building blocks of kinesiology, the way our body responds to the stimulus we place upon it with strength training, cardiovascular exercise, nutrition, sleep, and other stressors, and how to relay that information in a way that resonates with our clients comes from different modes of education. Each of our educational backgrounds will differ. Most trainers tend to have some sort of degree in exercise science or kinesiology but some very successful trainers that I have known have business or chemistry degrees. Some trainers pursue certifications and other forms of formal continuing education, while others simply take matters into their own hands and self-teach through reading articles, seeking out new research, and shadowing experienced fitness professionals. Regardless of where or how you receive your education, know that because this industry is based in science, it is ever-changing and that requires us to adapt and learn alongside it. When we choose to continue our education through an assortment of avenues, it allows us to see so many different perspectives and how we choose to use that abundance of information as tools to help our clients is truly what matters in the end.

By educating ourselves, learning how to apply the information we learn, and tailoring each experience, workout, and plan of action to each individual client, we have the real opportunity to help our clients reach and exceed their fitness goals, as well as set them up for additional successes outside of the gym. At the end of the day, our field is a result-oriented business. If we are great at connecting with people but have no ability or interest to strategically and intelligently help them work towards their fitness goals, we aren't providing the service we promised. We can't be one or the other. We must take it upon ourselves to learn the information necessary to help others, connect with them in a manner that helps them open up, be vulnerable, and trust you to guide them towards what is best for them in their journey, and then apply what we've learned to piece together the most efficient and effective training plan for our clients.

CHAPTER 24

Why Do People Train With You?

W hy do people decide to buy into the idea of exercise, specifically with you as their coach? It may sound like a simple or even rhetorical question, but when we think about it, the answer usually lies somewhere within the range of a few of these areas: health, self-improvement/confidence, community, recognition, attractiveness/sex, and the influence of loved ones. We all have our own reasons and those reasons aren't always set in stone. Why you started working out and why you continue to do so may differ or evolve over time.

The simplest and most common answer to the prefaced question lands near a health-related response. Exercise has its obvious benefits of improving body composition, building muscle, helping our bodies move and feel better, and working our heart. Fortunately, there are many other health benefits that aren't quite as obvious. "Health" is a broad, but encompassing term that includes the mental, physical, and psychological outcomes stemming from exercise. Oftentimes, this definition seems like the "correct" answer when explaining your purpose as a trainer with clients or prospective clients. This is an easy answer. Yet, the real reason individuals may choose to begin an exercise regimen could lie even deeper.

In our business, Collin and I see a very wide range of ages, genders, and goals. When narrowing down to the topic of personal goals, there typically seems to be a deeper meaning behind each person's thinking. Many people, including myself, have struggled with confidence, self-belief, worry about what others think of them, and some sort of insecurity. The gym can be an intimidating place. At my own gym, a main pillar of training is to make the weight room a familiar place, where every person can walk into with confidence, feel at home, and know they will not be judged or put down inside of those walls. When we are able to help people feel that sense of belonging, the chances of them sticking around and continuing to show up day after day, week after week increases. When attendance increases, the hard work and consistency of your clients builds up and results begin to show. When it comes to training, it's crucial to have a pattern, a routine, a set of behaviors that allow you to live your life, while working towards what you want to accomplish. When people know your doors are open and they are at home within that building, routine is significantly easier to establish. Create a space where people can find comfort and enjoyment in the gym for the rest of their lives.

Whatever the reason for working out or approaching a trainer about working together, make your people feel part of the inner-circle. If they want to truly just improve their health and well-being, kudos to them. If they have a deeper meaning and they step into your gym with the desire to work on self-improvement, build more confidence, or become more "attractive" (whatever that means to them), be part of a community, gain recognition, feel better about their appearance, or to work alongside or set a positive example for their loved ones, make sure you support them in their quest. Their reasons may change throughout your time together, but with your encouragement, support, consistency, and intentional goal setting, clients will recognize the value of staying with your program for more than a few weeks.

CHAPTER 25

You Get Paid for the Value of Service You Provide

Although the old adage "Time is Money" is a valuable senti-ment, as a personal trainer, you must be aware that you get paid for the value of service you provide, not necessarily your time. If you provide a 60-minute workout, but it doesn't end exactly on the hour, don't sweat it. Preparing for and implementing each individual's session grants them the quality of service for which they are paying. Our training sessions are advertised as 60-minutes long, but in reality, some workouts may end earlier or even run over the time, depending on an assortment of factors that go into our planning process. As long as you are checking the boxes of what your clients are looking for, the final timing of individual workouts should not be a huge concern. That's not to say you should ever intentionally end sessions early, but if your estimated workout comes up a bit shorter on timing or runs over, do not panic or beat yourself up over it. Note the timing differentiation for future use, so you can better plan your workouts during that specific individual's time slot. It's an ever-evolving task personal trainers must attend to while trying to fit in what we want to ac-complish in our clients' workouts, while being most efficient with

PERSONAL. TRAINING. BUSINESS.

our time. Understanding that the flow of each workout depends entirely on a variety of factors, starting with each client's needs and expectations and how quickly they work all must be accounted for when planning your training schedule. If clients are used to cycling through exercises with little to no break, you can use that as an opportunity to educate them on why rest periods in certain scenarios can actually be beneficial. For those instances where it becomes difficult to get anything accomplished because someone may have shown up as a bit of a Chatty Cathy that day, incorporating workouts that require them to start on certain times of a running clock or with more definitive start and/or stoppages can be useful to make sure they are getting a workout in between their conversations. Use your best judgment with those clients because sometimes they may even enjoy the time spent with you more when they are able to vent and converse as opposed to doing a heavy workout that day. Obviously, you still want to provide them with a workout, but be strategic in how you structure their regimen so they can receive some of what they want, with what they need.

The same goes for the other side of the spectrum. When your training session concludes, do you rush your individual out of the gym or is it a cohesive environment where they feel that just because their allotted hour workout is finished they can still be part of the community? This is obviously situational and dependent upon prior obligations you may have after that session. However, if you have free time after their session is complete, what you do outside of that "hour" clients believe they are paying for can strengthen your relationship with them and can also be used as a chance for you to share some additional tips with them in or out of the gym. Again, the client believes they are paying you for an hour, but when you go above and beyond that time limit, it increases your value in their eyes. When that value increases over and over again, the return-on-investment clients get from your services improves. Your value goes up, their return-on-investment increases, clients tend to reap more training benefits, and all parties are satisfied. The way you make others feel, the quality of the training session/product you provide, and the way you serve others is more important than the time you spend with your clients. The quality and value of service is what people value and are paying for, not the time.

CHAPTER 26

Provide Resources For Your People

In the spring of 2022, Collin and I attended a virtual International Society of Sports Nutrition (ISSN) conference. This conference had some of the greatest minds in this field, including Jose Antonio, PhD, FISSN, Erica Goldstein, PhD, CISSN, Trisha VanDusseldorp, PhD, FISSN, and Nicholas Tiller, PhD, among several other very intelligent presenters. This was a day-long event, so we actually had to hop on the Zoom call while we were still at the gym on that Saturday morning. The guest speakers touched on a wide variety of topics related to nutrition and how it can affect exercise performance. Some of the topics were more relevant to us and our clients than others, but all presentations were noteworthy. After the conference was over, we compiled information gathered from the presenters and put together a laminated packet that we have sitting next to the front door of our gym. This grants our clients the opportunity to learn more about certain topics of personal interest from accredited professionals, any and every time they walk into the gym. Right next to the ISSN packet is another laminated resource with a page full of mobility exercises broken into different areas on the body. In referring to this resource that we created, our clients are able to find the area they want to work on and identify a recommended exercise (or grouping of useful mobility drills) with a suggested set and rep count for them. Strategically placing these at the front of the gym allows every client access to these extra pieces of information.

The goal is to educate and inform everyone who steps into the gym. The more information we are able to provide our clients, the better. Everyone learns in different ways, so oftentimes we need to get creative in order to get our points across. A few techniques that we use to help our clients better conceptualize what it is we are looking for include drawings on the white board and comparing videos or photos of before and after adjusting technique to a specific exercise. Neither one of us are particularly good artists, nor are we tech savvy but neither of those are required to help demonstrate and break down what we are discussing with our clients in a way that they may better understand those concepts. But if our diagrams, pictures, and comparisons help our clients learn and progress, then we should continue utilizing different modalities to help them retain that information so they can apply it at a later date. With our training service, we provide our clients with numerous versions of different content so they have resources available and at their disposal if they ever need them. If one person uses the materials and learns from them, that is a win. If materials go unused, so be it. It's beneficial to continue learning as the trainer, so you can take that information and pass it onto your clients and members.

CHAPTER 27

Educate Your Clients on the Reasons Behind Training

"Andrew is a great trainer and great person. His focus on proper movement and maintaining a pain free lifestyle is only exceeded by the quality of his education. He's not going to throw you into some cookie cutter workout. He's going to make you feel well, move well, and achieve YOUR goals. As someone who is also in the fitness industry, it's easy for me to recommend Andrew Seymour. He really knows what he's doing and more importantly, why."

Most people have a general idea of the benefits of regular exercise. Having an educational background provides us, as trainers, the chance to pass on in-depth explanations and reasonings behind the science of a successful workout routine. As you introduce an exercise to your clients, share the reasons why each movement may affect their daily lives or how it relates to their specific individual goals in the gym. Teach your clients about the impact resistance training has on bone density as they age, tissue resiliency, rehabilitation and reducing the chances of recurring injuries, hormones and confidence, getting out of pain, and decreasing the effects of aging. The majority of your clients want to utilize exercise as a tool to help them get out of pain and discomfort, look better, and feel better about themselves. There are so many more positives to the services we provide than just building strength so make sure you figure out what is important to each individual client and direct your guidance to them using those benefits as reasoning for why you're having them do what you prescribe.

Share with your clients your reasoning behind the programming you choose for them. Why did you choose front squats over back squats? Why are we performing pause or tempo squats versus regular speed? Why are we doing only four power cleans instead of 21? Why are we starting with lower weight than we usually do? Why does one client get to do barbell overhead press while another is currently doing landmine presses and a lot of overhead mobility drills? Whatever you decide, however you choose to create your programs, have a purpose and reason for doing so. Using your platform and expertise to tie your programming and the choices within each individual workout to your client's goals is crucial. You want your clients to buy into your program and if they understand the rationale behind the creation of your program, there is a better chance of them seeing true benefits and progression without getting discouraged. When they have questions around your program, answer them. Be honest. Tell them the science behind your program. Phrase things in terminology they will better understand. For example, when a runner asks why they do so many lunges and other single leg exercises while everyone else seems to back squat more, how do you respond to that? Do you have an answer? Since you would have knowledge of your client's physical ability, as well as limitations and past injury history, your response should be related to the client's personal goals. A reasonable explanation would include something to the sort of "because with your goals of running the Des Moines IMT

Marathon this upcoming fall, we want to be sure that we are strengthening both of your legs equally. When you run, you're spending the entire race on one leg or the other so preparing for that race by taking the time to work on single leg strength is huge in injury reduction and making sure that you are at your fastest and strongest on race day. This is also why we work so consistently on improving your ankle dorsiflexion and hip flexor strength. Ankle mobility and hip flexor strength directly correlate to injury reduction and improved performance for runners. Squatting is a great exercise and has so many benefits but for where we are at in your training and for you to stay healthy throughout your longer runs, lunge variations would fit better in this portion of your training program so you can perform optimally on the day of your race."

A snippet of one day of my client's strength training program for this exact position has been added below. Each and every choice from exercise selection, sets, reps, overall load and volume, and training frequency had been thought out and tailored to this individual with where they were in their training, what their goals were, and based on their body's abilities and restrictions:

Warm Up:

8/8 Toe Elevated Wall Knee Taps
20 Alternating Banded Hip March (band around mid-foot)
:45/:45 Band Distracted Foot Elevated Ankle Dorsiflexion
3x

Workout:
6/6 Front Foot Elevated Split Squat
:30/:30 Copenhagen Plank
4x

8 Chin Ups
:30/:30 Isometric Pallof Press
8/8 Landmine Twists
4x

Showing the thought and effort you put into each client's personal program will help them understand your long-term plans for them. This simple conversation of explaining your exercise selection can remind them that you do personalize each program with their goals and wants at the forefront of your mind. This proves intention and dedication to them and again, creates the possibility for them to further buy into the service you provide.

If you are just guessing or randomizing the workouts, you are doing your clients a disservice. They can Google a workout and get that. You have the education. You have gained, and are continuing to gain, invaluable experience. Use that level of expertise to prescribe an intelligently, well-thought-out program that makes sense for your client on that day in that phase of your program with them. If anybody ever looks at a program, whether it be theirs or somebody else's, you should have a reason for the direction you've chosen. Having a rationale for each detail of each workout is part of the product you should be delivering to your clients. Expanding on the reasons why you choose certain details of the exercise program can be a great way to improve the value of your service. Helping clients better understand the thought process and background that goes into the workouts you provide for them equips them with a better understanding of what their bodies need. Be cognizant, though, that not everybody wants to know all the nitty gritty details of why they're performing every exercise you implement with them. Share your knowledge, if your clients are open to such information. Pride yourself in backing your programming with science, rationale, and tailoring them to what it is your clients want and what they need.

From one trainer to another, know that it is important to provide your clients with more than just a good workout. You're being sought after, talked about, and pursued because of the experience you provide, the value you offer, and the way you make other people feel. From the minute your clients walk into the gym, to the door closing on their way out, their allotted workout slot should be catered specifically to what they need and what you've agreed to help them with.

Let's start by deciphering what makes a good workout. That is a very subjective phrase, so it does and should differ based on the individual. What we've been taught to separate a good from a bad workout by society isn't necessarily what qualifies a workout to be productive or unproductive. Again, this is dependent upon the individual and what they are looking to receive from you in your services., but when someone says they have a good workout, that looks different for everyone. For so long, it's unfortunately been characterized as a good or bad workout based on how sweaty, out of breath, or physically exhausted one is at the conclusion of a workout. There are still countless trainers and coaches who still abide by this philosophy and their clients and athletes are suffering as a result. If exhausting end results are the main goals of any exercise program, ask yourself whether or not that is the most intelligent way to go about helping someone else attain their goals. Individuals training this way will have more injuries. They will have more difficulty remaining consistent and enjoying their workouts year after year because of the constant maximal effort not quickly leading to sustained results. They may sweat more or even burn more calories, but are those factors indicative of the quality of workout? Burning calories doesn't automatically mean you'll lose more fat, gain more muscle, or accomplish whatever fitness goals you may have. There is so much more to a successful training program than that. Keep this mantra in mind: Train your clients smarter, not always harder.

That being said, nothing can replace hard work. Pushing yourself to new heights should always be rewarded, when done correctly and intelligently. Hard work is what will separate people. Those not willing to put forth the same effort cannot go unmatched with those who will. Hard work is a quality everyone should want to have. There is a time and place to push athletes to levels of physical exhaustion through hard work and determination, but when you do, be smart about it. Working the heart and entire cardiovascular system at a higher intensity does have an intentional place in training. It is a great way to push your anaerobic threshold and raise your maximum heart rate, so you can more comfortably perform at higher heart rates without experiencing the negative effects resulting from an inefficiently established cardiovascular capacity. Is this intensity recommended for people working with personal trainers in Suburbia, America consistently? Definitely not. Most people would benefit much more from less intense levels of cardiovascular exercise that emphasize more of aerobic conditioning because it is a more efficient way to burn fat, which typically is one of the goals of most of our clients. Working the heart at lower levels, with the occasional higher-intensity workout, can be a great way to continue to burn fat on a regular basis, while challenging the body (and mind) in a way of progressively overloading the cardiovascular system. Just like our skeletal muscle needs to utilize progressive overload as a strength-training principle, our heart needs to continue to increase volume, intensity, or duration to train for continued growth.

When we thoroughly think through the way we program for each individual, it is another way of proving our support, commitment, and using our resources to provide them with the best service we have to offer. Explain to your clients, in terms that make more sense for someone who's unfamiliar with this field, why you chose the exercise variation or intensity that you did. Use the explanation of your client's workouts as a way to lay out the plan, tell them why you chose what you chose, and how it applies to them.

Even those applications may be different. Let's take Bulgarian split squats, for example. These can fit in a variety of individual's workouts, but we can explain them in different ways to connect them to the goals of each individual. Even though they aren't the most enjoyable exercise, they're great for unilateral strength, balance, quad and glute muscular growth, anti-rotation (especially when holding only one dumbbell), and are a great overall, multi-joint exercise. Saying all of this to some people may not make any sense. Some people may simply want you to tell them how great it is for the way their legs and butt will look. Others may want you to explain how it can benefit them as an athlete because it helps them be strong on one leg, which is crucial because of all of the running, planting, changing of direction, and balance required in their sport. However you explain it, at least make sure you have a reason for choosing the exercises you did.

The reason why you do something is sometimes more important than the actual action taking place. Your intent behind exercise selection can help clients understand your rationale for prescribing those exercises. Explain the three energy systems used in different methods of cardiovascular exercise. Share how the simple strategy of resting between sets of strength exercises can refuel ATP and invite more energy in their muscles for the next set. Clarify how protein plays a role in muscle hypertrophy. Teach them how to adapt a workout when certain areas are limited for some reason. Give them numerous exercises they can perform with minimal or no equipment, so they can workout on vacation, with no access to a gym, or whenever their schedule allows. Disclose the importance of foot stability (you'll find a lot of people who have flat arches and foot stability can help create a sturdy base for any exercise). Justify the importance of posterior chain strength and postural mobility, especially for those who work in a sitting position at their jobs all day. Educate people on the reasoning behind also strengthening tight muscle areas instead of only stretching them. Divulge to your clients how steady state cardio may be a better option to align with their goals, as opposed to more modern fitness crazes of high-intensity interval training (HIIT). Sharing and explaining the reasoning behind each chosen exercise will better enlighten your clients of your purpose in helping them achieve their goals.

Each exercise you choose, each rep count, each number of sets, each length of isometric holds you pick should be backed with logic. People will call you out and ask why they have to do certain exercises or why you picked one exercise to be supersetted with another. Be prepared. Have a real explanation for your planning. If you can't think of one, maybe it's time to rethink why you're selecting the exercise you are for that person on that day so you can refocus on their goals and your role as their coach. Once clients recognize you are putting extra work in behind the scenes to build their personalized program, rather than showing up empty handed, their belief in you and your service will continue to grow. Be prepared before the session begins. Be prepared to answer questions. Be prepared to adjust as needed. Being prepared will show your clients you care and know how to help them attain their goals. These are exceptionally important attributes in our business.

One little note to add, especially to those who pride themselves in their educational approach to this industry: Stop making clients do so many burpees! Avoid using your workouts as a time to punish your clients. Burpees are often a filler exercise to elevate the heart rate of the individual doing them. There are better ways to get your heart rate going through smarter exercise choices, such as running, jumping rope, biking, skiing, rowing, and pushing or pulling a sled. If you want your client to do cardio, be smart about the way you program. You're well educated and should feel no need to do constant filler exercises. Take the time to provide a thoroughly programmed workout to better serve your clients.

CHAPTER 28

Produce Results

Get quantifiable results for both your clients and your business. Results don't always have to be scale or weight related. Body composition changes. Proper squats to full depth can be attained. Bench press weight amounts are added. A first pull up victory is celebrated. Enjoyment and confidence have been reached by simply showing up to the gym. Celebrate those little victories and recognize that growth is a reward for all of the discipline and hard work. Target your programming to help improve the health and fitness of your clients, but use those measurable results to remind your clients of how far they've come.

As with any fitness related goals, simply showing up to the gym can be the most difficult aspect of working out for some people. This can be especially stressful for clients when they first step into a gym for the first time ever or the first time in a while. When a new client starts training with you, make sure you pay attention to their comfort level. Walk around the facility with them to gauge their knowledge of certain machines or equipment. Introduce them to other trainers who they may encounter around the gym. Familiarize them with others who may be training at the same time as them or may be working out in the same class sessions. Listen to their needs. Find ways to make them feel like they not only belong, but they are part of the community and culture created in your gym. Feeling welcome, regardless of being at work, the gym, or in any group, can play a huge role in confidence, motivation, and commitment. Our job is more than programming workouts. We need to do everything in our power to create a culture where our clients feel comfortable working out, talking to us, opening up to us, and being transparent with us in all avenues of life. Trust between our clients and us is essential in building a quality relationship and ensuring compliance within the health and fitness aspect of training. Creating a relationship where both parties benefit and consistently complying with the program can be considered two of the most important aspects of working with a personal trainer. These two go hand in hand, as once you enjoy the process of working out, the dedication to bettering yourself, and you see results begin to come, it can be much easier to get on board with what someone is trying to teach you. Obviously, results don't happen overnight. Before those physical and mental changes begin to take place, we have to provide clients with an obscure product. This is where it is important to lay out your plan, discuss your expectations, and dive into the goals you have set together. People like having a plan, especially one which takes the thinking out of their hands and makes things as easy as possible on their end. It is our job to provide a step-by-step plan to keep our clients focused and refrain from overwhelming them.

Creating big, elaborate, life-changing goals are great and definitely attainable. However, for some, extensive goals can be extremely overwhelming. Oftentimes, people are deterred from making real progress because the changes they expect to happen take time and a lot of hard work. Working out consistently isn't easy for some, while cleaning up nutrition is hard for others. Battling the internal dialogue clients may be experiencing can become a challenge in itself. To alleviate any feelings of being overwhelmed or discouragement you may observe in your clients, first decide on a big goal together. Spend time working backwards to break that main goal down into little stepping stone targets. These smaller goals will feel more achievable and realistic to your client. Once each step toward the main goal is attained, it will provide for little victories in which to revel. Celebrating these little wins allows people to pat themselves on the back, and get ready for the next step toward the big goal. They begin to understand and better visualize how all these little goals add up, and recognize they are inching closer and closer to the greater target.

Applauding your clients when they eclipse these smaller milestones can help them when they may feel like they are in a rut. As trainers, we need to be cheerleaders. Not everybody needs or wants you to be the stereotypical cheerleader, where you are overly cheery and very jovial, but we all need someone to have our back. Being a cheerleader for our clients means we don't only get excited for them when they accomplish large goals they have set out to achieve, but also celebrate every small accomplishment. Drinking more water, finding ways to relieve stress at home or work, walking on a regular basis, prioritizing you ahead of always giving to others, or other exercise-related wins are all things that should be celebrated. These may not be major goals we set out to work toward, but creating and acting on little daily habits allow for us to live healthier lives and provide us with a better chance of attaining determined larger goals. One example that comes to mind is a gentleman I've been working with for a handful of years. He loves lifting heavy, with goals of eclipsing 400 lbs. on deadlift and 225 lbs. on bench press. He also has the goal of losing a certain amount of body weight for a variety of reasons. His weight loss goals became more difficult because of personal challenges he was experiencing. As a result of these road bumps and in recognizing this client's most immediate need for workouts to be an enjoyable part of his day, we focused on his weight lifting goal, so he could use our gym as a mental getaway. Lifting weights can be a good way to improve all sorts of overall health. We incorporated steady state cardiovascular exercise into his program to get him progressing towards his weight loss goal, even though to him rowing, walking, or biking aren't as fun as lifting some big weights. As it does, time helped heal some of this client's emotions, which allowed us to reshift our focus on the initial goals we had created together of still lifting heavy and losing a certain amount of weight. With most clients, you will find that once the stressors in life are lowered, they will be able to focus more on themselves and their intended goals in the gym. Fortunately, this client was able to expand his and his families' goals to include prioritizing their nutrition, incorporating at-home workouts into their weekly routine, and walking regularly. Less than four months into establishing and sustaining these little habits, he had already lost 15 pounds. Water weight and decreased inflammation from substituting out his regular processed snacks with fruit and nuts were contributing factors to this loss, but either way, the fact that he recentered his focus on himself and his health needed to be acknowledged. Those little habit changes he put into place, the dropping of body weight and the regained enjoyment in his workouts, were all applauded by me, as his trainer. We celebrated him getting back on a positive path in life. A good trainer can put together an exercise regimen that perfectly fits all of the pieces a client is looking for, but connecting with people and being a leader, while also guiding them in that same direction, even if the path isn't linear, is what makes a great personal trainer. Help your clients navigate their goals in the gym with the life they live. In a perfect world, every little area of each of our client's lives would go according to plan and everything asked would fall perfectly into place. But life happens. We all go through rough stretches with ups and downs. The perseverance from your clients, and having you as a steady rock in their lives, can be what gets them through difficult times and allows them to get back to who they are and what they want for themselves.

Revisit the importance of obtaining quantifiable results. These results can help people remind themselves of how far they've come. As trainers, we can use these promotions as a testament to the service we provide. For clients, but really anybody, seeing change can take some time. We see ourselves in mirrors every single day. From yesterday to today, we may not have physically changed all that much, but from a few weeks ago to today those changes may have been drastic. Tracking numbers such as exercise load or heart rate at rest or during cardiovascular exercises, not solely body weight, and taking permissible photos and videos can be great ways to remind your clients just how far they've come.

Unfortunately, when we think of improving health and fitness, for some reason our society automatically jumps to weight loss as the primary health measurement. Although the number shown on the scale does have some importance on overall health, body weight and BMI (Body Mass Index) are two types of dimensions that shouldn't be used as frequently as they are. Body weight is partially correlated to health levels, but doesn't take into account body composition and therefore, isn't the best way to measure wellness. In my years as a trainer, I have tried to preach over and over again that we shouldn't solely focus on body weight. The problem with focusing exclusively on weight loss, is there are so many more important factors to being healthy than simply how much you may weigh.

Weight loss can be a great goal for some, especially for those who have excessive weight and are at a higher risk of other health issues. Having too much weight can be linked to Type 2 diabetes, high blood pressure, heart disease, liver disease, kidney disease, and other dangerous disorders. For this reason, it is very important to remain at a healthy weight. Working toward losing weight can be a great starting point, but should not be the only factor of concern for people. At some point, your body finds a weight where it feels comfortable and performs at its best.

Aside from losing weight, another common health measurement is Body Mass Index (BMI). The Body Mass Index screening plugs the individual's height and weight into an equation, yet it does not give a full perspective of one's overall health. This type of assessment is (thankfully) becoming more and more outdated, as it does not take muscle mass into account while calculating. Because this only takes height and weight into account, a very muscular person who is the same height and weight as an obese person would have the same body mass index. This disregards all aspects of health because those two completely different people are clearly of different body types, even though they have the same BMI. BMI is beginning to be replaced by more accurate means of measuring, such as the use of Skin Calipers, Bioelectrical Impedance Analysis, Hydrostatic Weighing, BodPods, or DEXA Scans but the problem there is that some of those can also have their inaccuracies and can be difficult to come by, because of their availability or pricing. Although these types of tools can be used to create and understand statistics, depending on their accuracy and how much stock we put into them, they can be very detrimental to the health of the individual. Just because a tool to measure is popular doesn't mean it is always accurate. As it relates to BMI, the categories are underweight, normal weight, overweight, obese, and extremely obese. Think about the names of those titles. Would any of them make you feel good about yourself? The names are based on a mean amongst all humans. With our profession, we need to understand that people reach out to us for all sorts of reasons, and regardless of those reasons categorizing humans into BMI sections as the sole way to quantify their health isn't going to do anything but knock them down. Although some people are motivated through quantitative measurements, err on the side of caution and shift your thinking away from placing people in such categories. Do yourself and your clients a favor. Avoid using BMI and other potentially harmful health measurements if you don't truly believe they will provide any useful outcome to utilize in your programming.

That being said, a healthy body doesn't look the same for everybody. There are definitely some areas that can and should be addressed to help our clients become the healthiest version of themselves. As a society, we have created this skewed vision of a healthy body. Just because someone has visible muscle or a lower body fat does not mean they are healthy on the inside, as they may simply have low subcutaneous (surface level body fat) levels of fat. Some subcutaneous fat is healthy and beneficial, as it can control body temperature and act as a buffer to protect your muscles and bones. We should note that managing these levels is important in reducing the chances of certain health concerns, such as diabetes, heart disease, and other life-altering conditions. We have the ability to control this type of fat through diet, exercise, managing stress levels, and prioritizing sleep to help regulate hormone levels. Unfortunately, with how consumed our society has become over the way we look, we may not realize how important it is to also take care of our visceral body fat. Visceral fat is the adipose tissue that is deep within the belly cavity and surrounds our internal organs. Too high of visceral fat levels can also be cause for concern, as it wraps itself around the organs and can lead to health problems, such as diabetes, atherosclerosis, and heart disease. Fortunately, we can usually manage this type of fat through diet, exercise, and lifestyle. There are definitely certain factors outside of our control but if we focus on those that we have influence over, we give ourselves a good chance at finding and remaining at healthy levels of both subcutaneous and visceral fat.

Health is much more than the perception of an attractive aesthetic. We could look healthy on the outside, but our insides may sing a different song. Being healthy inside and out is so important. This is why we must emphasize the need for a well-balanced nutrition program for our clients to follow to parallel their desire to be healthy inside and out. When we can get past assuming someone is healthy based on how they look or what the number on the scale shows, we will be able to progress further into our health and fitness journey.

As with anything, if we zoom in too much, it's hard to see the bigger picture. For example, when we weigh ourselves every single day and base our mood, progress, self-worth, and belief in ourselves solely on the number staring back at us, our health begins to revolve around that number. In reality, somebody could notice drastic changes in muscle mass, strength, fat loss, body composition, athleticism, and confidence, not to mention other very important health indicators such as heart rate, blood pressure, cholesterol, and organ function while that number may not budge. Helping people understand realistic expectations of weight loss and the importance of using other methods to track progress is part of our jobs as personal trainers. Reminding clients that their quality of health is more than just their weight or aesthetic, and that patience is crucial to sustained success, are two main aspects of a strong fitness program. When not relying solely on the numbers of a scale, the fitness journey of your clients can be much less stressful, more empowering, and will take the mental anguish out of the equation.

Once we wrap our heads around the idea that one's health is based on more than their looks or weight, we can acknowledge that obsessing over the scale is an unhealthy behavior, which will allow us to find so much more joy and satisfaction in our everyday lives. When we get past shallow thoughts, we allow ourselves to open up to enjoying the little things. Coming to a trainer can be a very intimidating and uncomfortable situation, as more clients are taking on new habits and altering their entire life with that choice. It is our job to make the process as easy and comfortable as possible for them. Choosing the right ways to motivate each individual client and push them along can really help build their confidence, ensure their adherence to your program, and to ultimately allow them to succeed. Some constants we can always rely on to remind our clients of how far they've come include photos, videos, recycling previous workouts as benchmarks, and being there to cheer them along.

Photos can be a great tool to show clients the growth they've made. If your clients are comfortable taking pictures of themselves and understand they will be used in a motivational manner, that's a route to take. If pictures could possibly discourage your client and make them unhappy, avoid this approach. Regardless of the tactics you use to keep your clients motivated and progressing, make sure they approve of, and feel comfortable with them.

Photography can be great as a means of taking before and after shots and capturing them performing exercises, but sometimes video is an even better strategy. Taking videos of clients exercising, with their permission of course, is an effective way to help people better understand a correct technique and learn why and what we are trying to accomplish. Our job is to educate and teach people how to improve their health and wellness, all while guiding them along and pushing them when they need it. Utilizing videos has been extremely helpful in allowing clients to better themselves, as many people are visual learners. Videotaping an exercise, breaking it down, and analyzing it can be a helpful technique to teach clients how to improve their exercises to perfect form, get stronger, and avoid injuries. One of the other benefits of using video is you are able to slow down the motion, which may allow for you to pick up on something you might have missed in real time. This allows you to give feedback to your client through the use of a "cue" that could potentially result in a smoother and more comfortable lift. These videos can also be a great tool to remind clients how far they've come in the time you've been working together. Nobody moves perfectly every single time, although that is the goal. When clients get frustrated and have difficulty seeing their own progress, showing them old videos and photos is an easy way to boost their mood, keep them inspired, and remind them of how far they've truly come, even though they may not give themselves enough credit. Additionally, videos can be utilized to help clients understand exercises when they're away from you. For example, if you have a client message me that they are battling with a tight muscle or a minor ankle, we have the power to map out a rehab plan, write it on the board, and videotape ourselves performing and walking them through those exercises so they can have some tangible material to put to use to help them work through whatever they are dealing with. Over time, we can create a library of these exercises to recycle and reuse or we can continue to personalize the videos and send a more individualized video to each person as that situation arises. Videography and photography can both be useful tools to help our clients in so many ways.

Another tactic to remind clients of how far they've come in their health journey is to teach them and help them understand the concept of progressive overload, while also knowing when it is time to back off. Progressive overload is a principle that essentially involves continually pushing the musculoskeletal and cardiovascular systems in order to eclipse previously attained levels. This includes increasing the intensity in one way or another in order to continue getting stronger or better at whatever task you are attempting. With progressive overload, you will oftentimes see programs created with the same exercises week after week, with simple adjustments, typically seen through increases in weight and decreases in reps in order to get stronger. This can be a productive means to build strength. However, remember every program should differ, based on the client's goals, capabilities, and commitment levels. Set up your programming on a week-to-week basis while still keeping the client's end goal in mind. People vary so much from week to week. Their workouts should be adjusted based on how they feel, what stressors are in their lives, and other factors, which are not taken into account when planning out weeks or months at a time. Pushing people, in an intelligent way, may not always mean you have to up the weight from the previous week or jump to a significantly higher intensity. Sometimes what clients need is to have a deload week or higher volume or even a mobility day because certain things are going on in their lives. As your client's trainer, you need to make adjustments to keep people on track without pushing them too hard on days they may not need to have highly intense workouts. The majority of clients are people who have families, work full time jobs and most likely have many added stressors in their lives. This is expected. Exercise is a stress on the body, as well. Many don't view working out as a type of stress, but any additional force placed upon the body or mind can elicit stress. Stress isn't always a bad thing, as there are clear and obvious benefits to a healthy, thought-out training program. Just remain aware that the stress of exercise, with someone who is full of other stresses, could actually become a setback to their health and fitness goals. It is our job, as trainers, to seek out when people need a less intensive day, which could make them feel less overwhelmed when they leave the gym. Conversely, when you observe the client may have pep in their step, this could be a day you push things a little more. Reading your clients and being transparent with them through trust and conversation can help you recognize when you need to call an audible to switch things up on the fly.

Using a day to take a step back may act as a way to move forward. To some, easing up on a workout may seem like an unproductive use of their paid hour. Yet, it is our job to educate about the importance of listening to our bodies and rewarding them for what they crave. Don't confuse this statement with what the mind craves. We may feel guilty for not working out or pushing more than we normally would, but if our body is feeling beat up, using a day to limit ourselves is a way to step back in order to move ahead. This conversation may be one you have on a regular basis, as so many people enjoy the concept of pushing themselves to the point of complete exhaustion. Although you may be drenched in sweat and gasping for air, you may not have done your body good. There are definitely times when it is important to push yourself to the limit physically and even using hard workouts as a mental reset, but figuring out when to utilize those types of workouts is important in our growth in the gym. It's important to realize the truth behind the phrase "learn to live another day." Or, in our case "learn to lift another day."

When you do use workouts to push yourself and test your abilities, it can be fun to recycle former workouts, or benchmark workouts, as a means to compare to what you've done previously. This can be another great way to remind clients of how far they've come, especially when they're having a difficult time in between the ears. The use of quantifiable results allows you and your clients to realize the progress you've made, especially on those days when it may not seem like things are going in the direction you want. Whatever you and your clients decide are the best ways to measure growth within their workouts, use those as ways to remind them where they are, how far they've come, and where you're ultimately headed. Seeing visual and physical jumps can keep people on track and remind them of the results they've already attained, to avoid them becoming frustrated and fading away.

CHAPTER 29

Some of What They Want, Some of What They Need

Help your clients understand that good training isn't always the fun, sexy exercises they see on social media. Exercises can feel repetitive and boring, but those are the best ways to stay pain-free, healthy, and obtain sustainable results. Now this doesn't mean we recycle and reuse old workouts over and over again, but rather create a main focus on a handful of exercises (generally multi-joint exercises) and use accessory exercises to help supplement. These accessory exercises are where you have a little more freedom to get creative. If a client wants to try out a new exercise they saw on social media, by all means let them try it, but attempt to incorporate it into the session in a thoughtful and constructive manner. We have clients who want to try new things, such as learning how to do the splits or walk on their hands or do a bar muscle up. We would almost never program these into a workout for most of our clients, but if they have a desire to try a new exercise, we can find time at the end of a session to help them achieve their new goal. When it comes to training, try to stick to the motto of giving your clients "a little bit of what they want and a little bit of what they need."

That being said, there is a time and place to do a lot of what people want and very little of what they need. Some individuals enjoy a good bench press and arm day. Some people love a hip thruster, glute circuit, and core workout. Is that exactly what they need to stay aligned with what their goals consist of? Possibly not, but if they really want to do it and it completely makes their day, throw them a bone here and there. Have some fun with them. Make sure you have your sessions that make the most sense for the goals at hand. Imagine being somebody who dreads performing upper body exercises and really likes the way they feel after doing lunges, hip thrusters, banded fire hydrants, reverse hypers and then a long burning ab circuit. If you were that person, and you walked in the gym doors after a hard day to find your trainer programmed everything you enjoy with nothing you don't, your mood flips 180 degrees. The deep burn in the stomach from doing flutter kicks, bicycles, and hollow rockers may not be as effective as some Pallof presses, suitcase carries, hollow body holds, and stir the pots, but chasing that satisfying burn is what some people thoroughly savor. Enjoy. If that is what keeps them loving your workouts and also allows them to still progress in the gym, what's the harm? We see it all of the time. There are the best exercises for building a certain muscle group or the warning that you should never do this specific exercise, but at the end of the day, there are no perfect or terrible exercises. There are smarter ways to go about programming for people based on a variety of factors. Even though social media may tell us differently, there is no perfect workout. The better way to view this concept is to acknowledge there are individual workouts that might be best suited for each person. Every single detail of the workouts we program should be connected to each individual client for one reason or another. Some of those reasons may be scientifically backed to serve a purpose toward strengthening a weaker link in the posterior chain, for example, while other reasons may simply be that your client wants to get an arm pump on a Friday afternoon. Find that balance and learn to realize when to program what people want and what they need.

CHAPTER 30

Progress is More Important Than Perfection

Progress is more important than perfection. This is a great statement to continually remind yourself and your clients of. Not every day will be perfect. Not every workout or meal will be perfect. Allowing some guilt-free flexibility within your routine, as long as you stay on track by putting one foot in front of the other in pursuit of your goals is much easier and significantly more manageable than expecting perfection day in and day out. Perfect reps, perfect execution, perfect nutritional choices, and the perfect mindset are all good in theory, but in reality, not feasible. Repeatedly emphasizing that consistency over time overrides short-term or temporary perfection can help engrain that progress is more important than perfection. It is important we push this narrative, but also follow through on our actions and reactions when people stray from the course. We cannot punish imperfection because that instills a fear component that creates a definitive line of belief that if you're not perfect, it's failure and you're imperfect. That belief isn't true. Progress is not black or white. There is some gray area accounted for as part of the plan, so people are allowed flexibility. Being able to remain cognizant of your long-term goals as a way to motivate yourself to implement the necessary steps required to achieve those with the understanding that you will have to remain consistent and continually work hard will get you further than chasing perfection. This goes against every narrative of fairytale sport movies about only accepting perfection, but in the real world, consistent progress will take you to much higher heights than short-term perfection.

CHAPTER 31

Personalize Workouts but Find a Framework That Aligns with Your Style of Training

Formatting workouts is a topic that creates great discussions amongst trainers and strength and conditioning coaches. What we all learned in basic strength and conditioning courses about exercise prescription was they should include type, frequency, intensity, and duration. You will discover there are so many different ways to format your workouts for each individual client. As your career takes shape, so will your exercise prescription format. The substance of each workout should be individualized. Creating, adjusting, and settling on a framework to format your workouts should allow you to be efficient, timely, and set your clients up for success. Once you have settled on a framework that suits your personality and needs, it will be helpful to stick to that for the majority of your sessions. For instance, if doing a resistance training day for clients to sustain a most efficient workout, stay energized throughout, and accomplish their physical goals they are focused on, you could break the workouts into three portions.

I would suggest starting with a warm up that concentrates on preparing the muscle groups you will be working, getting some mobility at the joints that will be utilized, and get some blood flowing through core, lighter loads of your main movement, or some sort of cardio machine. Following the warm up, it is time to dive into the meat of your workout, which tends to include the exercises that elicit the greatest stimulus, whether that is a multi-joint lift, such as squats, or an Olympic lift, like snatches. By having your main exercises earlier on but after you have properly warmed up, you will likely get the most out of those exercises while having the most energy available because they require the most focus and attention. After that segment has been completed, it is a good time to sprinkle in your accessory or assistance exercises, such as single-joint exercises, additional trunk and core work, or some areas that need extra improvement.

If we dive further into the makeup of each of those portions of a workout, we can better understand why I like structuring my workouts in this manner. As for warm ups, think about more effective ways to warm up your body for an individually-tailored workout than running a few laps, doing generic static stretches, or hopping on the bike for five minutes. As a field, let's be more conscious about the precious time clients are paying for and provide them with a warm up that better fits their needs. To provide clients with a well-rounded warm up that makes sense for them, include about 6-12 minutes of exercises focused on activating and getting the muscle groups moving that will be utilized for our main portion of the workout, along with some core work, and/or some mobility. For example, if I have somebody front squatting, we would do some sort of single leg quad work, toss in a Copenhagen plank, some thoracic spine and latissimus dorsi mobility drills, and some band distracted ankle dorsiflexion so they should feel prepared to front squat while feeling loosened up. These chosen exercises should not be overexerting clients before the focal point of the workout. The exercises selected for that warm up should be

100% based on the individual in that session and should be specifically catered to what they need to get their body feeling best. This will vary person to person. While working with somebody new, take note of what works best for them, what areas in which they struggle, and how much is too much for a warm up so they aren't wiped for the meat of the workout.

After our warm up, we typically stick to one main lift that tends to provide a high bang for their buck. Squat variations, hinging, horizontal or vertical pulling and pressing, Olympic lifts, or lunge variations tend to be the main categories I choose for a lot of my clients as their main lift. Having one of these choices as the focal point of our workout is great because, assuming they are properly warmed up, they will be prepared to maximize the benefit these multi-joint exercises provide. These choices will elicit the most change, require the most concentration and focus, and challenge us in many ways. At this juncture, we want to make sure we have them at a point in the workout when they are fueled, prepared, and not overly fatigued. At times, you may choose to superset that main lift with some sort of core work or an antagonist muscle group. Pairing an exercise with your main lift can again provide you with more bang for your buck, but that should depend on the person, their goals, and if that decision fits what they're looking to accomplish through your programming.

The final portion of a sample strength workout would be accessory movements. Pair or even group these together as a superset or in somewhat of a circuit style of training where all of the movements are completed, and then rest is taken before starting the next set. Before moving to this step, take note of your client's ability and activity level. You may notice that after the main lift is completed, clients tend to be a bit more tired. Piecing together a few exercises that complement each other well and align with the goals of the client, can check the boxes of the needs and wants of the client while not burying them into the ground by making them work overboard. This is also a good time to sprinkle in exercises that work muscle groups your clients really want to focus on. If somebody wants to have more definition in their arms or glutes (which are both very common requests), give them fifteen minutes of biceps and triceps or a hip thruster, starfish plank, and banded fire hydrant circuit. Those are all useful exercises. If it makes your clients enjoy the workout a bit more, while getting stronger, and doing exercises they look forward to, don't be afraid to do that here and there. They will appreciate it, and you never want to lose sight of enjoyment in the weight room.

This three-portion style has proven to be a good strategy to get people moving, feeling better, lifting some good weights, and enjoying their workout. Obviously, there will be fluctuations and some workouts will differ, because not every workout is strictly strength training. With my background in strength and conditioning, I believe that depending on the client there should be a balance between strength training and different types of conditioning to help them optimally obtain their health and wellness goals. Unfortunately, sometimes people in our industry forget about the second half of that pairing, which is crucial for athletes and general population clients. Conditioning can be accomplished in many different ways but for the general population, mixing in regular cardiovascular exercise that includes steady state, interval, and higher intensity options can be useful in progressing them towards their goals and expectations. Cardiovascular exercise is a big part of our training prescriptions too because of the amazing benefit it provides as a base for all exercise. The physical benefits include working our heart, decreasing the chances of certain diseases and conditions, decreasing cholesterol, as well as being an aid to fat loss. This is why communicating with your clients is a crucial piece of your programming. Some days, for some clients, are deemed as cardio days. Some clients do more cardio on their own, while some clients are given little bouts of cardio on a more regular basis in our workouts. It all depends on the person and what we set as our goals with each other, as well as the accountability that they need to do it. Some people love it. Others hate cardio. Finding a way to get it in for those that need it but don't enjoy it can be difficult. Be strategic in your style of making them work on their cardiovascular exercise because it is so important for each and every one of us to incorporate it into our routine.

CHAPTER 32

Adapt Your Training to What Your Client Needs

"Andrew is extremely knowledgeable across all aspects of health and fitness. He has helped me with my rehab that had previously kept me out of the gym. Now, I am able to perform workouts tailored specifically towards improving my individual areas of weakness."

As your career lengthens and the relationships you create with your clients become stronger, you'll begin to notice some individual's sessions may evolve into a different purpose. When programming for each person, we must take into account what their health and fitness goals are, but we also need to account for what is going on outside of the gym in their lives. Are they overly stressed with work? Do they have family problems or a sick loved one? Are they high on life and everything is going their way lately? Thinking about outside factors can help you program in one direction or another. Some workouts need to be toned down if things are negatively impacting or wearing on your clients. Some workouts need to be adjusted up to match the energy or bump up the intensity if people are feeling strong and full of enthusiasm.

Some workouts need to be adjusted on the fly based on certain factors that may come to light as a session progresses. It is our job to have that internal dialogue to make sure each client's workout checks the boxes of what our people need in a given day.

Programming, just like your clients, should differ based on their goals, genetics, drive, and other factors. People are unique; therefore, their workouts should be too. You are paid to help clients accomplish certain goals. When you zoom into what that looks like on a daily basis, it includes personalized workouts each time you see them. Avoid cookie cutter programs. Understand that putting individuals through a cookie cutter program made for the masses is not the best use of their time. Are you making the most out of the hour together, or are you wasting their time/money? Clients are spending a great deal of money for a high-quality service. They not only deserve your time in the gym but also your time out of the gym where you are putting forth the thought and effort that goes into programming their workouts. If all you provide is a cookie cutter program for them, how is that going to help them reach their goals? Keep notes of each client with the different exercises they like and in which they want to see progress. Also, identify pre-existing injuries or areas of concern. Keep these notes easily accessible, so you can refer to them while setting up your programming, as well as quickly before or while working with clients. This allows you to add in exercises to help rehab from injuries, prevent future injuries, all while still giving them the product they deserve and helping them reach their goals in the most efficient way possible.

CHAPTER 33

Personalize Your Coaching for Each Client

"SHF has always prepared individually tailored workout plans for my goals. They truly adhere to the "one size does NOT fit all" and make sure you are getting what you want and need in a program."

Figure out what your clients respond best to and what keeps them motivated. Some people respond better and demonstrate repeated behaviors on a more regular basis when striving to accomplish quantitative goals or specific goals. For those people adjust your coaching and be sure you check some of those boxes to help keep them involved, interested, and invested. This may be shown as keeping track of certain maximum weight numbers, cheering them on as they try to reach 10,000 steps per day, or supporting them as they go through the process of tracking their food. Make note that all of these are not necessary to sustain success in the gym or in our lives. If your concern is always getting 10,000 steps just to say you got your 10,000 steps, it might be time to revisit the reasons why you set your goals and decide if those reasons make sense for what you're trying to accomplish.

That being said, if somebody performs better and remains more accountable when you tell them to reach for a certain number of steps, keep track of their food, or base your workouts on their one-rep or three-rep maxes, do so. That should be subjective and used as another tool to help keep your people satisfied with the results they're achieving as well as the service you're providing. Each little accomplishment and victory lead your clients more toward attaining their goals.

The same goes in the other direction. Not everybody needs those numbers or that quantitative data. If they don't, use other methods to help keep them accountable and ensure they stay on their goal track. In the past, I've found success in helping with accountability in many ways. One way is by having clients write down their goals and then the necessary actions they'll have to take to get there. Another good accountability measure includes inviting clients to send a photo of their meals to me to simply get them to be more conscientious of what they're putting on their plates. My clients have also sent me a checkmark after doing their at-home workout, run, or yoga class to make them feel a sense of belonging. This helps them be honest with me and themselves of what they're doing to work toward their goals.

The key is tailoring your coaching and programs to the needs of your clients. Finding different ways to reach your clients is another training method that will allow you to really connect with them so you can be the best asset to their health and well-being. Either way, it is important to figure out what matters to your clients and relate their progress in the gym, kitchen, and between their ears with their true reason for working with you. Reconnecting your clients with that golden nugget reason of why they're working as hard as they are helps them be consistently reminded of their ultimate goal and refrains them from becoming discouraged.

Having something to look back on and have some sort of measurement or recognizable change from then is helpful to remind ourselves that even when we get discouraged or find ourselves plateauing, we are still trending in the right direction. That measuring tool may look different for each person but it is our job as trainers to find out how to utilize that to keep our clients happy with what they've already accomplished, while also striving for what they want to tackle next.

It is part of our job as hired fitness professionals to assert ourselves into the lives of our clients to ensure that they are consciously making strides in the right direction, in and out of the gym. We have to be strategic on how we go about this because some clients have different needs and responses than others, but it is our job to help them help themselves. Being a leader in this field requires us to provide others with the tools, resources, and support to find the type of success they are seeking out. In coaching each individual, we need to set boundaries, dependent upon each person, that allow for some leeway and room for error, but ultimately push them to long-term improvement. One of the best ways to help others is by educating them, understanding the expectations each of your clients have for you, which may differ depending on the client, and through empowering them to use the tools and confidence we help instill in them to apply those areas to their lives. This doesn't happen overnight. This tailoring can be subjective based on who you are working with, but until your members and clients are ready to take that next step of accepting responsibility with the tools you've given them, you must lead through asserting your theories and demonstrating how to best carry those out. For example, as it relates to choosing to make healthy habits outside of the gym, we all know how important it is to establish healthy behaviors the other 23 hours not in the gym. So, you can guide your clients in the right directions by showing them what you do and how to make those choices easier. By being transparent and honest about what we do as trainers, the difficulties we actually have ourselves, and how imperfection is part of the process, clients can better wrap their heads around the process being more manageable and not as intimidating. Through you adding in those little suggestions and being a good source of guidance and leadership, you can show your clients more efficient ways to create and sustain healthy habits, which can lead to business retention and better results for our clients.

Remember that for some of your clients, their hour with you may be the highlight of their day. Ultimately, planning and programming this hour is up to you. You get to decide how invested you want to be in your clients, in and out of the gym. Whether you're providing them with a good sweat, lifting some heavy weights, or just being good company so they can enjoy spending time away from the craziness of their world, you may find that most people genuinely look forward to seeing you. Remember this, especially when you may be having a long day or are dodging distractions in your own life. It can be hard to set those aside for the moment and it's a very selfless thing to do because your mental health is important and should not be discredited. However, making each individual hour spent with each individual client tailored to be all about them will put your quality of service at the top of the tier within your community. For example, as I'm writing this, I have 13 hours of clients and a business meeting to attend. My 5:00 am session should be just as personalized, attentive, and high energy as my 7:30 pm session. Both people should receive equal and individualized care. Continue to put your people at the forefront of your service, and they will continue to look forward to being with you. Do what you have to do to make each session a highlight in their day. Be prepared, be conscious of your thoughts and word choices, and bring positive body language to each session. These are all nonnegotiable. If you control each of these, your clients will recognize you are there for them and their needs. Take pride in serving others with the top product.

Providing that top product and tailoring each session looks different for each trainer. To me, it looks like setting a few hours each weekend aside to program for each individual that upcoming week. Thinking about their goals, the way their body and mind have been feeling lately, as well as what our previous workouts consisted of and how they responded to those all contribute to building a framework for each individual and all of their upcoming sessions. Typing these plans into my phone, then transferring them onto our big white board at the gym lets my clients see what they will be tackling. This also ensures I don't have to pull out my phone to check the workout details. Preplanning and being prepared will avoid you from appearing scattered and trying to make up workouts as clients are walking in the gym. Personalized, thought-out programming, adjusted based on a variety of factors progresses clients further toward their goals.

After workouts are all planned out and written on the board, it comes down to the intricate details of the training session. Begin each session with personal verbal interactions with the client. In other words, start with friendly conversation and create a space that allows them to recognize that you're interested in them and what is going on in their lives outside of the gym. Recalling details about each person and catching up on their lives by asking questions about areas of interest, invites them to feel more comfortable in conversation. When speaking, do so with respect and make sure you read what your client is saying and meaning. As we are professional business people, it's recommended to watch the language we use around our clients, especially children. Avoid swearing or using inappropriate words when clients are present. It's best to NEVER listen to music that swears when you have kids in the gym. They will learn those words at some point, but it doesn't need to be from us. If they want a certain type of music that typically does use vulgar language, find a clean version of those songs and play that playlist. Everybody wins. Other than that, it can be appealing to cater your music to what your clients prefer. By making them realize the entire session, from the workout selection to the music to the time of day to the business of the gym, is all about them, they should feel right at home in your work environment.

The hours of a personal trainer can be long; therefore, you are going to get tired at times. Figure out what helps perk you up during your training sessions with clients. For me, I drink coffee in the morning and plenty of water throughout the day. Water keeps me hydrated, giving me a reason to go to the bathroom between clients. That small break has been a good tool to take a breath between training sessions. It may not seem like much but getting out of the gym area, even for two minutes, taking a few breaths, resetting to be sure you're attentive and present for your next person, can do wonders for your self-care and for the product you give your client. Clients will respect your need to visit the bathroom before their session starts, so utilize this opportunity to give your mind and body a brief reprieve from work. Small breaks between client workouts are important in making sure you stay on top of each session and bringing out the best version of yourself.

Stay engaged with your body language during training sessions. Your body language will tell people around you much more than your words sometimes. Lean toward clients when they are talking, to assure them you are engaged and listening. Align your posture in a way that demonstrates you are present and active in their workouts. Avoid slouching and keeping hands in pockets, as that may send the message you are not excited to be working with the client. Keep a respectful distance, but be in close proximity to guarantee your assistance with any proper technique, heavy lifts, or handing them equipment for a new set. Express enthusiasm through hand gestures, high-fives, and other ways natural to you to show a human connection. Smiles and eye contact are two other ways to enforce positive body language with others in the gym. Being present and professionally engaged with your clients through your body language goes hand in hand with preparing and planning for each individual's session.

These all may seem like small details, but by controlling each of these variables, we can provide the best service to others. When we do that, there is a good chance clients will thoroughly enjoy their workouts. That is a double-doozie. If they work out with you and enjoy the time spent with you, their process to accomplish their goals speeds up, their intrinsic motivation improves, your relationship strengthens, and client retention rates are maintained for your business. Intentionally try to make each session enjoyable for each person, and everybody will win.

CHAPTER 34

Be Coachable

Be coachable. Unfortunately, when some coaches reach positions they want to be in, they perceive that as a certain hierarchy and view themselves at the top. First off, viewing your position of leadership as a position of power evokes the sense of solely wanting to be in charge of others. A solid personal trainer should help lead clients in the direction they want to go. BIG DIFFERENCE. Be a servant leader and learn to guide your followers by providing them with the tools they need to become successful, rather than letting your ego guide you to subpar coaching tactics that eventually put your followers in harm's way. When coaches view themselves as the focal point of a team, they've already lost. The same goes for the training world. A personal trainer should be there to guide, lead, push, challenge, and be there for their clients. Conceptualize your clients as the centerpiece of your business. They are there to learn from you. You are there to make sure their needs are met.

Even though we are in the position of leadership, we all have areas in which we can continue to improve. In order to grow, we must be open to growing and be willing to put in the work, hear where we could be better, and never settle for doing things the way they've been done because that's what you were told. Keep an open mind. Don't be afraid to admit when you've gotten too comfortable. It can be easy to get comfortable and honestly, it's a safe space to be in. Comfortability is nice because there isn't the unknown. Becoming complacent in your education and growth will lead you to a dead end. Being open to being coachable makes you the best coach for each of your people. You owe it to them. You owe it to yourself. And you'll thank yourself down the line when you realize how far you've come and how much you've grown since you entered into this field. I am not the same trainer I was when I began in 2016. Make sure you find time to talk with other trainers, learn from others on social media, do research online and through books, and work to improve your knowledge on topics such as sport psychology. Each little resource will help you serve others better so they have more tools to become successful.

There are instances in your career you will probably look back on and shake your head at the way you used to train. Do not be not embarrassed or afraid to admit that. That tells you that at that time, you didn't know as much as you do now. Eventually, in recognizing your growth path, you will feel thankful and proud. Every so often, give yourself opportunities to reflect on your most recent growth as a trainer. These reflections allow you to appreciate how you have grown and developed in your profession. They also emphasize the importance to never become complacent. Continue to learn and further progress yourself, professionally and personally. As you know, being coachable and seeking out different methods to improve yourself as a person, trainer, and coach will continue to positively separate you from others in our field.

CHAPTER 35

Avoid Complacency

Don't get complacent. Step back, reevaluate from different angles, allow for a fresh mindset. Reassess and make sure you and your clients are improving and remaining focused on the right path. If you catch yourself going through the motions, recycling workouts for all of your clients, and not making a conscious effort to improve your programming, do better. Your clients are paying for your services to help them improve their health and well-being so neglecting to upkeep the standard of your quality of service is unacceptable. Don't let them down because you decide to slack off and get lazy with your programming, education, or resources. Whether you work for another company or are self-employed, in this field our business really falls on our shoulders. The success we find is determined by how much effort we put in for those who invest in us and how well we connect with those around us.

One easy way to avoid complacency is through that little computer we all have in our pockets. With having the internet at the tips of our fingers, and when used correctly, it can provide us with such a great chance to stay up to date with the latest findings in our profession. There are so many helpful resources available to those willing to look for them. For example, one thing I really admire about Collin is his constant desire to learn about different areas within the health and exercise world. With no prompting or anyone keeping tabs on him, he makes a point to find, read, and decipher one new scholarly article each week. Does he apply everything he learns, or does he agree with everything he reads? No, he doesn't. However, intaking information is beneficial. It's up to you to decide whether or not it applies to your own clients, your business, or your communications with clients.

One way our business reaches out to clients and the community is through bi-weekly electronic newsletters. The newsletters are another way to keep us up to date on what is an ever-changing field. Each newsletter focuses on topics ranging from the misconceptions of 10,000 steps to squat variations and benefits to why the body needs rest. In sending out these quick and informative reads, we hope to not only help educate our subscribers on different areas of the health, fitness, exercise, nutrition, and strength and conditioning world, but to also keep ourselves accountable. We don't receive any monetary value in sharing our newsletters, but we become more knowledgeable, more reputable, and hopefully we can help educate our followers in ways to improve their lives. When you work in a field based upon science, there are constantly new findings and new ways to go about certain things. Science is not set in stone and continually evolves as we proceed to learn and apply more and more information.

In regards to education, there can be great value in degrees and certifications. In fact, Collin has his BS in Kinesiology through Drake University, has worked to get his Certified Strength and Conditioning Specialist (CSCS), which is widely known as the gold standard for strength and conditioning coaches, as well as his USA Weightlifting certification. At the time of the publishing of this book, he is also wrapping up his Master of Science in Health Science with a Sports Performance Concentration at Rocky Mountain University. I have a Master of Education in Positive Coaching and Athletic Leadership through the University of Missouri, BS in Exercise Science and BS in Human Performance & Fitness from St. Ambrose University, and my ISSA Personal Training certification. These accomplishments have provided us with a wealth of knowledge to share with our clients and integrate into our program, but degrees and certifications are only as good as you apply them. Sometimes people strive to get certifications, but their only purpose of working toward those is to get more certifications. If you're going to work to increase knowledge and expand on what you can offer others, invest in those areas to continue your education. There is the idea of theory and application. We can ingest all of the theories in the world and become well-versed on the latest findings to obtain and hold all sorts of information. Yet, if you choose not to apply that information to better the lives of the people you are working with, the theories, content, and all of those certifications become useless. This bridges the gap between what we know and how we use that information. Degrees and certifications provide us with a foot in the door and access to more knowledge, but it is our job to use those tools to help our people through applying what we actually learned to real life scenarios.

Another way to avoid becoming complacent is to set aside time to study more than just the science of kinesiology and biomechanics. Personal training has an art to it. Our occupation creates opportunity to those who understand the ins and outs of the textbooks and of the human body in motion, alongside numerous other additional components. Learn human behaviors. Research psychology and learn to become more socially aware so you can navigate conversations from every person you come in contact with. Find out ways to connect with people with whom you may not otherwise bond. Ask questions. Discover what piques your clients' interests. When you are able to create an environment where people realize you are truly interested in their livelihoods, they will continue to open up to you. When people feel comfortable enough to speak freely without the fear of being judged, they can be themselves, thus furthering that relationship and bond.

As it refers to the human body and biomechanics, learning the textbook and understanding how the body moves is crucial. This information allows for you to have the knowledge base necessary to then use that material to create a program and realize what is happening in the body at more than just surface level. What we also need to do is take that information and really understand how to apply it. Information is great, but until we realize how we can use that to actually apply change, it doesn't mean much. This again ties into the idea of theory versus application.

Obtaining and applying the tools and information necessary to benefit your people is the real way to help coach and lead others. Colleges and companies that offer certifications can be a great way to better educate yourself. If you're willing to do the research, find quality resources, and apply information in a way that works for you and those working with you, you will be able to continue to better yourself and increase the tools you have in your mental toolbox. Your curiosity will help you avoid complacency in a profession that already experiences too much burnout.

CHAPTER 36

Know When to Adjust on the Fly

"Everybody has a plan until they get punched in the face"
-Mike Tyson

Mike Tyson's famous quote is a sentiment to adapting on the fly, regardless of how you planned a certain situation to go. In any circumstance, we must know when to push things, but also when to dial them back. When training, we can go into each session thinking we have the absolute best workout for a client but the fact of the matter is that life throws us curveballs. For example, if a client enters the gym for their session on that specific day and their job kicked their butt or they were bogged down with a relationship issue, that program may no longer fit the needs of that client on that particular day. This job requires fluidity. This job involves making adjustments based on the situation at hand. Because we work with humans, there will often be unexpected factors that come into play which require us to recognize those unforeseen circumstances and learn to adapt accordingly. Learning to read the room and to understand the body language of your clients is something that takes experience and cannot be learned in a text book. You must take it upon yourself to note when clients are having difficult days and when they are feeling their best. Based on your client's moods and other factors, you need to learn how to alter your program on any given day.

Use your best judgment, communication skills, social awareness, and previous knowledge to decide whether or not to adjust your original programming. If you suspect things may be off, physically or mentally, with your client, ask them. Talk with them. They may be up front and tell you, or they may have things buried deep down. It is up to you to decide how to play that. The right choice may not always be evident, but the wrong ones can be destructive and make a situation even worse. Be careful and learn to read your people to the best of your abilities, based on what they do and don't tell you. Listen to what they say. Then do your best to gather information from nonverbal cues to adapt your programming to best fit your client's mood.

The same set of rules can apply when a client shows up fired up and ready to get after it. You have the choice to continue with what you had planned for that session, or maybe take advantage of that energy and push the limit a little more than usual. Be smart about how hard you push or the height of increased intensity. When your client feels good, it can be okay to use that fuel to get in a more dynamic workout. Again, use your discretion and be smart about your adapted program. Also, don't second guess your original plan. You're intelligent and that session was planned that way for a reason. Be smart, adapt when needed, and learn to read your clients as best you can.

CHAPTER 37

Most Efficient Way to Eliminate Body Fat from Stubborn Areas of Your Body

If the title of this Chapter snagged your attention, I'm here to apologize. You're not going to read about some quick fix or magic pill that will help you or your clients instantly lose excessive body fat in those stubborn areas. In the perfect world, after identifying a spot of your body you wanted to improve or weren't necessarily happy with, you would work on that area a handful of times, and voila, perfection would ensue. However, in reality you realize the good things take time, patience, and a lot of hard work. In today's society we get caught up finding the easiest way to skate by and reach our destination as fast as possible. Although efficiency is great, taking the easy way out when improving one's health is completely different. When it comes to exercise and accomplishing whatever muscular or body fat goals you may have, you can't expect instant gratification. That mindset needs to be refocused to get away from the concept of immediately reaping the benefits that truly take time.

First and foremost, let's set things straight. We've been fed years and years of incorrect information through all types of different outlets in the fitness industry. SPOT REDUCTION IS NOT A THING. The thought that you can work a certain area in order to only burn the body fat in that area is simply not realistic and there is not enough evidence to support that as a theory. In order to burn general body fat, you need to comply with a program of weightlifting, cardiovascular exercise, and eating a highly nutritious diet. The key to long term success is to do these things over and over again. When you start to burn body fat by figuring out what equation works best for you and your lifestyle, you may notice you will burn body fat easier in certain areas. It is common to start noticing leaning out or definition through spots, such as the arms, whereas it can be more difficult to burn the body fat around the torso. It's important to let clients know they aren't the only ones having trouble with this. Many people have a difficult time shedding centrally located extra weight. In order to come out on top and get your body looking, feeling, and performing the way you would like, it all comes back to those main attributes of being patient, consistent, and working hard.

To improve the way a certain area looks, targeting that area isn't a bad idea but it should not be the only type of exercise you prescribe. For example, if a client were to have the goal of getting more definition through the arms, it is okay and definitely recommended to spend more time doing arm exercises. Bent over rows, pull/chin ups, bench pressing, curl variations, dips, and skull crushers are a few examples of how to build lean muscle and improve muscle hypertrophy throughout that area. In order to notice definition from all of the hard work, you have to remind clients to have their nutrition on point. Exercise and nutrition need to go hand in hand to see long-term desired results. You'll also notice if you incorporate cardiovascular exercise and weight lifting, especially a program that includes working the larger muscle groups (legs, back, core, and chest), weight will fall off faster. As a fitness professional, if given the choice between two different programs for a client to reach the goal of losing body fat in a certain area, 10 times out of 10, I would prescribe full body, multi-joint exercises that would recruit more musculature to improve the entire body composition. Utilizing multi-joint exercises, such as deadlifts, squats, lunges, pull-up variations, pressing variations, and core exercises will get results faster than simply doing isolation exercises while neglecting the bigger muscle groups. Finding the balance between multi-joint exercises to hit more body parts and isolation or single-joint exercises will help clients reach their goals more efficiently and effectively.

The path to any goal, in or out of the gym, may not always be linear. Whether attempting to lose stubborn body fat, hit a new personal record on a certain lift, or even improve consistency in the gym or kitchen, there will be setbacks. Clients may hit plateaus. They could get frustrated with becoming stagnant. When stumbling upon these hardships, you need to remain focused on the end goal. It's up to us, as trainers, to keep our clients' spirits up because not every day will be a victory. Keep pushing one step at a time, regardless of how frustrated or uncomfortable it may make us feel.

Stepping outside of the comfort zone is where your clients will really start achieving growth and seeing results. It can be uncomfortable in new waters. When starting something new, a client may question the whole process. Stay the course. Help clients understand that to see change they need to push themselves more than before. We need to help clients welcome difficulties because when persevering through uncharted territory, they will begin to understand they are capable of more than originally thought. Health and fitness programs are unique in the sense that they often look very simplistic and tend to revolve around some type of quantitative goal. There is nothing wrong with setting number related goals, but learning to understand the importance of that qualitative side of the journey (technique, form, motivation, determination) will allow clients to celebrate steps in the right direction and better understand that the end goal isn't the end of the journey. Each little stepping stone goal is a minor victory and the real triumph is found along the ride. People learn so much about character, patience, and work ethic when progressing through the journey of an exercise routine. Actively making a conscious effort to improve upon these aspects will keep your clients dialed in on their goals. There isn't a magic pill. There isn't an easy route. Work hard, stick with it, and keep on keeping on.

CHAPTER 38

Train Who You're Good at Training

Find the demographic of clientele you enjoy working with and with whom you are passionate about coaching. Some trainers have very specific types of clients. Some trainers excel at coaching athletes. Others specifically work with a certain age group, while others have a range of clients. Collin and I find ourselves in that latter category and we wouldn't have it either way. Like I expressed early on in this book, my initial intention was to use personal training as a stepping stone to build up my experience and work my way into the strength and conditioning profession. Training such an amazing assortment of people carved out the decision in my mind to work with more than just athletes. I still have a sweet spot for training athletes, but working with general population people who have either retired from athletics or were never in that realm in the first place now is just as enjoyable to me. Collin is in a similar boat. He began with the intention of wanting to strictly work with youth, high school, collegiate, and professional athletes. Although he still gets to do that in a 1:1 setting in the gym, in addition to partnering with the NE Gold softball team, CY Select Wolves girl's AAU basketball program, and previously leading the strength and conditioning program for the Iowa Prospects baseball program, he also works with others simply interested in becoming healthier individuals.

Having a range of clientele to train may not always be the norm in our line of business. The purpose of this section is to state that whatever group(s) of individuals with whom you end up working, lead with passion, dedication, loyalty, and the intent to continue to provide what they need day in and day out. If you have a certain niche you prefer working with, be the best trainer for your particular clients. Work so hard that you're the person people in the community think of when looking for a trainer of certain interest. Regardless of the area in which you choose to specialize, the way to be the best trainer is to treat your people the way they want to be treated, help them work towards the results they want, and really research how you can better serve those people in their training sessions. If it's working with elderly, maybe you spend more time on balance; exercises that will help them get up off of the floor if they fall; or work on coordination drills. If you are with athletes, help them pursue perfection with their running mechanics; improve speed and agility (especially reactionary and changing direction); and help them become more explosive. If you are working with a group of people who just enjoy working out together to socialize, catch up, and feel good about themselves, hype them up; help them work certain areas they want to "tone;" and make it an experience they want to tell their friends about. At the end of the day, find what you're good at and passionate about and be the best that you possibly can be. Personalize workouts and conversations. Invest in those who invest in you. Lastly, give every client a training experience they feel good about and will leave them wanting to come back. Finding the area of expertise where you feel most successful as a trainer will shine through in the success your clients experience with your programming and execution of their individual goals. Consistency and catering to your clients' specific goals will help them see results, which will lead to client retention.

CHAPTER 39

Stick With a Variety of the Basics

Don't try to reinvent the wheel. Personal training is helping people and providing them with the tools to successfully adhere to a training or workout regimen to accomplish their goals. The same goes for strength and conditioning. In this aspect, personal trainers help individuals get strong and work to improve their conditioning through an assortment of tactics, but with a focus on the three main energy systems (Creatine Phosphate/Phosphagen System (ATP-CP); Anaerobic Lactic (Glycolytic); Aerobic/Oxidative). Don't neglect strength or conditioning. Get strong, improve the health of your heart through intelligently programmed cardiovascular workouts, improve mobility, listen to the body, and learn to fuel yourself with quality foods. Focus on the basics, while tailoring the programs you prescribe to the wants and needs of your clients. Keep things simple and stick to what works. In our world, social media advertises nonsensical exercises, flashy new short cuts, and the latest and greatest fad diet. Be curious but remain optimistically cautious because the basics stick around generation over generation for a reason. Flashy new exercise variations might catch people's attention or get you likes on Instagram but sticking with the basics will get you results. Provide your individual clients with the best opportunity to succeed, while remaining safe, and make those the focal points of your programming. Doing and perfecting the boring, basic movements over and over again will do far more for you than any unscientifically proven new exercise. As much as you may aspire to become famous through social media, realistically you will better serve your clients through sticking with the basics on a consistent basis than trying to chase likes on Instagram. Social media is a great platform to get your business additional exposure and to reach new audiences, but using it for the right reasons will determine whether a potential client scrolls past or decides to stop on your page.

We have all seen ridiculous exercise creations on social media. As a matter of fact, there have been Instagram and Facebook accounts specifically created to comedically show this type of content. We've all seen something laughable like a man juggling lacrosse balls while doing an overhead squat on an exercise ball. This may seem a little far-fetched, but it probably isn't too far off. Some client's needs may require you to get more creative with your programming, but any collaboration of movements that increases your client's chance of injury should be thoroughly thought out and justified before moving forward with them. Safety comes first. Although some people are capable of doing extreme mixtures of already difficult exercises, that doesn't mean these should be done on your watch. Be careful to not risk your client's safety. Pushing them to certain physical limits can be acceptable but when they toe the line of danger, it is time to back off.

Even though there are basic exercises all intelligent trainers and coaches should recommend to their people, there is plenty of room within a program to set yourself apart and carve out your niche in this field. Create your brand to uniquely express you and your beliefs. The core movements of squatting, hinging, lunging, pushing, pulling and doing core have been around forever. Find what exercises you believe play the biggest factors in helping your clients improve. Educate yourself on how to cue those movements to all audiences, perfect the movements yourself, and make them a staple in your programs. One of those movements for me is the hollow body hold. This core exercise is such a simple one, yet so demanding. For the majority of our multi-joint movements, they require our torso to remain stable. Every one of my clients understands the importance of bracing the core properly. During all of the multi-joint movements, whether you are bending at the knees or hips, or pushing or pulling at the shoulders, your core remains a constant. The entire belt region is our core, not just the abdominals. Front, back, and sides of the core are essential to strengthen and stabilize in order to maximize the main multi-joint lifts. We have all done ab exercises that we really feel that deep burn, stemming from crunches or sit ups. Although these abdominal exercises can have a time and place in some programs, we owe our clients a better product. Cranking their necks and allowing them to use their hip flexors to knock out hundreds of crunches are not worthy ways to build the belt region safely. For the most part, my clients can attest to how frequently we work on rotational core, anti-rotation exercises, hips, low back, and isometric core movements, especially plank variations and the dreaded hollow body hold. These options are my personal preference to prescribe to clients (and to do myself) because it is now the societal norm to sit and work at desks for more than eight hours a day. When you step back and think about that, collectively as a society we spend 1/3 of our lives at a desk. On top of that, we are seated on the couch or at a table a chunk of our other time and asleep for roughly the other third. Spend time improving posture through choosing better core exercises and addressing areas of discomfort by strengthening and mobilizing those areas and the surrounding joints. It is important to help your clients understand that just because they feel "tight" in the hips and back doesn't mean simply stretching those areas will help alleviate discomfort. There is something to be said about satisfying your client's craving for immediate gratification so I've found some ways to check that box, while also helping them with longer term solutions. One example of this is giving my clients some stretches that help those "tight" areas temporarily feel better, while also prescribing them with strength and mobility exercises to the surrounding areas in different planes of motion to help permanently fix what they may perceive as just being tight muscles. What they feel is real to them but if we can determine that their feeling really may just be weakness or fatigue, by strengthening the surrounding areas, we can help them get out of that discomfort and hopefully avoid any future issues. With the hip flexors being a commonly reported "tight" area from clients that do spend the majority of their days sitting at a desk, I would confront that issue with a combination of groin and hip flexor stretches to help them feel those areas they are complaining of. I would then work on some banded hip strength, combined with some low back and/ or adductor strengthening exercises, and potentially some bridge variations, anti-rotation oblique exercises, or a hollow body hold. Not only could a formula like that help them feel better in the moment, but in doing so, it may help them piece together that a similar combination of exercise choices done on a more regular basis can help combat their stationary lifestyle, which can elicit habit changes throughout their day at work. Getting someone out of pain or discomfort through some simple exercise choices like that can do wonders for the trajectory of an individual's fitness journey.

When guiding your clients through these basic exercises, be sure to explain the reason why you're choosing the exercises you are and give them certain cues that help them feel and under-stand the exact stimulus you want for them to get the most out of that movement. Let's use the hollow body hold, for instance. The hollow body hold is a very easy set up and requires zero equip-ment. With so many other ab exercises, the low back arches and hip flexors take over. It is important we strengthen the hip flexor muscles but for this movement, the main objective is to prevent that from happening. While laying on your back, pretend you are a puppet with your head and shoulders being drawn towards the sky with strings, not cranked so you have a double chin. Already you may feel your abdominals contract. Think about pushing your belly button into the floor and bracing as if you are about to be punched in the gut. From here, raise your feet off of the floor, keeping your legs straight, and really force your low back into the floor. You will notice when you keep your legs locked out, the higher they are, the easier this exercise becomes. When you lower your legs closer to the floor, it becomes considerably more strenuous and your low back may peel itself off of the floor. When this happens, reset your back to be in contact with the ground beneath you, and raise your legs up slightly so you can still feel the abdominals working. The stomach area may be trembling a little bit. Hold this for as long as you can. If it becomes too vigorous or your back arches, take a breather and try it again.

You'll notice this isometric contraction doesn't necessarily give you that same burn as you'd receive from doing 100 straight crunches, but it is much more effective in allowing you to understand what proper bracing technique feels like and to learn how to create a better mind-body connection through focusing on different body parts at work. This is a very underrated exercise and something that I have just about every one of my clients perform on a regular basis.

The hollow body hold looks like a very simple exercise, but so many parts of the body need to be manipulated in a specific manner to make sure the right muscle groups are working at the proper time. Lay yourself on the floor and walk yourself through that paragraph. Do each of those cues make sense? They should all be understandable for just about every audience and should allow for each person to comprehend exactly what they should be doing. Can you describe each and every exercise that you prescribe in a comparative manner? If you can explain every little portion of each exercise, your clients will have a much more thorough idea of how to properly execute the exercise, giving them the best chance to learn how it assists their body and fits into their program.

Some clients you work with will pick up on exercises relatively quickly, but some clients may have difficulty understanding certain movements. Some may understand what you are trying to say, but then they aren't able to translate that comprehension to move their body in the proper manner needed to execute the movement. By repeatedly coaching them through those core movements, using cues they understand, and walking them through each exercise to the point of them feeling comfortable and confident to execute it on their own, they will learn better from you and will retain that information. In order to progress so clients feel more comfortable with those crucial, multi-joint movements, repetition is going to be a huge determining factor in eventually learning to move the proper way. Doing variations of those movements, fluctuating the tempo, limiting the range of motion, or decreasing load are great ways to enhance a client's ability to become more educated and comfortable performing difficult movements. It may seem arduous to do certain exercises over and over again, yet that repetition builds confidence. My clients spend a majority of our time squatting, hinging, lunging, pushing, pulling, or doing core work. These six movement patterns allow for variance and ensure we are not leaving any muscle groups behind. Sticking to the basics and adding in accessory movements to address missing links or to improve certain weaknesses is my biggest remedy when training my own clients.

When you get clients in a routine of learning and refining those exercise choices, it can become monotonous and may be difficult to recall the importance of such movements. In those times, remember that our discipline is so important in achieving lasting, long-term results. Trust the process you have laid out. Take the programming one day at a time, and encourage your clients to continue to show up on days they may not have motivation to push. When we lack motivation, because it will happen to each and every one of us, we need to be reminded of the bigger picture. To achieve significant change, you must make significant changes. When not feeling up to the task, it is important to ask our clients if that sudden desire is more important than the long-term goal. Enjoy consistency, keep it simple, and strive to give your clients the best product through your selection of exercises. Vary the repetitions, sets, tempo, and intensity, and always remember to stick to the movements that allow each individual client to progress towards their goals in an efficient manner.

CHAPTER 40

Count on Your Fingers

Throughout my years of personal training, I've found that some clients are more talkative than others. Some enjoy chatting between sets, some converse during every repetition of every exercise. Others prefer small talk, allowing the gym to be a place for them to focus on themselves and the exercise at hand. Whatever your clients prefer, our job is to roll with those punches, allow the client to somewhat dictate the conversational direction in which their session goes, and do our best to match their energy. No matter which direction the conversation takes, we still owe it to our clients to serve our purpose of providing them with and getting them through the planned workout. We must focus on the exercises while also concentrating on the conversation. This may sound simple but when somebody is talking while doing lunges and you're trying to hear what they're saying, it can be easy to lose track of their reps. We program our workouts for certain reasons, meaning we choose a certain number of repetitions for each exercise. If our clients are relying on us to count for them and we lose track of those reps, we defeat the purpose of programming our workout because the reps didn't equate to the plan. Is one rep here or there the end of the world? No, but by finding ways to count while still staying attentive to conversations, we can avoid the issue all together.

One simple way to help you keep track of reps while multitasking during a session is to count on your fingers. I frequently stand upright with my hands behind my back with one hand clasping the other wrist. It is very easy for me to pay attention to the conversation with my client while counting on my fingers. You can very easily count on your fingers while remaining engaged and actively listening to where your conversation with clients is going while still providing them with the absolute best service.

CHAPTER 41

Not Every Day is a Good Day

Working out can be frustrating. Not every day is a personal record day in the gym. More frequently, we will all just have average days. Occasionally, we will have bad days. The important thing is that we don't get burnt out, frustrated, or too down on ourselves. The fact that we keep showing up, in an attempt to become better versions of ourselves, is what makes the daily trips to the gym, establishing and sticking with healthy nutritional choices, and prioritizing your physical and mental health worthwhile.

As a trainer, not every day will be your best professional day either. If you're a trainer, you're well aware that we have a pretty great gig of throwing on shorts and a t-shirt, working at the gym, and being around some amazing people but it would be ignorant to say that we don't have parts of our job that we don't enjoy or that every day is perfect. You've probably experienced your own rough days at the gym and in life at some point. We are regular people. We can be optimistic and see the good in just about any scenario, if we decide to have that mindset, but that doesn't mean we don't come across our own hurdles. We have hard days outside of work. We deal with family issues, broken friendships, tough times in relationships, and some days we just may be cranky for no reason at all. During those times, it is important to remember our role and that we are providing a product. If you're a good trainer, the product you are providing is held to a high standard, for which your clients are thankful. A good trainer has built a regarded reputation. But even you will find these aspects difficult to sustain at *all* times. Showing up to a desk job after you had a tough day or night, burying yourself in a cubicle, and isolating yourself are luxuries we cannot afford. It is important we show up to every session, every day with the same high-quality service for each and every client. If you are dealing with difficult situations outside of work, you owe it to your clients to not let those outside circumstances negatively impact the service you provide. Focus on giving them their deserved time and workout, and never dump your emotions onto them during their paid time slot. You certainly can be transparent with them and honest about what is going on in your life. Yet, if we risk that trickling into a venting session for you to your client, you are not upholding your training agreement for your service that particular day. Our job duties include providing our clients with relief from their crazy lives through creating healthy behaviors and exercising. Because of this, if you need to find a way to compartmentalize those feelings and emotions to temporarily push them out of your current state, that could help your service as a trainer. Opening up to clients and confiding in them when you have a problem is not a bad thing, but don't upheave everything onto clients who aren't looking for that. If you have established relationships with clients with whom you can have those chats, consider yourself fortunate. Always remember though, your clients shouldn't have to be your therapist when they are paying you for a product.

One prime example for me was in the early part of June 2020. I had a full day of clients and midway through my schedule, I felt my phone going off in my pocket. I am never on my phone during training sessions, as that would be rude to steal time away from my clients, but it kept buzzing and I could tell I had a few phone calls and a handful of texts coming in. With about a five-minute gap after that training session wrapped up and before my next client came in, I had enough time to check my phone. I read my texts and my heart sank. My great aunt had suddenly passed away. I was in shock as I had just been scrolling through social media the evening before and got a good chuckle out of a post she had shared. She was a saint of a woman and every time she saw us, she always bear-hugged each of us and planted a big ole smooch right on our cheeks. I didn't know what to do. My world stopped for a minute. I was caught completely off guard and all of a sudden, my next client walked in through the door. I quickly wiped my eyes, grabbed a swig of water, and gathered myself. I was very close with this next client, but not to the extent where I felt comfortable opening up about my aunt when I hadn't even been able to reach out to my family members yet. I composed myself and finished my training day as originally planned. The second I walked in the front door of my house following my final client, I balled. Being in my own space, I was finally able to let my emotions run freely. If I had told my clients about my great aunt passing away, they would have been more than understanding and would not have taken any offense to me canceling our training sessions that day. With many miles of distance between my family and relatives and COVID-19 shutdowns, there wasn't much I could do at that moment. Deciding I didn't want to throw a wrench in the plans of my clients, as they had scheduled their day around the workouts, my personal choice had been to finish out that day of training even when my heart was somewhere else. Opening up to clients can be a special bond amongst the trainer-client dynamic, but most clients don't show up to the gym for a session with you and expect to be bogged down with your personal issues. Understand when it is the right time to get into personal conversations with your clients. Finding connections like that is special and can build trust, but we must remain aware of the client's purpose in being in your gym. Communication is the key to a successful relationship of any kind, but with that, we need to understand when to have certain conversations.

When we do have a bad night of sleep or a difficult scenario in our home lives, whether we decide to open up to our clients about those topics or not, we need to provide every client with the same exceptional service. Whether it is with your client at 5 am, 10 am, or 8 pm, each one should receive the absolute best from you. It might be your twelfth hour in the gym but you need to remember that it is likely your client's first. Understanding this is within your control is the first step in providing that type of service. When you have a very early morning client, get your sleep. Prepare beforehand. Be sure to be at the gym before your client. Show every client you care by respecting their time. If your session begins at 5 am, and you stroll into the gym at 4:58 with none of the equipment laid out and nothing set up, they are really not getting the full product for which they had originally paid. Following through on providing quality service is a great way to ensure you retain clients and make people happy with your product.

Setting that standard of how prompt you will be, how you will act, and what you will wear is important in creating your brand. When people think of your business, they should only have positive thoughts. Once a client has a negative experience with your business, that will remain at the forefront of their minds and will outweigh any positivity you may have provided previously. Creating a brand that promotes you, sets you apart from the competition, and reflects your philosophies is massive in your training growth. How far in advance do you report to the gym when you have a client? Do you program ahead of time? What do you tend to wear during your training sessions? Do you make each and every session about them? How you present yourself on a routine basis has the ability to drive clients through your door, or it could force your clients to slowly fizzle away. Set a standard, take responsibility, and always, always, always take care of your people. At the end of the day, you may never know what they are truly going through, so being a reliable constant in their lives is reassuring to anyone. Be respectful, understanding, and tackle each session with individualized programming, but the same effort, for each client. Remain the constant that provides clients with the product you mutually believe in and agreed upon.

CHAPTER 42

Live the Lifestyle

Live the lifestyle you believe in. It isn't a requirement for every personal trainer to post skimpy, flexing mirror pictures with minimal clothing to their Instagram account. Nor is it a requirement to eat a diet consisting of nothing but bland chicken, steamed broccoli, and plain rice with no condiments. You don't have to be the motivational speaker that tries to instill fear by being condescending to your social media followers. As a matter of fact, please don't feel like you have to do any of those things. Those are some of the reasons personal trainers can receive questionable reputations. It is essential you take care of yourself, your body, and your mind through the habits you preach to prioritize your own physical and mental health. Through exercising and living out those healthy behaviors on which you educate your clients, you are proving to them you believe in the product you offer. Taking that into account, people are not coming to you and seeking out services because of the photos and videos you post of yourself working out. Clients seek you out because of the reputation your brand of business has, the quality of service you provide, and the way you treat others and make them feel. Demonstrating that through your marketing, social media, and with each client every single day will create a ripple effect throughout your community that tags you as the person who puts others at the top of your priority list. Living this lifestyle and continually proving to others that their investment by training with you is looking out for their current and long-term health.

Through living the lifestyle you want to portray to others, you will be able to find what you believe in and who you truly are at your core, which may take time. It is easy to be influenced by so many different resources. It's okay to not be entirely sure the exact persona you want to give off. Take in the content you want, remove the stuff that makes you feel bad, and learn from those with differing opinions. When you find the path you want to lead within your career, buy into that. For me, it took some time. I tried different workout styles. I fluctuated with what I ate. It took me some time to realize who I wanted to surround myself with. Since then, I have found my circle, created a sustainable variety of foods that work for my lifestyle, and realized what type of workouts I like which allow me to be consistent with the demands of my life.

What worked for me may be different than what works for you. It takes some trial and error. You may even look back at the way you were doing things a few years ago and wonder what you were thinking. That's normal. It's called growth. There is nothing to be ashamed of for the way you used to perform in your job. If you continually work to improve, of course you will see changes. One of the beautiful things about this job is you are in a certain Chapter of your own fitness journey, but also may be in a completely different Chapter of your career path. You will continue working with some of your clients, and you will see growth in them just like you see growth in yourself. Sometimes those trajectories grow parallel with one another, as the growth in your knowledge, experience, and desire to improve will help them grow, and vice versa. By being true to yourself and continuing to want to improve while buying into the product and lifestyle you genuinely believe in, can actually become your best asset to marketing the type of personal training you provide.

The way you train, the way you eat, and the life you live may be completely different than those areas with each of your clients. It shouldn't be the same. Their programming, nutrition, and goals should all be different from yours because they are different people with different lifestyles at different points in their lives. Despite those differences, you can market your business through demonstrating that the dedication, patience, and hard work necessary to work towards and accomplish fitness goals actually pays off. You are a walking billboard for your business. When others recognize that the way you go about things elicits results, it is proof that what you're teaching actually works. This creates buy-in and makes your training services much more appealing to those interested in possibly working with you.

What it comes down to is the message you're trying to express. Your message and the lifestyle you live should exemplify those qualities through your words and actions. Whatever your message, be sure you are showing others you wholly believe in what you are saying and actually live the lifestyle. Collin and I constantly preach on the importance of creating habit changes that cultivate sustainable behaviors to encourage healthy, wholesome lifestyles. If we are doing everything within our power to demonstrate the importance of these habits, we need to practice what we preach. Why would our clients buy in and take our message to heart if we don't believe in the product we are trying to sell? Does this mean that as a trainer or some sort of health coach you have to have minimal body fat, a six-pack, and lift ridiculous amounts of weight? Not at all. Living the lifestyle does mean you should lead by example through eating a well-balanced diet, exercising regularly, living by the rules you advise to your clients, and creating a positive mental space that allows for a healthy mindset. If you are a slob when it comes to nutrition, only lift weights when it involves bench pressing and curls, and party every weekend, your clients will be less likely to instill the behaviors you recommend to them because you are doing the complete opposite. Why should someone pay for your services when you live in a completely alternate universe with how your actions are conflicting with the message you are speaking?

This doesn't mean you can't go out for ice cream, pizza, or a few drinks, but if you are always doing the opposite of what you are trying to get your clients to do, you may lose some credibility. Encouraging the balance of doing the majority of what you need and a little bit of what you want is a good way to keep your progress on track, all while enjoying the process and not going overboard, one way or another. When we find that equilibrium of enjoyment while bettering ourselves, we are much more prone to continue on a productive path. Seeing results and having fun are two of the keys to not losing focus in training. Doing what we can to lead our clients by embracing and epitomizing those behaviors will create an environment where they will want to imitate those habits to achieve the same successes that we will. Sometimes you may need to put yourself into the shoes of your clients to give them the best possible experience with you. This might mean you have to test out a workout plan prior to having them try it, just to see if it would be effective and if you would have to make adjustments along the way. It could also mean you need to be an accountability partner for them by trying out some new forms of exercise simply to help them reach their overall health and wellness goals. These small undertakings will set you apart from others and are an easy way to express how to effectively live the life to your clients.

As a coach to your clients, expressing what your personal goals are is a good way for you to remain accountable. Giving your clients the opportunity to view the methods you use to tackle your own personal goals models the work and discipline needed to accomplish said goals. We know health and fitness goals can be very difficult and sometimes they seem far out of reach. Being transparent with your clients by acknowledging you have goals and are maybe even experiencing difficulties in getting over the occasional hump can allow them to understand not everything goes as perfectly as one would expect. We all have hurdles we encounter. As a trainer, being up front with your clients about failures you've faced will help them see failure as a normal part of the process, not as the end of the road. Leading from the front, despite missteps, will help both parties remain accountable. Taking this stance will help your clients recognize that even trainers trudge through the mud at times. Living the lifestyle will also show them that perseverance during difficult trials will create a stronger, tougher version of yourself on the other side.

CHAPTER 43

Failure Isn't Always Bad

Failure is not always a bad thing. We all have goals. Expressing how paths to success more than likely will not be linear is important with improving the mental and emotional side of our health journeys. Failure can come in all shapes and sizes. We can blunder a lift. We can slip by completely derailing our nutrition. We can simply decline to even show up. Failure will happen. When we fail, we must do so gracefully. When miscuing on an exercise, fail safely. When failing in our nutritional plan, recognize that and hop back on the bandwagon as soon as you can. When failing to physically or mentally show up, figure out why and decide what you can do to be more present next time. Nobody is perfect, and we will all experience these snags over and over again. Failure may come in different shapes and sizes. As long as you recognize those failures, create a plan to step over them. Come at them head on next time, and you will continue to grow.

One minor, but also extremely important part of physical failure, is teaching clients how to fail the right way. Whether they are deadlifting, front squatting, dumbbell benching, doing pull ups, or any exercise, they should feel confident in knowing how to remove themselves from the exercise in a safe manner before doing the exercise. As their coach, safety for your clients is your responsibility. While explaining how to properly execute an exercise, wrap the explanation up by also telling them how to fail correctly without hurting themselves. This isn't because of your lack of confidence in them properly performing the movement, but rather because if they do fail, they shouldn't walk away battered and bruised. For example, if you fail a 400 lb. back squat in an empty gym on a Saturday night, will you be trapped under the bar or limping away with back issues? Through the experience, knowledge, and the education you've received, you should know to dump the bar behind you and fall forward in a safe manner. You also know the best way to deal with the disappointment of not hitting the lift is to unload the bar, put it back on the rack, load it back up, and then proceed to lift again. Retrying the lift with the chip on your shoulder and some additional motivation of not succeeding initially may be just what you needed to eventually complete the task.

We all fail in the gym. Our body and our mind will both quit at some point. When that happens, rather than trying to muscle through it and drastically increase the chance of injury, show your clients how to fail the right way. This teaching strategy is something you should address early and often. When we teach our clients proper technique of an exercise, never conclude that education session without informing them of how to fail in a safe manner. Not every single lift will be a success. Learning to lift with proper form is more important than lifting heavy with poor technique, which is a concept oftentimes get overlooked. Spotting your client while they are with you, but equipping them with the knowledge to understand how to fail properly when they are on their own, will instill confidence in them. This will help rewire their mindset in accepting failure isn't a setback, but rather the recognition that your body and mind were truly pushing their limitations.

This should be a staple in our coaching. When we step in the gym, it can be very intimidating to see some weightlifters moving obscene amounts of weight. For a novice, that can be an automatic turn off and can deter people from ever wanting to take another step into the gym. That fear could stem from an assortment of reasons, one of them being the fear of failing with that quantity of weight on their bar. That is a very real and scary thought. Before our thoughts snowball and get too out of control, speaking to gym safety can help calm the nerves of many, especially the new gym goers.

Personally, I believe that every person who steps into a fitness facility should be taught proper form and proper ways to fail. Form is so important and should be taken seriously by all. Trainers often forget to teach people how to safely fail, for when those situations appear. As a trainer, be sure you don't overlook the importance of this portion of teaching exercises. For example, when teaching proper squat technique, explain how there may be a time where you may not be there to spot your client. This especially pertains to clients who are new to squatting with a bar and weights. If they are unable to bring the weight back up and are essentially trapped at the bottom with a loaded bar on their back, they need to understand that shooting their hips or trying to muster the bar up by any means necessary is not the right choice. Possible injuries that can occur from incorrect squat technique or misjudging your capabilities can range from a minor low back strain to torn ligaments, muscle strains or tears, or even spinal issues. Push yourself to the limit, but understand that getting injured during one session and having to rehab and sit out for an extended period of time may not be worth that one additional repetition.

To help clients prepare for a possible situation of failing their lifts, a good rule of thumb is to create space between them and their weights. For back squats, push the bar backwards and fall forward. For front squats and deadlifts, simply dump the bar. We will all fail at some point. Understanding how to avoid being trapped under a bar is for the betterment of our clients' health. This begins with you, as a trainer. Your clients will be so focused on learning how to properly execute a lift and they may not even acknowledge the lift could fail. Erasing the perception that all failure is a negative thing will keep your clients safe and happy.

It is human nature to question ourselves when we fail. Becoming frustrated and rethinking our choices can bring us down. Changing your frame of mind, realizing that a missed exercise is not indicative of who you are as a person, and showing your resiliency by climbing back under that bar to finish on a high note will show you, as well as your clients, how powerful the mind really can be. Coaches and clients alike will run into situations that catch us off guard. Being up front about those difficult situations and not pretending that you are Superman to your clients will help them realize we all have problems with certain things. Leading by example and being honest to your people will again create that relationship of trust and will help both sides buy into the bigger picture.

CHAPTER 44

HIIT vs Steady State

There has been so much debate over high intensity cardio and low intensity cardio. **High Intensity Interval Training** has become a household term that floats in all gyms around the world. HIIT workouts can be useful, but let's dive into them a bit more to see if they're actually what you should be prescribing your everyday clients if their goals consist of burning fat and living a healthier life. The way HIIT workouts work is doing a very highly intense bout of cardiovascular exercise, followed by a rest, and repeated for a certain frequency. Depending on the ratio of rest and work, you may be sweating, gasping for air, and burning a bunch of calories, which might be beneficial but that ultimately depends on what your intention was behind that cardiovascular choice. My point being, exercise isn't just about the number of calories you are burning; it is about the fuel source from which those calories come. We have two main fuel sources in our body, fats and carbohydrates. What we eat acts as our fuel and it is stored within our body until it is called upon to act as energy to help us perform. When exercising, our body calls upon either fat or carbohydrate stores to use as its main fuel source. Most of our clients want to burn fat, so choosing exercises that do just that, burn fat, makes most sense. Although HIIT workouts burn a lot of calories and can push you to levels of exhaustion, they surprisingly utilize more carbs as their main fuel source. The fact that harder exercise may actually not burn as much fat may shock some people, but HIIT workouts can still be utilized and have their time and place to provide health benefits.

In order to burn more fat, it can be beneficial to do more steady state, lower intensity cardio than working too hard and raising our heart rates to a heightened pace. Reread that. Before you call me crazy, hear me out on why simple daily walks, steady state rows or bike rides, or lower intensity swims (or any other form of cardiovascular exercise, for that matter) elicit a fat-burning response from our body. Think of a graph. There is a Y axis and an X axis. Along the Y axis, we have fuel sources and along the X axis is exercise intensity, which can be measured by an RPE scale (Rating of Perceived Exertion), heart rate, or other measurements. Along the Y axis, fats will be at the top, with carbohydrates at the bottom. Again, these are the two main fuel sources the body uses as energy to allow our body to function properly and maximize performance. The line starting on the Y axis at the top by fats goes out parallel to the X axis as the exercise intensity increases to a point where it drops to the bottom of the Y axis and then again runs parallel to the X axis at a much lower point along the Y axis. Going back to the carbohydrate along the Y axis, there is a second line that starts low along the Y axis as exercise intensity increases and then as the fat line drops, the carbohydrate line elevates, they cross each other, and then it runs parallel to the X axis at a much higher level. There is an inverse relationship between carbohydrates and fats on this chart and it resembles a sideways H.

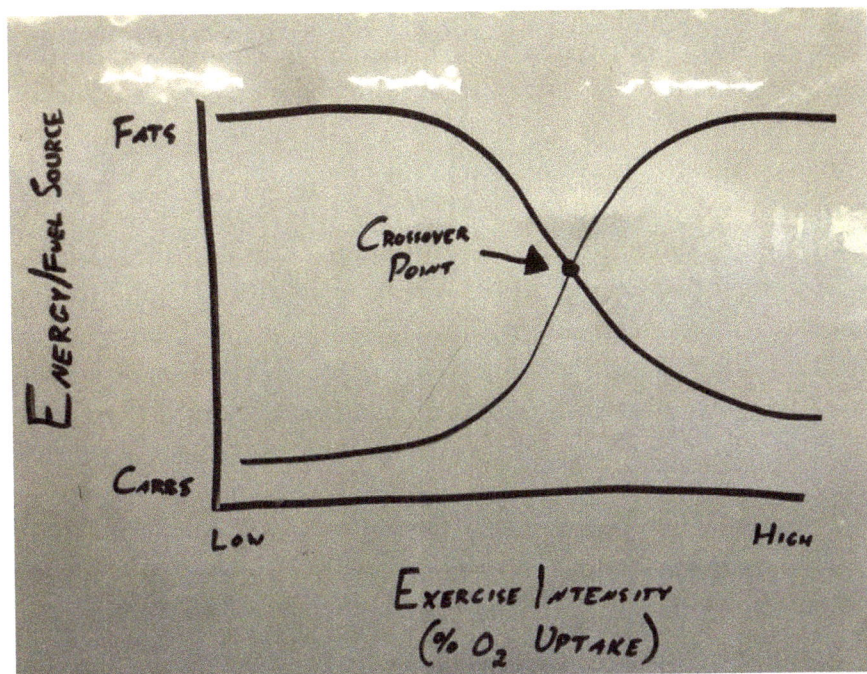

Energy/Fuel Source vs. Exercise Intensity (% O₂ Uptake) graph showing Fats, Cars, and Crossover Point from Low to High.

What that chart can demonstrate is how efficient the body is at utilizing different ratios of fuel sources at different exercise intensities. For example, when performing lower intensity exercise in longer durations, our body dips into the usage of the fats it has stored up. This stems from our body not stimulating the breakdown of glycogen at those lower intensities, so we rely on the oxidation of available fatty acids to act as our main fuel source. As exercise intensity increases, our body relies less on the fats and more on the carbohydrates it has stored up. At maximal intensity levels, such as HIIT workouts, we may be burning a high number of calories but carbohydrates will actually make up the large majority of that fuel source our body is calling upon. Now, that intersection point where our body transitions from using more fat to more carbohydrates is a very important point and has been referred to as the crossover point. It is the point where our body shifts from using the energy from fat to using the energy from carbohydrates and is clearly affected by exercise intensity. The crossover point can also be impacted by endurance training and overall cardiovascular shape. The goal is to shift that cross-over point further and further to the right on the graph to allow your body to be a more efficient fat burner, but to also improve our cardiovascular adaptations. If you can burn more fat while working less intensely, you're being smarter about your training, recovering quicker, and probably reaping additional benefits that cardiovascular exercise provides. There is a time and place to find that dark place, buckle down, and really challenge yourself to the point of physically exhausting yourself. As trainers, we owe it to our clients to better inform them and stop prescribing that type of exercise for our general population clients so frequently. It tires them out and makes them sweat, but may not get them any closer to what they are wanting to accomplish.

Burning fat and burning calories can be different things. Burning calories for weight loss is important. Being strategic through planning and programming in how we help our clients go about burning those calories, can lead them to be more efficient in learning how and when to push the threshold with burning more body fat and not overexerting themselves to the point of exhaustion.

CHAPTER 45

Strengthen Hip Flexors and Posterior Chain. Improve Ankle and Thoracic Spine Mobility. Learn about CARs.

Spend time strengthening hip flexors and posterior chain, help your clients improve ankle and thoracic spine mobility, and dive into some material on controlled articular rotations. Obviously there is so much more to your client's health and fitness goals than just focusing on these areas. But incorporating these into their programming will alleviate some common discomforts and hopefully will get your clients out of pain, which should always be a top priority. These specific areas seem to be commonly overlooked by a lot in the industry. We are so used to stretching areas that may feel "tight," but the hip flexors, which are a frequent concern of people who work at a desk for the majority of their career, can actually benefit from strengthening them instead of automatically jumping to stretching those areas. The entire backside, known as the posterior chain muscle groups, can always use some extra attention. Many people who workout on their own revert to working muscle groups they are comfortable with, which oftentimes include the "mirror muscles," those seen in the reflection of the mirror. These muscles include the quads, abs, chest, and arms. While these are all very important muscle groups to tone, if we primarily focus on only strengthening those, we not only create some wild imbalances, but posture can also be neglected because of the lack of working to build muscle throughout the back of the body.

The ankles and thoracic spine are also crucial areas to emphasize the importance of mobility because some of the most common complaints from clients will be pain or discomfort at the knees, hips, low back, and shoulders. By improving the ability to create more mobile joints at the areas surrounding where pain is felt and helping your clients increase the range of motion in those areas, there will be a noticeable reduction of discomfort. When an injury or nagging pain is found, it is evident there is irritation of some sort at the specific point of injury. Looking at the areas above and below that location can be a good indicator of the reasoning for an injury. If you have knee pain, assess the ankles and hips, as well as the muscles that tie into that joint, such as the calves, tibialis anterior, hamstrings, quadriceps, and adductors. If you have shoulder pain, see how well the thoracic spine moves and how the surrounding muscle groups function. It isn't always going to give you answers, but the body adapts around imperfections. If we never seek out and find where the source of an injury is, but rather just address the point where it hurts, we may miss out on compensation the body has been repeatedly doing to make up for weakness in another area. By assessing the ankles and thoracic spine mobility, you can alleviate a lot of pain and discomfort of the majority of your clients. If you can get people to actually notice drastic changes that make them feel better, your training reputation will skyrocket.

Do your due diligence on Controlled Articular Rotations (CARs) to help increase range of motion and mobility at your joints. These types of exercises can be informative to your clients on simple ways to incorporate mobility into their daily routines without needing any equipment. The use of CARs can help clients access greater ranges of motion through their joints. This is useful because it can help get them out of pain and discomfort. It will also eventually allow them to strength train the muscles tying into those joints through an increased range of motion, leading to greater strength and stability at end ranges, helping with muscle growth, reduced stiffness, and feeling better working from those joints. Your clients will thank you for incorporating a focus on these areas, but the true reward will be alleviating your clients of any pain they have been experiencing.

Some of my favorite exercises for each of these areas are listed:

Hip Flexor Strength: Banded hip flexor march, banded hip flexor isometric elevation, kneeling hip flexor elevation, reverse Nordic curls, front foot elevated split squats

Posterior Chain Strength: Romanian deadlift variations (RDL), reverse hypers, hip thrusters, leg curl variations, single leg bridges, GHD hip extensions, Nordic curls, Sorensen holds, row variations, pull/chin ups, lat pull downs, rear delt fly, band pull aparts, farmer's carry, prone lying overhead press, prone lying snow angels, prone lying IYT, face pulls, calf/Achilles variations

Ankle Mobility: Toe elevated wall knee taps, deficit calf stretch, ankle inversion stretch, foot elevated band distracted ankle dorsiflexion stretch, three-way ankle strengthening series (inversion, eversion, dorsiflexion)

Thoracic Spine Mobility: Kneeling thoracic spine twist, side lying upper body clam shell, side lying upper body windmill, cat/cow, kneeling prayer stretch

Controlled Articular Rotations: Hip, shoulder, ankle, mid-back, neck, wrists, knee (basically any joint)

CHAPTER 46

Food and Supplements as Fuel Tools

Emphasize the importance of nutrition, sleep, and hydration. Cautiously avoid automatically reverting to the importance of supplements. Supplements should be exactly what their name implies, an addition to our normal routine to fill the gaps of what our regular diet/lifestyle isn't providing. Before directing clients to spend endless money on supplements, make sure they are getting adequate amounts of protein, veggies, antioxidants, water, carbs, fats, sleep, and are prioritizing effective recovery tactics. If you notice clients are solely relying on supplements, foam rollers, and massage guns each and every day, it may be time to have a conversation with them about permanent solutions versus band-aids. Foam rollers, massage guns, and supplements can be great additions to the main types of recovery techniques, such as getting enough sleep, properly fueling the body with nutrient dense foods, remaining properly hydrated, and listening to the body for when you need a rest day or to do some mobility. Once we begin substituting fitness constants for quick fixes, we start putting our bodies at a disadvantage.

It is very hard for the human body to ingest absolutely every necessary vitamin and mineral from a normal diet. Therefore, supplementation can be a useful tool to fill in those gaps where our diet falls short. Some of the more commonly suggested supplements include protein powder, creatine, Vitamin D, caffeine, iron, and some type of scientifically-backed powdered "greens." When you look at that list, all of those could very easily be swapped out for real foods or sunlight. If your clients ask you what supplements they should take, first be sure to have a conversation with them about what the role of supplements should be. Then, and only then, recommend ways to fill the gaps of their regular nutrition with supplements. If you're not sure what to suggest, refer them to a reliable dietician. This technically isn't our realm, so please don't guess and blindly prescribe meal plans you think are going to help. It's acceptable to give recommendations or suggestions, but mandating supplement or nutrition advice is serving an unacceptable service to your clients. If you truly don't know this area, find a dietician you trust and connect your people with them. This can be a great way to help them reach their goals, build your network, and it can speak wonders to the fact you are willing to send them in other directions to help them, instead of selfishly giving them poor advice on your own.

Protein powder can be beneficial because society, as a whole, tends to not get enough protein to accomplish the goals we set for ourselves. Protein is super important, as it helps strengthen bones, muscles, and also repairs body tissue. If we can't find ways to incorporate enough protein through real foods, adding in protein powder can be a good idea. Examples of high protein foods include beef, chicken, fish, eggs, turkey, lentils, legumes, and cottage cheese, to name a few.

Creatine has unfortunately received a less than ideal reputation, but is actually one of the few supplements that would not be a waste of money and can play a role in physical health and cognitive function. Creatine can help your clients build more strength and aid in muscle hypertrophy, with very few downfalls. If you don't supplement with creatine, you can find creatine in red meats, as well.

Vitamin D can be obtained by being outside for an extended period of time on a daily basis, but some locations and times of year don't make that the easiest thing in the world. If you are outside in strong sunlight or for extended periods of time, be sure to utilize a reputable sunscreen option to protect yourself from the harms of the sun. If you are unable to get outside regularly, supplementing with Vitamin D would be to your benefit, as it can help promote healthy bones and boosts your immune system.

Caffeine can be useful with boosting energy, but should not be used as a substitute for lack of sleep or adrenal fatigue. Masking a real issue, such as repeatedly not getting enough sleep on a regular basis by overcompensating with caffeine, is a recipe for disaster. Take care of your body and use caffeine as a pick me up when you need it. When you do decide to take caffeine, stay away from the high sugar choices and make sure to not intake it too close to bedtime to ensure you don't interrupt sleep patterns. Be smart about it.

Powdered greens can be a great addition to those who don't get enough vegetables in their daily regimen. If you need to use this in addition to your regular diet, do so to provide your body with the endless benefits greens do provide. Now, if you are completely exchanging vegetables out for powdered greens, know you are missing out on the benefits real vegetables provide. Ask friends, coworkers, the internet, or family to help you find new ways to prepare vegetables. Maybe discovering new flavors mixed with real greens which grow from the ground will satiate your palate more than just consuming a powdered green liquid.

Iron supplementation can be very helpful for people who aren't getting enough iron in their diets. Iron is found naturally in spinach, red meats, nuts, dried fruit, legumes, and oats. Therefore, if a person is not consuming these types of foods consistently, they risk the chance of becoming anemic. People who have anemia often struggle with tiredness, lack of energy, dizziness, and lightheadedness. This is commonly seen with high school and college females, especially. If someone is dealing with anemia or any sort of iron-deficiency, this type of supplement can be helpful to suggest. Have your client check with a professional before automatically taking iron supplements.

When in doubt, eat real foods over taking a supplement. If and when you do need more of a certain nutrient, supplements can be beneficial. Please be sure you are recommending supplements at the right time and for the right people. When in question, seek out a dietician, nutritionist, or even a physician to gather a more expert opinion. Always recommend your clients to check with a medical professional to avoid any adverse effects of mixing other medications they may be taking with suggested supplements.

CHAPTER 47

Speak to Your Clients About Mental Health, Focus, Positive Emotions, and Learn About the Broaden-and-Build Theory

"I have loved working out with Andrew. He has helped me in more ways than one. He has helped me become a better person and helped find a passion for something I love! I love coming to workout and Andrew is always there for me! I have also loved working out with Collin on Saturday morning when he has classes! They both have impacted my life for the better and I couldn't thank them enough!"

While pursuing my Master of Education in Positive Coaching and Athletic Leadership through the University of Missouri, I had the pleasure of getting to work with and learn from Dr. Greg Sullivan, my professor and my advisor. Through the program at Mizzou and in reading Sullivan's book *Servant Leadership in Sport: Theory and Practice* (2019), I gained useful knowledge I was able to apply directly to my personal life, relationships, and those involved in my business. A few of the most noteworthy subjects in the program revolved around mental health, focus, positive emotions, self-talk, and the Broaden-and-Build Theory. Included below is a paper I wrote for one of Dr. Sullivan's classes to show the benefits of these particular concepts. As you read, note how you can better yourself as a trainer when connecting to these approaches.

According to Sullivan (2019), the broaden-and-build theory allows us to feel positive emotions that opens up the possibility to then snowball into the mindset that the next situation we find ourselves in will be seen as positive which allows for us to feel more positive emotions. This upward spiral provides us with endless opportunities and a great mind frame to encourage those chances. In addition to the broaden-and-build theory, the theory of attentional control, which is controlling your attention by focusing on what is helpful and relevant, ultimately leading to optimal performance is another theory that allows us as coaches to lead our athletes in a better direction (Sullivan, 2020). The unique ability of athletes to engage in and improve their skill of focus is what allows them to achieve that peak level of performance, experience those positive emotions, and spiral upwards into more positivity in all aspects of our lives.

It is very important to expand on our theories by applying them to real-life situations that we find ourselves in. In the case of the theory of attentional control, focus plays a major role in being able to concentrate on certain helpful tasks. Focus, in itself, is a skill. It is a mental skill. In fact, it is a skill that involves drawing together, incorporating, and applying all of the mental skills introduced and discussed in this course (Lesson 5 Applicational

Content, n.d.). We are in such a busy world. Time stops for no one. If we aren't stimulated by our phones, we have music on. If we don't have music on, we need to be conversing. If we aren't convers-ing with others, we are on the go. It can be very difficult to slow things down and to concentrate on one task with the distractions and hectic surroundings we constantly are engulfed in. Learning how to focus and to focus on the right things can help us in sport as athletes, in coaching, or in any little facet of our regular lives by providing us with the ability to ignore all of the distractions. When we learn how to concentrate on the task in front of us, we can remain present in that moment and ensure to get the most out of it. We are only capable of selectively attending to one thing at a time, according to the idea of Limited Information Processing Capacity (Sullivan, 2020). For the specific example of an athlete, there are so many external distractions, internal cues, and such high levels of arousal that focus can be difficult, especially during game situations. It may seem that so much is going on at once but in reality, we can only handle one thought at a time, but when placed in rapid succession, it can become overwhelming. The ability to dial in, use our learned skills of focus, and to perform optimally is what all athletes desire and what coaches want for their athletes.

It is our job as coaches to take the knowledge of those theories and apply it to the way we educate our athletes. During practice, we need to help athletes harness the thoughts and concentrate on controlling those mental skills in the moment so that when it comes to gameday, those skills of focusing come as second nature. The way that we converse with our athletes and by putting the same amount of emphasis on the mental practice repetitions as we do on the physical practice repetitions is what will allow our athletes to learn to focus on a higher level. One thing that I do with my clients to help them focus on whatever task we have ahead is to create a checklist through my cues. I work very hard on perfecting coaching cues that allow for my clients to fully understand what I am saying and to put those cues to action. In creating some of those cues, I have used an autonomy-based approach so the cue sticks with the clients a little more because of their assistance in coming up with those instructions. When we create those cues together, they will feel a sense of belonging but they will also remember how to do things the right way, which is very important. That ability for them to focus on the little details allows them to perform the exercises with perfect form and with maximal load, while remaining safe.

In identifying those coaching cues that help my clients focus, they often engage in self talk. Self-talk is one of the initial reasons why I became interested in enrolling in my graduate program. I absolutely love the study of the body in motion, the depths of strength and conditioning, and helping people set, pursue, and achieve physical goals but what has begun to fascinate me more and more in recent years is what goes on inside the heads of the personal training clients I have. The conversations you have with yourself in good times and bad, are what will elicit your performance at a level above, at, or below what you think you're capable of.

Self-talk can be a real contributing factor in the mindset that we have before, during, and after our workouts. Self-talk is that conversation that you have with yourself in your head. More often than not, the productivity level of a workout is based on what goes on between the ears. We can't show up to every single session, week after week, year after year motivated to our max. We need to be disciplined and push ourselves, whether or not we feel our best that day. Self-talk determines the outcome of our attitude and effort in the gym, at work, and in all sorts of life situations. The way we speak to ourselves can elevate us or tear us down. Be kind to yourself. Be proud of yourself. Push yourself. Create that internal drive through focusing on improving your self-talk. As a trainer, our job is to program, listen, and push our clients using a variety of strategies but that external push from us only does so much if the internal voice is an opposition to the plan set in place. Positive self-talk can be a constant in an ever-changing world.

Specifically, as it relates to training, I engage with my clients to receive some snippets of insight as to what is going on with their body during our workouts by asking questions about what muscles they felt working, how the movement felt, or ranking the workout on a scale of 1-10 in physical difficulty. To get some idea of where their mind is, I ask similar questions about what was going on in their head at different time frames, how were they able to push through and persevere when I intentionally made it a mental grind, or if they even had the thought of wanting to quit. Learning that we have the ability to teach clients how to focus more and by using the broaden-and build theory to keep their thoughts positive, which can improve self-talk, and then lead to better outcomes during our training sessions is so exciting moving forward. Using this strategy to transfer the concept of me keeping them focused to them learning how to improve their skill of focus will allow them to understand that positivity needs to come from them to truly maximize their positivity and to improve performance to the utmost.

In continuing to learn how to improve the skill of focus, we need to find the optimal arousal level. Physical Arousal would be how "pumped up" you are; Psychological Arousal would be how "psyched up" you are (Lesson 5 Applicational Content, n.d.). In order to perform at the highest level, we must seek to obtain our optimal arousal level, which differs for each of us and can even differ depending on the day, environment, or even the task involved. Through attentional narrowing, which Sullivan (2020) describes as the ability to narrow or broaden attention as necessary, we understand that increased arousal can lead to a decrease in ability and that an increase in distraction can create a more difficult environment to perform optimally. Learning to narrow our focus and to find that optimal arousal zone will not only allow us to feel more comfortable performing while internal or external distractions are thrown our way, but we will then give ourselves the possibility to reach peak performance on a more consistent basis. Spending time learning to direct attention through attention control training is a great way to personalize the strategies needed for each individual to focus during their specific sport (Sullivan, 2020). Using this approach to inform my coaching practices allows me to hypothetically zoom in on each person to dissect their strengths, weaknesses, and determine the width and direction of attention that they need to ultimately become the best version of themselves during times of high distraction or of increased arousal. In working with athletes and being a former athlete myself, coaches often tell us to "practice like you play" and although that can be a good thought, more often than not, practices don't quite have as much on the line as in-game situations. In order to mimic that situation, some coaches do more scrimmage-like portions of practice, that allow for athletes to direct their attention towards game-like situations so they can practice focusing more often prior in preparation for game day.

The next step to learning to improve our skill to focus depends on concentration, which is improved by learning to observe a situation, strategizing your mode of attack, utilizing imagery so you can feel your future performance in your mind and trusting yourself (Lesson 5 Applicational Content, n.d.). Learning to use these four steps, in conjunction with my leadership traits to improve the skill of concentration of my clients with the limited time we have together will allow us to get the most out of our sessions. In using my optimism, positivity, and belief in my clients, I have the fuel I need to keep moving forward and drive results (Gordon, 2017).

The final piece to improve our skill of focusing is application and putting all of the steps together. Throughout this course, we are constantly learning theories and although those can be beneficial, if we neglect to put those to application, those theories don't mean much. The same goes for our ability to improve our mental skill of focus. We understand the process needed to improve our focus, but until we put that education to action, it isn't doing us much good. This idea of application is why I am so excited about this program. Using the connections that we've found between the tra-ditional sport psychology and positive theories, especially those that allow us to improve the positive mindset, and in turn, open up even more possibilities down the road, as the broaden-and build theory suggests, can help my coaching and leading practices, but hopefully help others reap the benefits of my learnings. In working to improve our personal focus and through helping others learn to improve their skill of focus, we are able to tap into a mental skill that we otherwise only guess how to replicate. Taking the guesswork out of a learned skill through applying our knowledge of theories can help transform my coaching and leadership practices, as well as provide a much-improved experience for my clients.

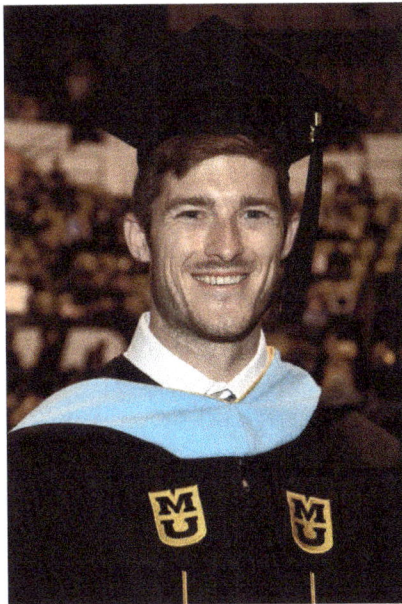

CHAPTER 48

Psychology and Imagery can Help You Help Your Clients

Psychology plays a big part in the personal training field. We all act, think, and feel differently than others because of what we've experienced, our mindsets, and how we internalize dialogue. As a coach, first understand there are different techniques on how to effectively coach clients. What may be obvious to us may be completely foreign to others. The brain is an amazing organ, and if we can educate and influence the minds of our clients, we can help motivate them and improve their chances of success, in the gym and all other aspects of life. Helping clients improve their mindset, focus, and confidence in themselves will benefit you and allow your clients to flourish with their performance. The same idea applies when working with athletes. By working to improve their mental practices, they can overcome obstacles, build resiliency, and cope with difficult situations. Just as we emphasize the importance of individualizing physical fitness and health, we must tailor the details of our imagery and mental practices to those we are tending to in order to set them up for success. As coaches and trainers, we should take pride in giving others the best opportunity to succeed long after our time together has concluded. Through educating those we work with on effective ways to incorporate mental practices to their regular routines, we can provide others with so much more than just physical fitness services. As personal trainers, our focus needs to be on both the body and the mind. By preparing our athletes with the tools necessary to succeed and assisting them in enhancing their physical and mental skills, chances greatly improve that they will boost their athletic performance and their well-being outside of our practices. One successful tool to use with clients to assure their minds are as strong as their bodies is a mental construct known as "imagery." Imagery involves the ability to use our memory and imagination as a way to formulate mental pictures in a way that allows us to connect our thoughts to our emotions without environmental input. When implementing the use of imagery as a construct into our programming, we can help positively affect psychological states thus decreasing anxiety and enhancing self-confidence, self-efficacy and concentration (Garza & Feltz, 1998; Post & Wrisberg, 2012). It is also beneficial for use as coping strategies, maintaining existing skills, and reviewing past performances (Thelwell & Maynard, 2002; White & Hardy, 1998).

One example of how to use imagery in the personal training field is through setting intentions and gathering the minds of clients at the beginning of sessions. The majority of our clients lead busy lives. Although they may need someone to lend an ear so they can get things off of their chest, we also need to set boundaries to ensure we accomplish our goals in a timely fashion. By taking a few quick minutes before beginning, to set intentions for the hour session, allows us to be on the same page of what we are trying to accomplish through the programmed workout. Taking this time also reminds clients to be present throughout their session. Oftentimes, full engagement in a session allows an individual to completely clear their mind and relieve stress from outside factors, even more than if they just spilled everything out to you. The simple conversation with clients about how they are feeling generally gives you an idea as to how that session will go. Even when your client may seem more distracted than usual, simple visualization of technique or load or speed has proven to help drastically in making the most out of sessions.

In two recent studies, Anuar and her colleagues (2016a/2016b) demonstrated that incorporating elements of the PETTLEP model increased the ease and vividness of imaged movements. As Sullivan (2020) emphasized, vividness is crucial to successful imagery as it is when we create as possible the actual experience in our mind. When we work to improve this skill, we can use that to improve imagery. Through techniques of trying to improve the skill of imagery, we can improve other aspects of our training/ practice, as well as competition.

Through using imagery training programs, such as the PETTLEP model to create the most functionally equivalent image possible, we can be more specific in our mental practices (Quinton, 2013). One example to apply this theory would be if we were to train a runner who wants to participate in a marathon in town.

Physical-We would have this runner run in the exact or similar running clothes and shoes they would compete in.

Environment-They can run the exact route, if possible.

Task-They need to understand that as a newly competitive runner, they should focus on finding a sustaining goal pace, concentrate on breathing, and not letting outside noise distract them from completing the race, despite their competitors.

Timing-With how long of a race a marathon is, maybe there is a goal time set or maybe the goal is to simply finish.

Learning-We began by building their endurance and fixing nagging injuries that possibly have flared up in the past. Then we learn how their body adapts to increasing volume and speed. Lastly, their ability to adapt in performance can impact whether or not we can focus on increasing our level of imagery.

Emotion-There will possibly be feelings of nervousness, anxiety, self-doubt, pride, and contentment. Creating an environment in preparation for the race to mimic a race day situation as a means to create a level of optimal anxiety without any added pressure is one way to help work through those feelings so they know at what level they perform best at. Also, there should be a sense of pride and satisfaction or contentment. When the race comes around, the hard work has already been done. This client is more than ready from a physical standpoint but now it is time to put all of the pieces of the puzzle together and go compete.

Perspective-Through honing in on internal visual imagery, they will be able to sustain their pace and breathing on race day, and ultimately enjoy their first race. Controlling the controllable portions are things that are important to discuss with each other and maintaining the perspective of the importance of each stride and breath will help them mentally slow things down to concentrate on the variables within their control.

There have been studies, such as the hockey and gymnastic athletes Smith et al. (2007) tested with different methods of imagery, that provide support for the efficacy of PETTLEP-based imagery over more traditional imagery interventions. Those athletes that utilized the PETTLEP-based imagery techniques improved significantly from pretest to post-test with their success of penalty shots and performance of attempting a turning jump on a beam. Incorporating forms of imagery during training sessions are beneficial, but by incorporating a PETTLEP model, we would be able to improve our client's progress and allow them to perform at higher levels more regularly.

CHAPTER 49

Habits → Behaviors → Lifestyle

"Andrew gives over 100% to each of his clients. He works very hard to build a customized program for each of his clients. He helps you set goals and meet them, coaching you through every step of the way. Andrew is constantly researching the latest information in fitness and nutrition and is extremely knowledgeable. His positive outlook makes it all challenging and fun!"

Help create habits. Habits turn into behaviors. Behaviors transform lifestyles. As a personal trainer, you will put in so much time outside of the gym to provide for your clients doing programming, planning, and researching. Extend that expectation to your clients to help them accomplish their goals faster and to create a better sense of accountability by giving them homework outside of the gym. That can include additional workouts, stretching or mobility, daily walks, going to bed earlier, eating more vegetables or protein, drinking more water, and whatever other tips you find each person can take and apply to their lives to make them feel better and reach their goals quicker.

You want to capitalize on the hour you have with your clients. If they're on board with doing additional work on top of that, it makes your life easier and they'll begin to notice changes much sooner. This test of giving clients things to work on while on their own also gives us insight into a few different things. How dedicated are your clients? How badly do they want to accomplish their goals? Are they buying into your program? Are they willing to allow their lifestyle to change by beginning to shift their daily habits?

We are all creatures of habit. We live years and years with certain routines and tendencies. When we get out of our normal routine, change can take time and will definitely take effort. If we want to see changes, we must first make the conscious choice to take initiative. When it comes to beginning a workout routine, it will take your clients time and effort to begin this new routine and for the programming to reverse some of the lingering issues from previous routines or habits. Stepping into the gym for the first time in weeks, months, years, or for the first time in their life can be a huge accomplishment. Walk clients through new routines bit by bit, so they do not feel daunted or distressed. The addition of a new habit can be intimidating and maybe even stressful. When you train somebody who is adopting new habits in their fitness journey, be patient and don't overwhelm them with too much all at once.

As someone who grew up with the gross habit of being a nail-biter, I've come to understand how difficult it can be to permanently halt a habit. My grandma offered to pay me to stop. I did. Then I didn't. I very briefly stopped and then unconsciously started right back up. It's a disgusting habit. The first time I ever trimmed and cut my nails, because they were growing out to the point of needing to be cut, was when I was 27 years old. It took me a long time to get past that habit. Habits are hard to break and sometimes even harder to pick up. When people approach you and want to start working out, understand the courage it took to make such a choice, and the first time stepping back into the gym is a big deal. Analyze your client's frame of mind when first starting out together. See how prepared they are physically and mentally when deciding how to immerse them into the culture of the gym, their workouts, and the path they are willing to take to achieve their goals. Don't bog clients down with drastic changes you're expecting them to make down the road. Help them set realistic goals for the future, but also make your main focus about the controllable factors in the present moment.

Once the gym becomes a more regular staple in their lives, then it can become manageable to introduce additional habits. For example, when a new client begins with me and we agree to workout three times each week, that's all that we need to start. They don't need to do three additional cardio days, completely alter their food intake, and cut out all soda or dessert. That may be too much to ask a new client who wants to become healthier. If your goal is to help them instill better behaviors to live healthier lifestyles, doing too much too soon or restricting certain enjoyable parts of their life goes against what you're trying to teach them. Take things one step at a time and read the situation to learn when each person is ready to incorporate that next stage to continue progressing. Don't have clients bite off more than they can chew.

We encourage our clients to have patience. When we are coaching, we must adhere to that idea as well. We have ideas we want to push across to our clients. Learning when and how to address them will allow for better reception, and our clients are more apt to take those recommendations to heart. In order to see drastic changes, we must take the steps necessary to build to the point of those larger changes being more realistic. This may seem simple, but in order to achieve that large goal at the end, we need to take little steps to get that ball rolling. We won't reach our goal overnight, but that doesn't mean we can make minor changes on a daily basis. When instructing your clients, start small. Don't put them in a state of chaos where they feel dumbfounded with how dramatically they have to alter their lifestyle. That will cause some clients to stop before they even get started. Use your intellect and suggest one habit change at a time. When that proves to be attainable, add in another. Repeat that cycle and eventually you and your client will look back and notice the leaps and bounds you've taken together by simply making one minor change after another.

When it comes to adding in new habits, think adding, not subtracting. Whether you are discussing exercise, nutrition, sleep, recovery, mindfulness, or anything health and fitness related, first have your clients focus on addition, rather than subtraction. Rather than overwhelming clients and having them remove parts of their lives that have been staples for a long time, have them focus initially on what they can incorporate into their routine. Not only will this help shift their mindset into taking in more healthy substances, but in doing so, they will naturally lessen the number of unhealthy foods, thoughts, and behaviors. Preach inputting minor changes through drinking more water, eating more vegetables, climbing into bed a half hour earlier, or making a conscious effort to actively move for 30 minutes a certain amount of times per week. Each of these suggestions are miniscule and seem rather easy in the grand scheme of things. Rather than completely altering their workout routines, sleep schedules, and nutrition makeup, these little changes will add up to those major transformations down the road.

When we program our training sessions, we should take into account the days we will meet in person as well as the days you won't see your clients. Working out with them one to three times per week (which is a typical frequency with one-on-one clients) is great but in the end, those one to three hours need to be complemented with a healthy lifestyle during the other 165-167 hours each week. With 24 hours in a day, an hour of working out can get us heading down the right path. Yet, if we eat poorly, don't get off the couch, don't drink water, and sleep inadequately, that hour of training realistically isn't going to be enough to elicit any type of noticeable changes. This is a good conversation to have early on in the relationship we have with our clients. On the first meeting, establishing these important factors as an all-inclusive health routine is important, but we must be cognizant on how we approach those subjects. If we tell a new client they have to completely alter all aspects of their life in order to reach certain goals, they will become overwhelmed and will more than likely drop out soon after. Although clients need to recognize lifestyle changes outside of the gym are important, as their trainer we should try to influence a change in one or two behaviors at a time. We must be strategic in what we emphasize and what we have clients focus on. Begin with simply having them move more. They can work with you once in the gym, then tell them to go on two 30-minute walks and do mobility one day for an hour on their own time. For a novice client, this is a huge step toward becoming more active and making a change in their routine. If they adhere to those instructions for a few weeks, then maybe you bump things up by adding more walks or an at-home bodyweight circuit to involve a second resistance training workout each week.

When clients take it upon themselves to assume responsibility for their time away from you, they make that hour of training a cakewalk for you. Clients who learn to take gradual steps and focus on little things outside of your sessions are the ones who are eager to learn and more likely to achieve their intended goals. Not every client will adhere to your suggestion, which means you may have to revamp the conversation from a different point of view.

Finding different ways to talk to clients about what each of them need to do in order to get where they want can be difficult, but it is why they are paying you. Your job is to not only prescribe them exercise for an hour, but to lead them in the right direction so they have the tools to make smarter, healthier choices consistently. I have had clients tell me that conversations we have had together will resonate in their heads for days at a time and will help remind them to make decisions, one choice at a time. These conversations have helped people make smart choices, move more, feel better, and lead happier lives. We, as personal trainers, have that power. We just need to learn how to unlock it and relay messages to those who want to listen.

The clients who do want to listen and make radical lifestyle changes are the ones that will buy into what you are preaching, especially if you show them the process will generate the outcome they're looking for. When your clients buy in, do extra homework, and make you proud with the steps they've taken, express to them how you feel. Voice your pride in their accomplishments. Acknowledge their ability to get through a certain difficult workout. High five them. Write them a thank you note or a message of gratitude for the time and effort they are putting into bettering themselves. If you are going to propose to your clients to go the extra mile and do homework, follow up with them and do your due diligence to see how it went. If they report back that they did your workout, celebrate their effort. Working out on your own can be difficult. We see it all the time with clients. Some come to a trainer because they don't know how to workout safely or effectively on their own or don't feel comfortable alone. If we can get them to go on a walk, do a bodyweight circuit, or swap out those French fries for steamed vegetables, we need to applaud those decisions. Establishing lifestyle shifts and turning positive choices into habits are the first steps in noticing sustainable change. Once healthier habits are formed and they begin to pile onto one another, they become regular behaviors. After weeks, months, and years of finding a sustainable routine of an accumulation of behaviors that align with what you want your life to be focused around, you'll see your new lifestyle take shape. It starts with one small adjustment, but when we build upon those little modifications, they become noticeable changes. Personal trainers have the opportunity to help steer people in the right direction to accomplish big changes in their lifestyles.

CHAPTER 50

Be Where Your Feet Are

While training, center your focus on your client. Be where your feet are. We live in a world with so many distractions and so much noise. Your eyes shouldn't be wandering around the gym. Avoid checking your texts. Tend to each client, as they've paid you for your time. When someone signs up and pays for personal training with you, do your best to maximize the value for which they are paying. Clients should receive in-person training sessions, time you've set aside devoted to planning and preparation for our sessions, as well as contact (via text, email, social media, etc.) after each session to address any further needs. Clients should know they have your full devotion when they contract you to be their personal trainer.

The fee people pay for your service includes the product and service you provide, but in order to maximize the quality of those, your work actually begins before you even have your first actual training session together. From the moment you are introduced to or meet a client, the wheels should be turning on how to provide them with the best quality of service. This includes the preparation of getting to know them, who they are, what they need, and how you can best serve them. Do your homework. Speak to them directly. Set up a consultation. Send over a questionnaire. Do some

PERSONAL. TRAINING. BUSINESS.

research into who they are. These little things may not seem like much, but if you can begin that relationship on the right foot by making them feel the most at home in your gym, the transition period, which oftentimes can be a bit awkward or uncomfortable, can be bypassed or at least sped up. Getting through that introductory period to the point where both parties feel like they can be themselves around each other is important. This comfort comes from you doing prep work beforehand to make sure you can be the best version of yourself as a coach and leader.

Once your sessions begin, your focus on the client should begin before or at least when they walk in the door. Having equipment laid out before the session can help the flow of each workout. At times, this feat can be challenging if you have sessions backed up to each other. Regardless, be efficient with the time between clients and shift your focus from whatever you were doing prior to the new client walking in your door. One suggestion to utilize in a situation like this would be to initiate conversation asking how they are, what's new in their world, and how their body feels. These are all open-ended questions to help you get a feel for what their mood is and how life is coming into that workout. You may need to call upon your interpersonal skills and social awareness but the way they answer those questions can give you a sense of how you need to approach conversation and if you need to adjust the workout based on how they feel.

From there, walk your client through the purpose of the workout and what your goals of that session include. This can help them get on the same page as you for how the next hour will go. As the workout progresses, check their form, watch technique, count their reps, critique and fix little things when necessary, but also understand when you should keep quiet and allow them to figure out some of the technique on their own. We don't want to overcorrect or be overly critical with every single exercise. It's important to prioritize form, but there can also be benefits in letting your clients learn to move their bodies on their own or

223

letting them notice those little things, as long as they won't put themselves in a higher-risk of injury.

Be attentive and focus on your clients and their individual needs for the entire duration of your session. Not letting distractions in during your training session with someone will show them you care and that you prioritize and acknowledge their time. Make them understand they are your main priority, as they should be during that time. Other things can wait until later on, as this is contracted time. At the moment, you are being paid to lead, teach, and help work through the program you created for your client. When you are distracted and not fully paying attention, your clients may take notice. Care. Pay attention.

We are in a world where we are constantly receiving texts, calls, emails, social media posts, and all sorts of other notifications. When you are working, put the phone away. Have a clock and a timer in the gym to keep track of any time-related exercise routines. If you absolutely must use your phone for your programming, as a timer, or any other inevitable need during your training session, make sure you ONLY use it as such. If your client is paying for your assistance and you have your phone out responding to text messages or scrolling on social media, refund their money. That type of behavior is inexcusable. You shouldn't be paid for that type of training. Your client's safety is top priority and if you are distracted by your phone, you are putting them and their safety as a secondary priority. Allowing your phone to distract you from training sessions not only shows your clients you value what is on your electronics more than them, it is also very irresponsible as a fitness professional, which could negatively impact your reputation.

Imagine you are working out in a gym and are thinking about investing in a personal trainer. You scan around the area scouting different trainers to see who is attentive, invested in their client, and prescribing an interesting workout. As you are looking around, you notice one trainer clearly not paying any attention to their client. They are on their phone and not engaged, whatsoever. Regardless of what you had seen this trainer doing previously, or how intelligent they may seem, that trainer should be automatically eliminated from contention of potentially obtaining your business. Not only does this trainer miss out on you as a potential new client, you may even inform other fellow gym-goers of that trainer's behavior. As a trainer, put yourself in a situation where others observe you doing your best for each and every client with whom you work.

In our business, we constantly have eyes on us and our behaviors. Whether you know it or not, people are always watching and judging. I have gotten new clients because they invested time in researching, analyzing and comparing trainers. One particular client of mine did just that. For weeks, she would come to the gym, hop onto the stair stepper, and look out for a trainer who would meet her needs. She watched a variety of trainers to see if they trained the way in which she was interested. As a former teacher, she was looking for someone who taught, educated, and took the time to explain why each exercise was selected. After weeks of observation, she decided upon the trainer who checked off those boxes. Together, she and he made huge waves to help improve her strength, stability, and overall health. When he was promoted to another gym in a neighboring state, she was concerned about who she would work with and even debated on not working with a trainer anymore. This trainer, thankfully, brought up my name and explained to her that my ideas and philosophies lined up with the way he trained and the qualities she was looking for. They approached me and asked if I was interested (of course I was). I shadowed a few sessions before her previous trainer left so I could help her pick up right where they left off. We connected very quickly and got along great. She frequently insisted she enjoyed the way her previous trainer and I taught the movements, versus simply demanding people do them. This confirms the importance of including an educational portion in a great training program.

In the same light of showing your undying support of your clients, it is important to follow up and be there for clients after sessions conclude. What this looks like may vary person to person. As their trainer, it is your job to keep tabs and check in on them to retain that line of communication. Shooting a simple text the day after someone had a tough workout, sending homework (cardio, stretching, nutrition suggestions, etc.), or a simple follow up message on something you chatted about during the session would be ways to extend your reach to clients. The way you go about following up can be personalized in your own way. Ultimately, letting your clients know you care for them as people, beyond their paid hour, can do wonders for your relationship.

This job doesn't necessarily allow for you to "clock out" as we have to train a certain amount of hours to make money; program for those clients in our down hours; as well as stay on top of marketing, advertising, and all of the other behind the scenes parts of this job. It's also imperative to make time for ourselves, our loved ones, workouts, meal preparation, and sleep. This job is very similar in the sense of what we preach, in that we need to make it a lifestyle. We tell our clients they can't just take a pill and accomplish everything they've ever wanted. They have to buy in. They have to do the little things that allow the big things to eventually take place. The same goes for us as trainers. Be present in your own personal life outside of your job. Your family and friends outside of the gym need to know you are present when you are together. They deserve quality time with you and you should enjoy the ability to have time with them away from work. "Be where your feet are" applies no matter where you find yourself. It is important to remember what role we are supposed to be playing for our clients as well as our families. Remain where your feet are to soak in and enjoy the present moment.

CHAPTER 51

Not Your Body, Not Your Business

When conversing with clients (or anybody, for that matter), be conscious of the comments you make that may be perceived to be about their body, habits, or nutrition/working out. Body image, body dysmorphia, and eating disorder issues are real and unfortunately, are so much more common than we may realize. We never know who is experiencing some of those difficulties, nor to the extent of which they are battling emotional obstacles. Err on the side of caution and stay away from commenting on other people's bodies, making suggestions that imply you need to work extra hard in order to earn or enjoy a meal/dessert, or even categorizing foods as 'good' and 'bad.' These types of phrases or comments can be very triggering, and we may not know the damage we are doing. If it isn't your body, just be conscious of what you say, even if you don't intend negative connotations. Replace the 'you look so thin/skinny' with 'you look so strong/powerful/confident/happy.' It may not seem like much, but to people around you, that small shift in the way you discuss the body and exercise can help them feel more comfortable in their own skin. Speak with empathy and understand even if your intent wasn't malicious, damage can be done to those around you based on their individual perception. Body image, eating disorders, and body dysmorphia can be very difficult subjects to speak upon, but doing research into it will be something you'll thank yourself for if you plan on continuing in this field. Find your resources, do your research, and begin to understand some of the areas surrounding body image, eating disorders, and body dysmorphia to help your clients feel at home around you. We are in a profession where we work closely with others and our work revolves around the body. Learning about, understanding, and having some background in these subjects can be helpful in navigating conversations or situations you may find yourself in with your clients and loved ones. We cannot ignore these issues because they are very serious. Being better equipped with knowledge on body matters and being cognizant of how we speak to others, can make people feel more comfortable around us and not feel judged for whatever they may be going through.

Notice that at no point in the prior paragraph did I mention any gender. So many people, regardless of gender or what others may perceive as fit or healthy, have concerns over the way their body looks. Body dysmorphia doesn't discriminate but for some reason it is often viewed as something only females struggle with. It's time that stigma changes because females aren't the only ones who deal with body image disorders. In my experience, I know of countless males who have dealt with or are currently battling body image concerns. It is a very real thing and as fitness professionals, we need to tread lighter and be sure that every individual we come in contact with knows that their time with us is judgment free and that we are there to help them work on whatever they desire. By recognizing that body image issues are spread across so many, regardless of gender, age, or any other characteristic, we can be intentional in our word choices and the way we view this mental health subject so nobody gets hurt.

CHAPTER 52

Celebrate the Quality of Work Your Clients Show in the Gym

Preach quality over quantity. In order to see results in the gym, progressive overload is necessary. Progressive overload is when you increase resistance, repetitions, volume, or frequency. In other words, you make your training slightly more intense through manipulating one variable or another over time in order to develop more muscle, burn fat more efficiently, build strength, increase power, and continue checking off little goals on the way to your bigger goal. People need to see continuous improvement over time to achieve quantitative results. As we continue to progress, it's important to not compensate for technique. Moving heavy amounts of weight is impressive. Typically, in order to lift those high amounts of weight, form needs to be somewhat decent, but form is something we should prioritize every single time we walk into the gym. Lifting heavy is fun and rewarding. Lifting heavy with perfect form is impressive. In my own training regimen, I have wrapped my head around that thought and over the past few years. I have gotten away from focusing solely on how much I can lift and pinpointing my workout more on how to lift with perfect technique. I have made it a point to make each and every repetition as near to perfection as I can. I pride myself in making working out look "pretty." When a weightlifter demonstrates proper form day in and day out, their numbers will climb. Focusing on perfect technique has not only helped my numbers naturally rise, but my body has never felt this good and my risk of injury has significantly reduced.

This realization may take some time. Being in the gym can be an ego trip. It's common to compare yourself to others, but recreational exercise, particularly weightlifting, really isn't about how much you can bench versus what others can bench. Rather, it is about how much a person can bench with perfect form and zero pain versus what that individual used to be able to bench. That being said, I enjoy lifting heavy (subjectively) to see what I am capable of, but when my form slips, I stop adding weight and ensure quality form. As a result of this shift in thinking about weightlifting, my training has improved, my excitement to workout hasn't wavered, and none of my joints hurt. Consciously working out with the purpose of showing perfect technique each and every rep will help you also feel this way.

When it comes to defining perfect form, it would be easy to state one certain way to perform a movement but in this field, and hopefully in other resources we have access to, everything is so personalized to the individual. There can be many versions of what perfect form looks like. Because of an assortment of factors, such as genetics and anatomical variations, some exercises can be done more easily for some while they may provide difficulties for others. One common technique issue can be seen when people squat. You'll note that although some claim there is one perfect way to squat, I would stand firm in arguing that perfect technique varies from person to person. There can definitely be different factors that limit squat form, such as lack of ankle dorsiflexion, weak hip flexors, inability to properly brace the core, or simply lack of confidence with the bar in certain positions but sometimes the reason a squat looks different from person to person is because we are all made differently. Each of us have a different anatomical makeup and we may have been dealt a hand that makes it harder for us to get into what some would consider to be perfect form. For example, I have a friend who is strong as an ox but he has a wider stance and squats a little more hinged over, which according to some may not be the ideal form. He has worked ankle mobility, continued to work on improving range of motion, and even tested out different stances but we've come to the conclusion that because of his 6'5" frame and long legs, he may just have longer femurs and his form may look different than someone who isn't as tall and has shorter legs.

Over time, as we gain experience and work with a variety of clients, we'll learn to not try to shape every individual into the same box. Some people and their form should be a bit more tailored to what their body and lifestyle allow. All the same, we can work around those individual differences while still prioritizing great technique and impeccable form. With that experience and as our career takes shape, we will get a better sense of when form slips, even with those contrasting techniques. What we should always look out for is anything that will put our clients in harm's way. We may not need to instantly correct every little detail, as I think there is something to be said about allowing others to figure out some of the ways of their body on their own without overloading them with cues and corrections but we must look out for the errors in form that raise their risk of serious injury. Lifting too much with the back when you're not intending, significant shifting of the hips, overarching of the back when core engagement is necessary, and unstable feet causing a ripple effect up the rest of the body while under load are a few important lapses in form that we should keep an eye out for to keep our clients safe.

As trainers, we need to do a better job of celebrating the perfect reps of our clients. Quality reps will lead to clients feeling better, improved mobility, and weight to pile itself on with lower risks of injuries. In your training, whether it is for yourself or while coaching your clients, emphasize the importance of form and technique. Get excited about that. Show your people how much you love seeing them perform those perfect reps. On the other hand, sometimes you need to be the bad cop and realize when it is time to strip some weight off of their bar to refrain from getting injured. It is your job to understand when it may be a good time to halt from throwing more weight on the bar while explaining to your client why it is the smart decision to do so. Through transparent communication, both parties can be on the same page moving forward with technique and range of motion rising to the top of the list of priorities. Feel free to share how you, personally, approach your own exercise regimen. When your clients learn what is important to you, they may be open to shifting what is important to them to align with what you believe is crucial to their long-term health.

CHAPTER 53

Give, Give, Give

While understanding your worth and the value of your service, don't be afraid to give, give, and give some more. The more you give to others, the more good will come your way. One way to give to others while training is to help people, even if they are at other gyms or in different cities. With the way the world works now, you can create programs for individuals from your hometown, across the country, or even overseas. Even from a distance, people properly executing your program will create awareness of your program and your expertise. The brand you are working to create and build can expand far beyond the walls of your gym. What most of you will realize, if you haven't already, is when you begin training, you'll have friends and family reaching out to you to help them with getting in shape, losing weight, or even finding some sort of new workout regimen. When approached, this situation should be viewed as yet another opportunity to grow your business and increase brand awareness. You should be proud you have people seeking you out to help them accomplish goals that are very important to them. This may come from simply helping a friend back home fix the form of their deadlift so they don't get hurt or writing a workout program for an aunt looking to find some consistency with her health and wellness. Your ability to help people and prioritize their health through their individualized programming is another way to spread and expand your professional name. The more people you are able to connect with, the more your network will grow. The more your network expands, the more people will associate you with being their go-to person when they need help in this field. When you help them when asked, they'll speak highly of you and recommend you to others in their lives. This networking is a web you have the ability to create. Even though it can be easy to solely focus on the demographic in your geographical area, imagine the opportunities you have to keep growing your product when people from outside those parameters contact you.

To piggyback on that, if it's something you're interested in, don't be afraid to dabble with the online industry. We all have friends and family who don't live in the same area as us. If they see you building a business in the personal training field and want to support and take your professional advice, think about using technology to provide service to them. Asking the central questions regarding their intents and goals for prospective workouts would be the first place to start with clients from a distance. Inquiring about the equipment or areas they will be able to access for workouts is another crucial aspect of planning for those with whom you will not physically be training. Identifying any health concerns also guides your programming in these instances. Once you are clear on your client's background and motives, start typing up their plans to be shared. Everything is at the touch of our fingers and having a personal trainer via an app, through Zoom calls, or at the convenience of your own home without actually having another person in your house can be very appealing for some. I've dipped my foot in those waters a bit through programming for my cousin for a few years, a younger cousin on Facetime workouts during COVID-19, and a friend of mine back home. Collin and our dad have done workouts over their phones to help him learn some new exercises and stay pain-free while running. There are so many great opportunities and if that intrigues you and you believe your strengths would bring an attractive product to people around your area and beyond, give it a go! You can decide if and how to actively promote or push online programming to be a larger chunk of your business. It is a great way to work on programming and keep your friends and family accountable and healthy even from a distance. If you do decide to give it a go, I'd love to follow along so let me know!

To bring it back to giving to others, offering your services for free or a limited offer at a special rate to begin your business is a reputable way to display the product you offer, the services you provide, and the knowledge you bring to the table. This worked well for me when I began training. Sales were hard for me. Not knowing what strategy was best to sell myself and the training services I provided, led me to give away free time. This approach was doubly beneficial because it not only got people in front of me where I could then show them what I knew and how I could help them, but it proved to them that although this is a business and money is necessary, profiting off of them wasn't my first priority. I let my services speak for themselves and never pushed a sale. Free sessions ended with simply putting the ball in their court and sharing my rate. Assuring these potential clients that if they wanted to continue training with me, I'd love to work with them. The best method is to avoid being too pushy and 'sales-y.' People understand you provide a service and when they approach you, they at least have some interest. When you give them a taste of your product for free, it allows them the opportunity to see if your product is what best fits their needs. People love free services. Give time away and watch how well you are treated by those interested. This is an unconventional way of getting a sale and your time is valuable. Yet, if you prove to a potential client from the get go that the value of service you provide to help others comes before the conversation of transactions, it shows where your priorities lie. Personal training is a business and we need to make money. But, if you give to others first and demonstrate how good you are at your craft and how much you care about them working toward and reaching their goals, your value drastically increases and the sales conversation becomes much easier. The scenario of training someone for free for an hour of your time allows you to create a first touch with potential clients, establish a level of trust, and give a taste of what you offer.

Giving away a freebie may not always be something you feel you must do to capture the attention of your audience. You may get to the point in your career where your name and brand do your selling for you. In those instances where you are approached by somebody who wants to start right away because of the reputation your business has acquired and you don't want to give away a free session, at least put forth the effort and time to ensure you are fully prepared for the first time you meet. Maybe that is a phone call, you meeting them for (and paying for their) coffee, or simply shooting an email their way with questions that will allow you to grasp everything they are looking for and expecting out of your services. Going above and beyond to prove that you care and through giving in various ways will help you attract more people who are seeking out someone who will return their investment to you in them.

CHAPTER 54

Use Your Position to Make Each Client's Day a Bit Brighter

We all have days when we need a little boost. Sometimes those days when clients seem to be dragging can be changed by an extra push from you, as the trainer. Each client will need a unique coaching style, similar to athletics. Some players respond better to a coach lighting a fire under them, yelling, and pushing them to what some spectators would say is too far. Others need someone to be a positive light in their lives and repeatedly show they believe in their capabilities. Every person's needs are different, but what is similar amongst most individuals is they all have a few days here and there that just don't go their way. Not only does the gym provide people with a lot of stress relief, which could be the release needed to turn a day around, but as trainers, we have the ability to help influence clients in a variety of ways. The role we play for our clients can mean we put on the mask of a counselor, therapist, coach, listener, and/or friend. We can also help directly boost self-confidence in our clients by setting them up for success in the gym in different ways. A simple method to help my clients if they're having a bad day is to modify their workout accordingly. This can be done through shifting the emphasis more towards prioritizing range of motion over weight, sprinkling in some exercises they thoroughly enjoy doing, and even sneakily helping them make more challenging exercises easier as a boost to their belief in themselves. For example, with the way our rig is set up, we have squat stations within the rig and each station has a set of movable j-hooks that hold the barbells. Or, in the case of assisted pull ups, we attach a band to both j-hooks so it lies horizontally between the squat station for people to stand on to help pull themselves up to the bar. By putting the j-hooks one notch higher, it makes the pull ups just a smidge easier. Pull ups are one of the most difficult exercises and the truest measure of upper body strength. When pull ups are easier for someone, their self-confidence skyrockets. When self-confidence goes through the roof and people feel stronger, the endorphin release can be mood altering. On a tough day, that little adjustment can change someone's day. Complementing clients on improvements or little victories, such as depth or weight moved for a certain exercise, can be small, meaningful ways to help boost their day. You don't need to be a superhero or cross the line too far to try to change the way people feel. Controlling little things within your abilities to hopefully provide your people with a better experience in the gym can make your clients happier individuals.

CHAPTER 55

You Do a Lot For Others. Take the Credit You Deserve.

Typically, most trainers genuinely don't accept any credit for the successes of their clients, since they are the ones who worked their tails off for what they've accomplished. That being said, take (some) responsibility for the successes of your clients. You might not have done all of the hard work, but you did have a part in their progress. Whether you gave them advice that stuck in their mind, provided them with the tools to take the next step toward their goals, or were their biggest fan and supporter throughout their entire journey, you play at least a sliver of a role in the success your clients achieve. Being proud of your job and the drastic lifestyle changes to which you contribute is amazing. Feel free to pat yourself on the back now and then. Not only do you have the ability to create strength and conditioning programs for people to follow, but you have the power to help them alter their mindsets to allow them to navigate their goals through permanent lifestyle changes. This ability to help persuade people to recognize what they are able to accomplish can build their confidence, which will lead to positive repercussions inside and out of the gym. When we help clients realize and perceive the importance of their health and wellness, we should celebrate our role in that milestone, and the many that will follow.

As easy as it can be to deflect compliments and deny credit for our client's successes, we play a major role in whether or not our clients progress towards their goals. Personally, I have a difficult time accepting compliments and tend to deny them or deflect them (something I'm working on). Acknowledge and accept compliments from your clients. Their gratitude is genuine. You have made a difference in their lives, and they appreciate the time, effort, and planning you have put into making them better, healthier individuals. As nice as it is to occasionally hear how appreciated you are, the best compliment to receive is when those you train find successes and are proud of their accomplishments. Seeing them smile and show excitement for all the hard work they've accomplished is what you two, as a team, have been working toward.

Once you have been in the field for a while, you will be able to reflect and recognize accomplishments for which you should be proud. Looking back over the years, it's hard to narrow down the most memorable moments that stand out as some of my favorite accomplishments as a trainer. The victories have ranged from people finding joy in exercise to helping someone simply get away from being in pain. One example that comes to mind includes a new client who came to me to help him climb Cho Oyu, the sixth highest mountain in the world located in the Himalayas. In preparing for his climb, we focused some of our training on getting him away from the nagging shoulder pain he'd been dealing with for years. After setting up and working through a program consisting of climbing specific exercises, such as lunges, step ups, calf and shin strength movements, and an assortment of posterior chain and core movements, but also some shoulder rehabilitation work. Those consisted of an assortment of mobility drills to regain full range of motion through the shoulder capsule, thoracic spine, and obtain more movement through different planes of motion at the shoulder. Once he regained a fuller range of motion, we introduced strength exercises to ensure he was building strength and muscle throughout the entirety of his new range of motion. This combination allowed him to get out of pain, although when he approached me to seek out training, that wasn't his main objective. Since then, his shoulder has never felt better. Alleviating this client's pain brought me more excitement than just helping him prepare to climb the mountain. Another example is when a high school soccer player was able to successfully return to play after tearing her ACL. Seeing her out there running around freely, after spending months rehabbing and then building back the muscles needed to return safely to the field, without any hesitation to help her team win back-to-back state championships, was incredibly satisfying. The pride of witnessing her resiliency and determination to come back stronger than ever from such a painful injury was immense. Another memorable experience with clients involved a high schooler who felt a bit intimidated by the gym. Creating a safe space, with nobody there to judge, allowed her to focus on what she wanted to work. After about a year of training with each other, she shared how she loved coming to the gym. Hearing her state this put a smile on my face. Other clients simply bring about good memories on an intellectual level. A client once told me that working together and talking about the science behind exercise and the kinesiology field have ingrained a thought in her head that an exercise related career field may be the route she wants to take in her own life. One last moment occurred when COVID-19 hit, and gyms shut down. The future of my business was in question, but I still wanted to help people. Collin and a few of his fellow Drake University football teammates planned to continue preparing for the upcoming season, but had nowhere to workout and didn't really have contact with their coaching staff. Having the gym equipment and a new house allowed my wife and I to open up our garage gym to anyone looking to train. Rain or shine, negative degree weather in the spring of 2020, or triple digit days after they got off work in the summer of 2020, those boys didn't complain and they showed up to work. They always said thank you before they left, and their special talents, in addition to being such wholesome individuals, took their football careers to new heights. Though I had nothing to do with the further successes they saw on the field, opening our home, writing strength workouts, and helping with speed and agility training benefitted them in bridging the gap in their training. The impact trainers have on others can be seen in many different ways.

Finding people who are looking to you for assistance may end up having as big of an impact on you as it does them. The influence you have on someone will help guide them in the right direction. You will come to realize the friendships you develop as a trainer emphasize a rewarding, positive career choice.

CHAPTER 56

Exercise Means Something Different to Each of Us

Weightlifting and working out can fill a void for athletes and non-athletes. The physical and mental benefit to weightlifting, cardiovascular exercise, mobility and stretching, and other practices, such as yoga, can help provide individuals with a newfound sense of identity. This pertains particularly for people who are no longer in team sports or have never been in sports at all. Not only can carefully programmed workouts help with self-confidence, intrinsic learning, and creating discipline among other values, they can be crucial in developing life lessons. One particular life lesson learned in the gym is that not every workout, not every lift, nor every run is going to be the perfect outcome. When faced with adversity in the gym, you learn to overcome hurdles or hardship thrown your way. One thing you will notice in this field is that most workouts are truly you against yourself. Your clients may get temporarily caught up in comparing themselves to another individual, but when they look in the mirror and compare where they are today to where they were yesterday, last week, or last year, it's pretty amazing to see their own personal accomplishments. When you are there to help your clients set out to achieve a certain goal and create sustainable habits which transform into behaviors you can both celebrate their new lifestyles.

When you're struggling in the gym, don't want to do or finish the workout, or simply aren't in the mood to put in the extra effort that day, the way you react to those struggles can dictate the reactions you have to parallel adverse situations outside of the gym. Overcoming the obstacles faced in the gym, both for trainers and clients, can promote leadership, resiliency, perseverance, determination, and even improve the ability to perform under pressure. This ability to overcome obstacles is a pretty special thing that gets overlooked. Helping your clients work through those difficulties can make a much bigger impact than it may seem at the moment. Sometimes it is okay to allow your clients to problem solve and navigate their way through those scenarios on their own. While other times it's important to hold their hand and walk them through how to overcome that situation so they know how to work through a similar situation down the road.

Regardless, being there as a supporter in one way or another, depending on the situation and the client, can be the best thing you can do for the people in your life.

Helping others reveal certain qualities about themselves in the gym they hadn't discovered yet is so satisfying. It creates enjoyment and can be a breakthrough when someone solves a problem or gets out of an uncomfortable situation that had been nagging them for what seemed like forever. The perfect example in the context of the fitness world is helping someone through an injury. When a client comes to you with fitness goals, and then slides in a tidbit about having a nagging injury that they just can't shake, don't neglect that. Quietly, make that a focus of your training. You can still work toward helping someone improve their fitness and live a healthier life while throwing in certain strengthening, stretching, and mobility exercises to help reduce pain in a previously injured spot. It might not have been the reason they came to see you. but with your background and the tools you have, if you can get them to be free of pain, you will be viewed as a magician. It will change their mood and even their entire outlook on what you do for them. When you are able to help someone get out of a pain they've been dealing with for a long time or a pain they just accepted to be part of the rest of their life, they will be so grateful for you, satisfied with themselves, and they'll realize just about anything is possible. It's a very fun, yet simple, part about this job and makes people's lives so much better.

BUSINESS

Whether you are running your own personal training business or working for another employer, set aside a few hours (if not more) each week to map out the route you want to direct the future of your business and services. Brainstorm, market, continue to seek out information that will help build your product, find areas of improvement within your services and come up with ways to fix those, and most importantly, do your best to avoid complacency. This job requires you to show up prepared for your clients on a daily basis, but you also have to be sure you're staying on the path you want to follow for the long-term success of your career. In this industry you will work many unseen hours. Putting in this extra time will prevent you from becoming overwhelmed in the day-to-day difficulties. It will also give you a greater vision of where you see your business down the road. You won't be paid directly for those hours. The time you work when you're not with clients (furthering your education, preparing for the future of yourself and your business, etc.) can be just as important as the daily operation of programming, providing for, and serving your clients. Taking care of your people day in and day out and helping them work towards, reach, and exceed their physical fitness goals are the mainstays of your job as a personal trainer. However, to sustain a successful business, it's imperative to set aside time to continuously improve your craft and build your long-term career goals.

Writing this book is one of those projects I've been working on behind the scenes. The goal of this publication is to provide others in our field with a framework to improve their skills, focus on the three pillars of personal training (personal, training, and business), and help set a new standard for the professional personal trainer. Unfortunately, a false narrative regarding trainers as egotistical has given people in our field a negative connotation. We want to break that mold. We want to use the experience of our years of training to help other fitness professionals grow in their roles and realize the potential they have to be true leaders and positive influences on everyone they meet through this career path. The personal training field is very saturated, which means we, as a unit, can help more people than ever. Just like any other abounding profession, there can be some bad eggs and people who are in it for the wrong reasons. You can be the trainer who is doing your job for the right reasons. Hopefully this book helps you recognize a new approach to training, using our experiences, suggestions, and advice to benefit you in your career, and in turn, the people you help. Now let's get down to business.

CHAPTER 57

Starting and Running Your Own Business

To give you a bit of background on my business experience, I want to preface this section by saying I've only ever been a personal trainer. Sure, I had other odds-and-ends jobs throughout high school and college, but after graduation, I started working as a personal trainer less than a week after I walked across that stage. I want to start with this because I want to make sure people understand that my advice, suggestions, and experiences are by no means the only way to do things. These are tidbits I've picked up on, gone through, realized, lucked into, and learned from others and they've all played a role in helping my clients, my business, and my personal life. I may not be as old as you. My experience and education may differ from yours. Therefore, I would love to hear from each of you reading this with your advice or strategies you have used which might improve my business. I do love learning, helping others, and continuing to grow and evolve to be an asset to those around me and those who mean the most to me. The fitness world allows me to do just that.

When I first began my career as a trainer, I viewed working for a corporate gym as a stepping stone to gain experience working with individuals. My ultimate career goal was to work in the strength and conditioning world. Boy, was I in for a surprise! The connections I created and the joy I found helping other people realize their capabilities and seeing them accomplish different goals in the gym truly reeled me in further to the personal training world. The relationships we created; the amazing people I've met; and the impact clients and other trainers have had on my life rerouted my pathway to remain in the training world. I fell in love with the fact that personal training is a people business centered around the relationships you create with others. After recognizing my employer and I had different values and ethical priorities, I knew it was time to move on. Logistically, I understood there were many things I had to take care of prior to branching off on my own. Being only 23 years old, I felt both excitement and anxiety in making such a huge leap of branching off on my own. The worst-case scenario of me falling straight on my face didn't have much risk because I could always find another job, even if it weren't my dream position. The thought of failing scared me, and soon doubt and questions began to creep in. What if my clients chose not to follow me? What could I have done more of leading up to this point to ensure they would follow my lead to another location? How does someone even create an actual business? How do I get insurance? Where am I going to train? Change is difficult because of the unknown. I am a man of routine. I create a routine and rarely waiver from it. When I am forced to get out of my routine unexpectedly, I can handle it but it does cause another layer of anxiety and concern. Due to that type of internal response, branching off on my own was even more scary. On the other hand, that was paired with excitement. I was eager to see what I could grow on my own, with the help and support of those who believed in me and what I valued in business. Having the freedom and independence to build a brand that would place others as the primary focus and priority inspired me.

Starting your own business can lay heavily on some, as the pressure of success is completely reliant upon you as the sole member of your business, but I grew to love that idea. I wanted to take on the responsibility of the different components that make up a business. Because there was no safety net, I worked extra hard to ensure I didn't fail. Because I wanted to accept that entire responsibility, I knew that I had to put my name into my business, which is how I landed on Seymour Health & Fitness, LLC. Legally, as a small business that would be collecting income, I would be required to pay taxes. For income tax purposes, you must choose a name, file for Certificate of Organization, pay a small fee, and register as a business. There are different business structures based on tax classifications and in order to personally protect myself from liability of the company, I decided to file my company as a Limited Liability Company (LLC) but was to be taxed as an S-Corp which offered me certain benefits while allowing me some additional flexibility on my income treatment. There are different ways to file your business and to ensure you're checking all of the legal boxes and not mistaking anything; I suggest finding a reputable accountant or professional to help guide you through this process. Choosing to use my personal name (Seymour) in my business title (Seymour Health & Fitness, LLC) meant I was putting all of my eggs in one basket.

The name of your product is nowhere near as important as the quality of your product. In order to offer your product, you must have a strong client base. My next step of action was to have honest conversations with my clients. Having signed a noncompete agreement at my previous employer, I was aware of the notion I was not allowed to solicit clients. This limited my options and forced me to be very careful about how I communicated with my clients to not violate those conditions. I spoke to them by informing them of my decision and told them that if they wanted to continue training after I left, for them to reach out to me. I didn't want to deal with any legal action so I was strategic about how I spoke and where I decided to rent from. Throughout our time training together, many of my clients became aware of my desire to build my own separate name and product. Therefore, when deeper discussions took place about moving my brand to another location, my clients were not surprised. Since we had always been transparent with each other and open throughout the entire process, it was a fairly easy conversation to have regarding my decision to move. Because of the relationships we had built on trust, honesty, and viewing each other as equal peers, I felt comfortable admitting my decision to them. Telling some of my newer clients was a little bit more difficult, as we hadn't created that same bond quite yet. Some had enjoyed our experience together and decided to follow me to my next location while others wanted to remain where they were at; no hard feelings. Although not everybody committed to joining me in my transfer, being honest and candid with all of my clients about my choice was something I will never regret. Having difficult chats with your clients will allow you to create lasting relationships, and you will grow closer because of them. What you'll learn is when you take care of those around you, they're not going to worry about where you work because they want to continue to work with you. In a sense, it's similar to the relationship between a customer and their hairdresser/stylist/barber. Once you find your person and they provide you with a product and service that meet and exceed your expectations time and time again, people tend to remain loyal.

As I began feeling more confident and comfortable with the amount of people that showed interest in continuing to train with me even if I changed my place of work, I could finally breathe a sigh of relief. This made me feel like there was less chance of me falling straight on my face upon me vacating my current position. That being said, talk can be cheap. People can tell you one thing and do the other. I was fortunate enough where my clients decided to follow, but know there is a chance that people will get cold feet and decide to stay put. If that happens, be understanding and make sure you don't burn bridges. Changing locations is a stressful time for you, but it is a stressful time for them, as well. People develop comfort where they are and beginning at a new location could be intimidating. In any change of circumstance, it's always best to be considerate and provide empathy. Your ability to be understanding in response to clients being hesitant could make or break the chances of you two working together down the road. That brings me to another lesson I've learned: just because someone stops working with you at the time doesn't mean they're gone forever. When people leave, thank them for believing in you and investing their health in your services. If they decide to hop back into training, there's a good chance they will contact you again down the road. By responding negatively or inappropriately, that last impression will stick with people and the chances of them returning or referring others your way will drop drastically. Positive responses keep your good reputation and open the doors for future positive referrals.

When looking for your next location to run your business, you have various options. You can rent, buy, independent contract, or even do in-home training. You don't necessarily have to pick one and stick with it, but having a "home" will help with convenience and ease for scheduling and clients. Finding a location where you and your clients feel comfortable, are able to workout without distractions and interruptions, and fits your budget are all important factors that will contribute to your decision. When I was originally searching around for a location, the intent was to buy a space and have it for myself. I quickly realized, as a kid less than two years out of college, that would be stretching my budget very thin, thus eliminating that possibility for the time being. I then looked into renting space from a local CrossFit gym. When I began with my first company out of college, I signed a non-compete agreement which disallowed me from relocating to anywhere within a five-mile radius of their company gym. I didn't want to deal with any legal action so a lot of strategy came into play to figure out what nearby areas I could rent.

Upon further searching, I decided upon a certain CrossFit gym, as it was run by gentlemen who proved helpful in my growth as an independent personal trainer. Making sure my clients did not have to travel too far to get to the gym was another factor in considering an ideal location. The building was outside of the five-mile radius and was a relatively close proximity for some of my clients. This location was a great starting space, gave me the environment I needed to run my business, and allowed for a level of comfort that was important for my clients. It granted me my own space for training, provided the equipment needed for workouts for my clients, and the rent was reasonable and within my budget. The atmosphere within the gym was conducive to expanding my clientele base and eventually, my business outgrew this space. While working in the CrossFit gym, I was able to better hone in on specific details I wanted to include in my future spaces. The agreement with this gym entailed rental of the space and equipment that they had, but because I was renting space and they had classes and clients that deemed priority over me, training involved some creativity and working around others, which was expected. Being around a successful gym owner allowed me to watch and learn from a distance. I learned a lot about making exercise fun and interacting with members. I also noticed things that I would have done differently, like making sure to utilize our heat on cold days and air conditioning during the hot and humid summers. Whether renting from others or owning your own space, it is good to note the things you do well and the areas where you can improve to provide a better, more homely environment for your clients.

Although I only stuck around that gym for about a year before deciding to reconnect with a past coworker who opened his own gym, it was a good initial experience upon leaving the corporate style of gym. In moving to my second location, many of the same factors came into play. Checking to make sure my clients were okay with the move, analyzing the distance of driving for all, negotiating rent, evaluating equipment, and assuring the atmosphere would be conducive to comfort and respect for my clientele were at the top of my priorities before switching spots. Having built a relationship with the new gym owner solidified the decision to move. Working with an owner can be a blessing and a challenge. Before you commit to working with another trainer in a gym, make sure you have similar views on how the business will be run. What are the rent expectations? Will rent stay the same or will there be potential for raising it in the future? What happens if equipment breaks? Who is in charge of fixing equipment and how quickly will that happen? Broken machinery means adjusting workouts, which can take time and extra effort on your part. How many other trainers will be using the same space? How will clients be scheduled so the gym is not too crowded for productive workouts? Who picks the music? Who is in charge of cleaning the gym and how often will deep cleaning take place? Having honest and well-thought-out discussions with owners when you have the option to rent from them can make or break your decision to pay them for their space.

After moving to this next centrally-located facility, we continued to build our client base. Note I switched to "we" in that sentence. My younger brother, Collin, had joined the SHF team. As a division 1 athlete, Collin excelled on the field and in the classroom. When he decided during his college years to switch majors from Environmental Science to Kinesiology to get into the strength and conditioning world, it was like I had déjà vu. Although we both envisioned a similar career, Collin's hope was to create a type of strength and conditioning business that was focused around youth athletes. After researching different approaches catering to athletes, the facility Building Better Athletes in Dubuque, Iowa caught our attention. The owner had built a successful and reputable sport performance gym that was well-known for advancing the abilities of athletes, youth through professionals. The impressive vision and outcome of the Building Better Athletes clients helped expand our own pathway as we added Collin as a new trainer to the business.

In maneuvering through this new path, Collin and I have found we thoroughly enjoy working with athletes. However, if that audience were to be the only clients we took on, we would miss out on building relationships with some amazing people and our entire business model would be different. Therefore, our services include working with everybody from athletes to nonathletes, all genders, and a wide range of ages. Some people are able to work in a certain niche and do very well. As a personal trainer, you need to be patient when trying to find your target audience.

When Collin began working for SHF, we figured experience trumped paychecks at the time. He was still in school, and we agreed he would dip his toe in the water by gaining experience as a trainer with an actual client. We figured the best way to find him a client was to offer free training. After posting a status on our Facebook page about the addition of Collin to the team and offering a package of personal training sessions with him for free, we were taken aback by the responses. Those interested simply had to be willing to sign a waiver, agree to commit to working with him with the understanding he was new to the field. There was no catch. There were no hidden fees. Collin would apply the knowledge he gained from school, and the willing participant would be his first experience. Nearly ten people wanted to participate. After some debate and discussion, Collin's first client became someone I had trained in my first year on the job. Though we had stopped training together, we kept in touch and maintained a good relationship. The fact that she wanted to get in with Collin and possibly reconnect as a paying client down the road were good signs. Since Collin was new to the game, this client's understanding and fun-loving personality encouraged him as he learned some of the ins and outs of personal training. After they concluded their trial package, she signed on to work with him and he was off and running. Giving away free time may not seem appealing at first glance, but showing individuals a glimpse into your product and services with no fee is a great way to sell yourself.

It can be difficult to start any business from scratch, especially one solely reliant on commission and bringing on people that would financially support your business in exchange for your services. When Collin decided to get into this field, if he wanted to work for my business, he would be at an immediate disadvantage. I had the fortunate opportunity to begin at a gym where there were constantly new people walking in the door with a gym membership, with some of them doing so with the intent to seek out a personal trainer. That made it easier because some people fell right into your lap with you just being in the right place at the right time. It was going to be different for Collin, as we had the business running, but ultimately that business was my clients training with me. I had a semi-notable reputation, but not even close to comparable to what the corporate business I worked for had in the metro. Because of this disadvantage, we had to rely on smart business decisions, unmatched service, providing the results people wanted, and lots and lots of patience. Word of mouth, reaching out to friends and family, and using social media to promote classes and sessions were the main ways we were able to build a strong client base for Collin. Collin had to work his tail off to bury any disadvantage from where he began and quickly filled up his schedule.

Starting out in a new business venture, Collin had to find ways to make ends meet. To save some money on renting the space from the gym owner, he mopped the gym floor daily, kept equipment wiped down, spent hours making sure the gym was clean and the appearance was up to par with the members. On top of working with his first client, Collin had some friends who were looking for a place to workout. So, he created a small group that met multiple times per week in the morning. Programming for these friends was easy, as Collin knew their individual abilities, personal goals, and preferences in the gym. In working with the group of friends, it gave him his first taste of realizing that clients don't have to just be connected to you through a business relationship. You have to keep things appropriate and professional but having people around you in your career that you genuinely enjoy working with makes business much easier. Shortly after that, Collin began helping coach some of the evening classes to take the load off of the gym owner's shoulders from whom we were renting. On his very first day of coaching the evening group classes, one of the classes consisted of one person. When you coach your first classes, you think about how to go about helping multiple people and speaking to a crowd. You don't expect that class to basically turn into a personal training session with a stranger who is paying for a service from a gym that you just recently started helping at. Depending on both of your personalities, that situation could either be very comfortable or super awkward and strange for both parties. Luckily, there was an immediate connection and things went well.

As he was coaching the evening classes, Collin began to establish a strong connection with a handful of gym members. They looked forward to working together every day and even spent time outside of the gym together. Their connection was much more than just a coach-athlete dynamic. Their support for each other in and out of the gym was a relationship which established a culture for that evening class and is what every gym owner and employee should strive for. The love for one another to succeed in class and in life was unique and hard to come by. Collin went out of his way to make each of them feel comfortable, spent time outside of his paid hours to work with them to improve certain areas within their health and wellness, and he didn't expect a single thing in return. He did, in fact, get plenty in return as these individuals continually showed Collin the respect and support he deserved. They were his biggest fans and made sure to spread the word of his ability to connect with and coach all of those in his classes.

It was Collin's expertise in the strength and conditioning realm that drew in his class participants but it has been his ability to connect with others that has created such high retention rates and success for those clients. Since Collin always intended to make youth strength and conditioning the focal point of his career, he introduced youth class sessions, which had a very positive response from the kids and their parents. Evening and summer classes were offered for kids ages eight through thirteen. Social media, word of mouth, and having parents as clients all contributed to the presence of children in these classes.

After two years of renting space from another trainer, it was time Collin and I took a leap of faith and got our own facility. Knowing that our company was expanding and many future opportunities were on the horizon, Collin and I agreed it was time to start looking more seriously into having our own space and equipment. Working with a realtor, scouting numerous locations, visiting many potential buildings, aligning our finances with our financial advisor, and listening to the needs of our clients all went into the decision of our new place. That opportunity came as we opened our new gym space in February of 2022.

Renting from other gyms was convenient for us and kept the overhead pretty low on our end, but it did create some limitations and restrictions on what we could do within our business. Opening our own facility would mean we could not only remove those limitations, but we could operate with our client's needs at the forefront of our decisions. We could create a gym layout that fit our needs and allowed for our clients to finally have a home they could call their own. I believed most of our clients felt extremely comfortable at the locations from which we rented space, but at the end of the day, we still had to configure our workouts around the members of the gym. We, in a way, played second fiddle to those members. Most gym owners and trainers are accommodating and make sure to communicate when there are any overlapping or conflicting workouts. For us to no longer have to worry about schedule issues; to be able to design our space in a way more in tune with what our clients needed; and to match the way Collin and I train was a big appeal to us when contemplating finding our own space.

Once we found our space, we were able to start envisioning the best way to set it up. We both entered into this field with a strength and conditioning mindset, and we agreed we like having open space to get creative and use in a multi-purpose fashion. We decided to line the outside of the gym with most of our equipment so that there was more room for us to use as we needed, which may vary day to day. We also wanted to have turf in our space. We didn't need 100 yards of turf but having the ability to work on agility, using sliders and sleds, and having a surface that better matched what a lot of athletes perform their sports on was something we agreed was important in creating our own facility. We had a free-standing rig along the wall, barbells, dumbbells, bands, exercise balls, a reverse hyper, GHDs, sleds, Row ERGs, a Ski ERG, Assault bikes, slideboards, medicine balls, hurdles, pulley attachments, boxes (both the standard sized wooden boxes and softer, smaller boxes to account for our youth athletes), and a variety of sport balls to incorporate into training or to simply toss around with each other. Piecing together our first gym set up was so much fun. It was all up to us and what we wanted to provide for the amazing people walking through our doors. I would compare it to someone who's always wanted their dream house and finally it was time to start planning it all out. We felt like little kids on Christmas morning as the process began.

There were a few delays on equipment and some hiccups along the way. Luckily, after months of planning, preparation, painting, payments, and hard work, we had everything we wanted and were able to function entirely on our own with the stresses of gym preparation behind us. Taking any leap of faith in whatever field or stage of your career you are in can be scary. Jumping to our own facility and paying off all of the equipment from the get go were big stressors. Having saved up and planned for this venture, as well as finding investors willing to entrust us with their financial backing, took some stress out of the money part of our move. Knowing that our new equipment was all taken care of and could be viewed as an investment and form of building up some equity was a sigh of relief. Paying things off right away was a no-brainer for me and it ensured we were able to focus on the main part of business: taking care of our people.

We found a centrally located building with an open unit right off of an interstate, which would be very accessible for our clients. With finding our new 'home' we wanted to ensure that we were still providing the same services to remain true to who we were at the time and who we are to this day. Remaining focused on the individualized side of things by providing budget-friendly group classes and loading up the in-between hours with personal training clients, has proven to be a great business model. A friend once told me, "You rarely see a rich gym owner." There are definitely exceptions to that rule. It can be very difficult to run group classes hour after hour, day after day, and not satisfy that personal connection we all crave. Personal training can accomplish that particular connection, while allowing you to gain more financially.

When we decided to open our own gym location, we wanted to be respectful of our previous gym. We made sure to explain to everyone we were simply leaving because of the opportunities we'd be able to open with our own space. We didn't want the prior gym owner to think we were trying to solicit any of their members. We did not ask anyone to come with us. We did not go behind anyone's back to attempt to steal members. We believed that the product we provided and the service we gave would allow us to fill our sessions with the group we wanted to create and the culture we dreamed of. The group members Collin made close connections with made their own decisions to follow and continue supporting us because of how well they all got along with one another and how much Collin helped aid them in their gym experiences.

There were many advantages to owning our own gym. With our own space, we had the ability to determine when classes took place, so we didn't have to plan our kid's classes around the other trainers or classes that were running. We were able to dictate our own schedules. Similar to how we schedule our client's training sessions based on both of our availability, we did the same for our Adult and Youth Strength and Conditioning classes. We polled current and prospective members to ensure the days and times worked best for them so that the services fit exactly what and when people preferred.

In addition to being flexible with initially structuring the group class times, we felt it best to also offer multiple payment options. There were the standard monthly rates that included unlimited classes at a reasonable rate. This made the most sense and provided the best bang for their buck but it also benefited us in several ways because it provided guaranteed income and consistent attendance. For those that wouldn't be able to make it to as many classes, we also offered a punch card that had ten classes which provided them with more flexibility and choice as to when our classes worked for them. This made more sense for those that travel frequently and could only make it a couple times each month.

When members would not attend, it could be easy to get stressed out or be offended as to why they weren't coming every time. Being understanding and reasonably recognizing that not every day is scheduled out around class times helped balance out those feelings. When this happened for Youth Strength and Conditioning, we understood because as much as we liked having them in the gym, kids need to be kids. We supported when kids decided not to come to class because they were playing a pick-up basketball game with the neighbors, for example. We really wanted kids to be kids but wanted to use our time together in the gym as a way to help them have fun, improve their mind-body connection, and establish confidence in themselves. We think there are numerous benefits to starting kids in the gym at a younger age, especially when there is a knowledgeable, fun, and personable leader (i.e. Collin) to safely guide the kids through an intelligently designed program. The way Collin structured his classes was by creating a balance between educating the kids on the basics of strength and conditioning, helping them learn to move and explore the way their body reacts to different stimuli, have fun in the gym, boost confidence and understand that the relationship with the gym should be a positive one, and to help athletes perform better while also being better teammates. It was perfect. Through a combination of creativity and assistance from outside resources, Collin was able to create a rolodex of ideas on how to best structure and coach those classes. He was constantly fine-tuning his coaching cues, coming up with new ways to help kids feel included, and did everything he could to make our brand well known as one of the best in the Des Moines area for youth strength and conditioning.

In the Spring of 2022, we also began our partnership with the CY Select Wolves,

a girls AAU basketball program. This partnership was conceived through a connection created while training a client, but it was another opportunity for Collin and me to both perfect our crafts working with a younger audience of athletes. The Wolves program consisted of over 120 girls ranging from second grade through high school. We were to work with a variety of girls, who literally just began organized sports all the way through Top-100 Division 1 recruits in the nation wrapping up their high school careers. When working with such a wide variety of kids, you not only had to adjust the way you coached and interacted with the different age groups, but you had to program differently and understand what was most important for each of the kids. The littlest kids needed to learn about exercise, but also play games, work on balance, improve hand-eye coordination, and have fun while exercising. The older kids may need to work on similar areas, but their programs might be a bit more specific to the areas of their game they wanted to improve.

When we began with the Wolves, it was definitely a team effort. I did all of the programming but designed the younger kid's workouts similarly to the way Collin did for his youth classes. We played games, taught them the ins and outs of basic strength and conditioning, and took turns leading those younger kid's sessions so we could each take the reins in working with them. For the older athletes, I led the classes, but we both floated around and helped the girls as we went along. 2022 was our first year partnering with the Wolves program, so it was a little trial and error but overall a success. The partnership was a way to help a variety of different athletes in one way or another, whether it be in helping them rehab injuries, improve strength and athleticism, or simply to enjoy working out and boosting self-confidence. Regardless, the main goals were to aid in their performance on the court, for the girls to have fun, walk away knowing a little bit more than they did before, and feel more and more comfortable in the weight room. At the end of the day, helping those girls realize the gym doesn't have to be an intimidating place, but that it can be a place of fun, growth, competition, creativity, and a place you look forward to going to, fulfilled our purpose. Creating a mutually-written contract with the owners of the Wolves was essential to ensure we provided a professional learning experience for the team, while assuring financial compensation for our time, space, and work. Business-wise this partnership was an endeavor which added a financial boost to our decision to branch off to our own building.

We also were able to provide Adult Strength and Conditioning classes at three different time intervals every week day. Our goal was not necessarily to mimic other gyms and load up on those classes, because it wasn't really our primary passion and what we wanted to make our sole focus. If people were interested, great. We had options available and soon the classes were filled with amazing people who made us all better. The participants in the groups played a huge role in establishing the culture of our gym to be welcoming, inclusive, friendly, and one where we all were there to get better. Personal training, partner training, and small group training sessions, all which we were justifiably able to charge more per hour because of the individualization we provided to those interested, rounded out our offerings to clients in our new gym space. By providing many options and opportunities to improve health through fitness programs, our gym and the services provided set us apart from other gyms. In establishing a place to call our own with clients we thoroughly enjoy interacting with on a daily basis while doing what we love for a living, we can honestly attest we find pride and fulfillment walking into our own gym every day.

As for the future of our business, at the time of this portion of the book, 2024 is here. The fields of strength and conditioning and personal training are areas which are going to play a massive role in the coming years, as will more health awareness in general. Mental health, physical fitness, eating well-rounded diets, and surrounding yourself with people who lift you up and push you to be the best version of yourself are some areas people are beginning to prioritize. With society becoming more accepting of the importance of mental health, the benefits of personal training have come to the forefront with many clients. Personal training is much more than just exercise. A good personal trainer is someone who believes in you, listens to you, and is a reliable, trustworthy friend with whom you can be open and honest. If you can encapsulate those traits, in addition to having the background knowledge of exercise science, kinesiology, and psychology, you can create a sustainable personal training business that positively impacts the lives of so many people.

You'll never know if you don't try. Whether you are contemplating jumping ship from a corporate gym (similar to what I did), deciding to install a new style of programming to a certain client's regimen, or working to provide a new service of sorts, the fear of failure can deter people from taking the necessary steps to successfully complete any of those tasks. If you want to take a new path, create a new product, or try out something that goes against the grain, do it. It's easy to follow the same path others have, but taking those leaps of faith can really pay dividends and may even be the propelling choice that leads to a greater future for you or your business. The last thing any of us wants is to look back at our lives and kick ourselves for not following certain intuitions or attempting something because we were scared in the moment. This profession can provide you with ultimate flexibility, happiness, and fulfillment, but it will require you to take some calculated leaps of faith. Be courageous, but smart, with your business decisions. Seek financial advice from those around you, as well as accountants, and bankers. Do your research and preparation before acting impulsively to avoid a risk outweighing a reward. The way we have paved our way through this industry has worked for us, but our situations may differ from yours. Come up with a plan, be patient. Roll with the punches, and continually work toward the type of business you want to create. Be open to the different paths you may be led down, as things may not turn out exactly the way you'd expect. Our vision has definitely fluctuated, but the success and fulfillment we have found as trainers in our own facility has been gratifying.

CHAPTER 58

Path Less Traveled

Take pleasure in creating a rare path in a difficult field. Throughout your years growing up into adulthood, there has probably been some sort of expectation or persuasion to find a pre-existing role, settle in, do as you're told to climb the ranks within a certain field or company, and work in a consistent job to elicit a livable wage. If that's the comfortable path you choose to take in your career and you enjoy what you do as well as how much you make, congratulations. That's a very good position to be in to take care of yourself, your family, and have a stable career. That path isn't for everyone.

Frankly, I didn't know what direction I was heading until I came to a fork in the road and had to make a choice. Upon graduating college, I wanted to get into strength and conditioning, which meant a formal setting of a high school or collegiate weight room, programming for large groups at a time, and playing my part in helping others improve their athletic abilities and maximize performance in their sports. That was a path that was already carved out by others, and there was a clear-cut path to follow to achieve that. While I was making some money as a personal trainer straight out of school, my plan was to pass my Certified Strength and Conditioning Specialist (CSCS) exam, the gold standard certification for those in the strength and conditioning profession, and dive into sports performance. However, after starting to train a wider variety of individuals, I began to understand there were many more alternative routes to take than preplanned, expected career paths. No longer wanting to be a strength coach in a school setting nor having any desire to conform to unwritten rules expected to follow in order to find a successful career, I decided to create my own path. Seeking out a job that allowed me to train the people I wanted, in the setting we all enjoyed, and on the schedule we created together was appealing. Therefore, taking a calculated risk, and leaving a corporate gym to branch out on my own, became my path less traveled. My decision didn't make much sense to many people, as they wondered why I would leave a comfortable job to take this risk of starting my own business with no safety net only a year and a half after graduating college. This new path was against the grain, out of the norm, and was seen as an uncalculated risk by a very new "entrepreneur" who didn't understand the way the business world worked. A lot of that is true. As previously stated, I had so much to learn about business. Regardless, I leapt into starting my own business. Seymour Health & Fitness started as a personal training business, but we've evolved into so much more than that. We get to interact and create relationships with people so they can feel more comfortable in the gym with us and in their own skin. By establishing those relationships and following up with helping produce results in the gym that apply to what our members are looking for, we are able to offer an unprecedented service that is unique to the area we are in. We are personal trainers. We are coaches. We are teachers. We are friends. We are what others need us to be in their lives to create healthy habits that can be sustained for the rest of people's lives. By deciding to start my own business, I got to establish what we stood for and what we provided for others. With the support of others and finding people who were interested in purchasing the service we provided, we were able to grow and remove some of the doubt about whether or not that once risky decision was all that risky. Taking an unprecedented leap to start a business on your own is a scary decision. There will be a lot of learning on the fly, if you choose to take this path, but deciding to go against the norm and seek out your own career path could be one of the best choices you ever make in your life.

To those in any health and/or fitness profession, it can be a very difficult field to find success. Sustaining that success can be even harder. It's easy to beat yourself up about day-to-day adversity you may face, but working in a field that allows you to help others improve their lives has many great rewards. There are plenty of ways to build a successful business in this field and just because the route you want to take or have taken hasn't been done before doesn't mean your business model isn't going to work. I challenge you to put all of those eggs in your one basket, commit to what you want to accomplish, and do absolutely everything within your power to create the best brand, best value, and best experience for other people. If you do your job with others' best intentions in mind, there's a very strong chance you will create a long, fruitful career while taking the path less traveled.

CHAPTER 59

Business Building Checklist

When contemplating the decision of starting your own business, there are a handful of tasks to undertake as you venture out on your own. When working for a larger company, they cover the liability, insurance, waivers, taxes, and churning people through the doors. When you are the sole provider for your company, and in turn, your paycheck and lifestyle, these responsibilities all fall on your shoulders. Having never taken any formal type of business class and essentially being considered a novice with the accounting and financial side of things, it would have been beneficial for me to have taken a course or two on these topics in college. Learning on the fly and putting a lot of trust in those around me helped me navigate my way to success. Receiving solid advice, having been granted amazing references, and working with supportive people guided me through the process of creating my own business. However, for those of you still in college, business classes would be a great supplement to getting into any field that remotely relies on running your own company. Having previous knowledge on topics relating to liability, insurance, taxes, and waivers would alleviate some of the stress experienced when starting a new venture. What this will provide for you is the knowledge to handle some of those roles on your own, or at least check in on the work you hire out to a secondary business to make sure you're being fairly treated.

As you settle into your business routine, you may realize there are certain roles that need to be filled, but it may not make sense for you to try to juggle them yourself. When it gets to that point, look into hiring others to make your life easier. Paying a CPA his monthly recurring fee to take care of your books, taxes, and other finances is worth the peace of mind knowing you don't have to worry about handling that area of your business. Locating an insurance agent to make sure you have liability and insurance, and employing a lawyer to write or look over your waivers are a few recommended professionals needed to start up and run a legal business without missing anything important. Relying on the paid help from such individuals and their businesses can make life more manageable. Finding business persons through referrals and client contact can be worth the extra expenses you may have to pay for dependable, honest, licensed experts in their field.

Finding people who are able to supplement your business can be a great way to expand your network, create a two-way street for referrals with other local businesses, and make your life easier. When I first began this business, saving money was a personal priority. Fear of not being able to stay financially afloat made me hesitant to go out of my way to hire others to help with specific business functions. Luckily, I decided to put my trust in professionals. Doing so freed my schedule for me to do what I love doing most: spending time training my people. Along with hiring professionals to assist with business tasks, self-learning through different resources online, with books, and through conversations with individuals in financial fields filled in many gaps as well. Personal training is comparable to teaching. We explain why we do what we are doing, so clients can actually learn, retain, and be able to repeat movements at later times. This shows they truly understand the exercises and aren't just temporarily memorizing the routine for that day. The same can go for business. Be an active learner when it comes to each aspect of running your own business. Learn how and why your accountant analyzes your financial status, prepares your taxes, and advises you on certain investments. Sit down with him or her to understand what expenses qualify to be written off. Make sure your insurance agent has you fully covered and is aware of liability expectations when owning a business using training equipment. Check in with this agent frequently to ensure you are always wholly protected, especially if you change locations, purchase new equipment, or simply if you have any questions. Meet face to face with your lawyer to lay out a waiver, adjust as needed, and keep communications open when running your own business. Surrounding yourself with knowledgeable, reliable professionals will allow you to properly take care of your business.

Starting a new business can be overwhelming. Breaking down tasks with a checklist will grant you a visual reminder of your accomplishments every time you cross things off once they're completed. Knocking out legalities should be a priority to make sure you will be protected. If you decide to claim your business under a new name, register your brand name and file for an LLC through your Secretary of State. This process ensures you legally hold your business name and nobody else could use it for their own. This can be as easy as a few clicks on a website and paying a fairly small price. Next, find a trustworthy accountant, lawyer, and insurance agent. They can help you obtain a business bank account, set up a tax ID, create waivers and learn about filing biennial reports. Ask family, friends, and even clients for referrals, if you are not sure how to contact these types of professionals. . Of course while you are doing these behind-the-scenes preparations you must also figure out how to fill your training schedule to continue making money.

CHAPTER 60

What Does Success Mean to You?

At the end of the day, we all view success from different perspectives. As it relates to business, my personal definition of success is finding something you thoroughly enjoy, working your tail off in determination to be the best at that craft, growing an audience you can help by providing them with the tools to grow on their own, and being able to appreciate those who believe in me. Defining your own vision of success as a personal trainer will develop throughout your career. Once you have found a formula which aligns with your personality, your following spreads like wildfire, and you will be able to pay the bills and make a comfortable living. This process becomes cyclical so as long as you maintain an intrinsic drive and do what you can to give your clients the best possible experiences, you can have a very long tenure in this profession.

This field is a tough one in which to make a lengthened career. If you find your niche and lead with passion for helping others, you can break that mold. According to a 2022 study by Zippia (*Personal trainer demographics and statistics [2022]: Number of personal trainers in the US.*), 57% of personal trainers have a tenure of less than two years with only 14% of personal trainers lasting more than eight years in this profession. You will most likely discover the first year is by far the most difficult, as you have to start from scratch and build up a clientele base from the ground up. The most challenging part is that word of mouth is our best ally when it comes to new business. When you don't have clients to speak on your behalf, that temporarily negates this particular mode of marketing. You need to get out of your comfort zone, give away free time, market yourself and your brand, and find unique ways to get your name recognized by the audience you want to attract. If you can generate leads and close on sales when people come into your facility, you can get the ball rolling and things will begin to trend in the right direction.

With the first year of personal training being the most strenuous, if you're able to make it through that without deciding to change career paths, pat yourself on the back. More than likely, through the past 365 days, you've been able to find and establish a balanced routine for you at work and in your personal life. Establishing that routine is crucial to long-term success. Years two and three need to be viewed as a continued time to grow your brand and business, while not being afraid to put in the necessary hours to build up your ideal schedule of clients. This can be very stressful because our field does not accommodate the societal norm of working from 9 am to 5 pm. If you can find people to fit within those hours, take advantage of that. However, most likely you will be working long days and many hours each week to meet your clients' needs. With burning the candle at both ends, it can be very easy to understand how we could potentially wear ourselves out.

In order to combat this mental and physical destruction, figure out how to cope and be efficient with your time between sessions. Take naps, deload, workout between clients, improve your time-management by programming for days and weeks ahead so you don't have to worry about those when the time comes. Regardless of how you spend your time, make sure you are efficient with it and find what works for you. Your friends and family may not quite understand why you work the shifts you do, but there is definitely some additional joy and satisfaction to getting up and being halfway finished with your work day before most people are even awake. Those strange hours can be difficult to establish and hard to maintain, but when you find that balance between work and life, you can make both enjoyable, which is what trainers need to find ongoing success and if they want to stick around this profession.

Self-accountability and discipline are pillars of success in this field. In order to remain on the path you want your business to go, you have to keep yourself accountable for your time and money, as well as remain disciplined on how to run your own daily life. One way to make sure you stay accountable and disciplined is to focus on efficiency. Make being efficient a new skill of yours by making the absolute most out of each training session and also maximizing the productivity between each session. If you need to veg out and watch television here and there to reset and get your mind off of things, do so but don't let that half hour show turn into a full season. Before you know it, 30 minutes of removing yourself from work has turned into an afternoon that you had a full slate of work to catch up on and clients to program for. Set aside time for work and set aside time for pleasure, whether that is with family, friends, yourself, and to get away for a bit. In order to build a thriving business, we need to go above and beyond for others but creating that boundary where we allow ourselves time to get away from work is huge in the long run. When it's time to work, work. When it's time to relax, do just that. Compartmentalize the two and keep them separate for your sanity and for the sake of those in your life. Work your absolute hardest to create the business you want, but when it's your down time, allow yourself to take advantage of that to avoid overdoing it and burning yourself out. When you mentally and physically allow yourself to temporarily get away from work, you may actually increase your overall productivity and get further than if you had continued without a break.

Creating and running your own personal training business can be a dream come true, but don't let any profession diminish your mental health or take away time spent with loved ones. Recognize when it's time to press pause and remember that you're playing the long game. This career path has its times to sprint, but we must view it as a marathon and pace ourselves.

Being the owner of your business, you have the power and responsibility to keep your own schedule. In that schedule, don't simply keep your training hours, but also keep track of specific tasks you need to take care of while you're not training. There are so many behind the scenes duties that we are responsible for with this type of business, so we must maximize the production during those hours when we aren't "working." For example, when I began writing this book, I had an end goal in mind of filling up 50 pages of Word documents that simply consisted of ideas. After achieving this and setting new goals, I figured out ways to efficiently use my time writing while continuing my work-life balance. Compiling and developing ideas for the book took a while, but it allowed me to continue my business with no distractions, remove myself from the physical side of training while dialing in the cognitive side of things, and provided me with an outlet to put my thoughts on paper. Not only was I productive while writing this, but I felt refreshed and accomplished by enjoying the process of brainstorming and writing. This strategy gave me a newfound pep in my step and continually jotting down all of those little initial topics kept my mind working through different parts of what this business entails.

Finding productive and (what some would consider) unproductive getaways are both important in ensuring longevity in this career. Regardless of your outlet during those busy days, if you are able to show up to each session, ready to help the client in front of you, and you have a long-term plan for your business, keep with that routine. We all have different hobbies, plans, strengths and weaknesses. Find what works best for you, your clients, and your routine, and create a schedule that allows for you to maximize your output through different avenues, while not overdoing it. We want to enjoy this field, and it is so rewarding, but it can be arduous. As with anything that has the capability to drain us, you have a choice. You can continue letting work get the best of you, or you can figure out a plan that allows you to increase your efficiency and create a much easier road for the future of your sanity and your business.

After hiring my brother, Collin, the plan was once he got his foot in the door by building up rapport and trust through working with people with any sort of health and fitness goals, he would have a better chance of working with clients' children or people they knew. The importance of word of mouth from clients shined its light again as taking care of his people led to an assortment of opportunities down the road. Although Collin wanted to work with youth athletes right off the bat, he had to be patient, get his feet under him by gaining experience working with anybody he had the opportunity to help, and then his sports performance business began to grow.

Collin's persistence and his ability to adapt to all of his clients are what have allowed him to find success as a personal trainer for people in the general population, as well as athletes. Initially being fresh out of college, he knew the information taught in lectures, but actual experience is a whole different story. Take opportunities to spend time learning from other personal trainers. Being able to observe and shadow other trainers and slowly start working with clients are good ways to approach the training aspect of this job. Notice how other trainers treat their people and identify how they gain positive results in the gym with their clients. Each personal trainer can attest to hitting bumps along the road of their careers. Try to brainstorm ways to overcome challenges with other trainers. Learn from their experience and their mistakes. Include lots of communication into your regimen, with other personal trainers, clients, coworkers, and business partners, as it is one of the most important facets of our jobs. Feel free to adapt characteristics learned from other trainers, utilize your education, mesh your program with your strengths, and you can make quite a name for yourself in this business. Being able to work alongside other trainers who aim to help others learn the tools that can aid clients in improvement in and out of the gym makes this job rewarding. Having a rewarding career is my definition of success.

CHAPTER 61

What is Your Brand?

What do you want your business, name, and reputation to be known for? What sets you apart from your competition? Take a few moments to really think about those questions. The brand your business represents is based on the product you provide, the way you treat others, and the perception of your business from current clients, prospective clients, past clients, and others in the community. Your brand is molded over time through each individual interaction and the culmination of what others say about you and your business. The outcomes of those situations are impacted by the results you garner and the relationships you create with others. While *working in* your business, you are unknowingly *working on* your business. Your daily habits and interactions all add up to reflect who you are and how others perceive you, which ultimately dictate what your brand becomes. Figure out who you want to work with; gain clients who are compatible with your goals and the person you are; and at the end of the day, be yourself. In trying to create a brand of business that ultimately revolves around you and your clients, the easiest way to provide a genuine brand of a product is to be who you truly are and base your business model around that.

How can you stand out? What can you do to go above and beyond to provide your clients with the best experience possible and continue to drive new leads your way? In this field, competition is endless, so we need to build a unique product and experience for people to enjoy. Think about that for a moment. Would you train with you? If so, why? If not, why not? When you sit down and line up your best qualities, especially when you're helping others or at work, these can be determiners of what sets you apart. My attentiveness; care for clients (in and out of the gym); willingness to listen; ability to adjust my coaching styles based on the individual; and ultimately my respect for individuals as a person first, client second is how I've established my clientele. Note that none of these descriptors have anything to do with exercise, science, or human physiology. Connections with my clients is what opens them up to me and allows us to be vulnerable with each other. We trust one another. With that trust comes responsibility. It is my responsibility to be there for my clients as individuals, while still accomplishing the fitness goals we have set together. This is how I stand out as a personal trainer.

Just because that has been what has allowed me to run my business well doesn't mean that is the only recipe for sustained success. Some trainers set themselves apart from others because of their attention to detail with preventative exercise, sport specific training, backgrounds in physical therapy, leading group fitness classes, or working with a specific age demographic. Finding what makes you stand out amongst a saturated field of trainers should be a centerpiece of your business model.

What are your strengths as a person and a trainer/coach? If you are a visual person, make a list of your capabilities as a reminder to keep those strengths a priority. Continue to utilize those to bring out the best in others and to be the best version of yourself, therefore being the best asset to people investing in you. Maybe you're a great listener, incredible teacher, very empathetic, a strategic problem solver, caring, or love the study of the human body and thoroughly know how to apply that information to clients to help them improve their bodily awareness. Pride yourself in your virtues, continue to sharpen those areas, and use them as a basis for the type of brand your business portrays.

What are some areas of your personality in which you can improve? Be honest and reflect on the notion we all can do or be better at something. Maybe you are great at talking, but have a hard time communicating (BIG DIFFERENCE). Possibly you haven't kept up with the latest findings within the health and fitness world. Do you just do the bare minimum in your job, relationships, programming, or planning? Have you become complacent or lost motivation for your career path? We all have areas to improve upon. The first steps to working on those is to identify them, acknowledge they require growth, and lay out the steps to get better.

Once you reflect on who you are, what you're good at, and where you can improve, you can make some personal and professional goals to build a better brand of business. Working on these areas will not only elicit better business results, but they will trickle over into your personal life, too. You are your brand of business. Who you are outside of the gym can be associated with who you are as a trainer, coach, and business owner. When working to build a reputable brand of business, always remember there are eyes and ears all over. Others may notice you, even when you are not aware, and word travels fast of your activities. Be true to yourself. Work on growing, learning, and improving yourself. Continue to reflect on where your business is and what you want your brand to be.

CHAPTER 62

Work on Your Business While You Work in Your Business

Don't neglect working *on* your business while you work *in* your business. What I mean by this is that as a personal trainer, our business staying afloat solely relies on our ability to obtain and retain clients. The trajectory of our business and the vision we have in mind for our business also should be on our mind. In order to find the balance required to handle the daily training sessions and stay on path with where you want your business to grow towards, we must be strategic in how we permanently include that into our routine.

One way to do this is through simply etching out hours each week to work on the business side of things, away from face-to-face client interactions. When you find yourself in the grind of your day-to-day operation, it can be easy to only focus on the people you train that day, which is also very important. When you create time to plan out where you want the future of your business to go, it ensures you stay on track with the long-term goals of the business. Although it can be difficult to do this in your "down time" away from clients, it is beneficial in making sure you are continuing on the path initially sought out. Set aside a specific day and time allotment each week to focus solely on marketing; evaluating and calculating payment plans; filing; updating client information; paying bills; assessing and ordering equipment; and any other tasks which accumulate when running a business. Make a list of tasks which have deadlines or due dates, and put a reminder in your calendar to ensure each one is taken care of in a timely manner. Letting tasks build up and not addressing them on a regular basis can eventually become overwhelming. Adopting these types of behaviors can also act as a form of motivation through reminding you of what it is you are trying to work towards and grow your business into but also as a refreshing step back to reflect upon how many people you've helped, how far you've come as a fitness professional, and what you want to continue to work on, in and out of the business.

Remaining present and providing your best self when working with clients and focusing on them as the main point of emphasis while training is something we all should do. When you have down time and you feel the need to relax, think about life outside of business, and enjoy time away from the gym, that is also important. We do need to prioritize our career path and if we don't set aside regular sessions to take that initiative, we may find ourselves stagnant with no sense of direction. Find what works for you with whatever structure that may be, but be sure to continue to work on your business while working in your business.

CHAPTER 63

Marketing

Specific strategies which have been useful in growing Seymour Health & Fitness include word of mouth advertising, giving away free time, social media, and connecting or even partnering with other businesses and professionals in similar fields in my area. When it comes to marketing your business, you should go into it with the intent of attracting your intended audience, demonstrating why your product is unique and worthy of their hard-earned money, and then retaining those clients to create a steady stream of business.

Relying on what I did best, taking care of people and helping them work toward their personal health accomplishments, is what has drawn the most interest in my services over the years. These simple beliefs, along with having a knack for connecting with people and a strong knowledge base within the world of kinesiology were the core of my marketing strategy. Figure out what you feel most confident in doing and make that the basis of promoting your business. Fine-tune parts of your business and cater your services to each individual with whom you come in contact, but most importantly, stick to what you know best and do so while being your genuine self. You and your ability truly are your best marketing tools.

Word of Mouth

Because this was the main route I leaned on to grow my business, word of mouth became my most effective means of spreading the word of what I did and what my business consisted of. Word of mouth is one of the best, most reliable forms of marketing because it comes straight from the individuals already investing in your product. Most people would promote a business to a loved one because they believe wholeheartedly it would be beneficial to the interested person. This notion is based on trust. Trust is a huge part of this business because people seeking you out trust you to do your job and put them in a position to accomplish their intended goals. The people with whom you connect, create relationships, and prove to be honest will trust you. They will tell their family and friends of the positive outcomes received during sessions with you. Although these extensions of your clients may not have met you personally at that point, they already know how you treat their loved ones. This recognition makes it an easier commitment on their end and an easier business opportunity on your end. Taking care of your people and working on prioritizing the personal side of this business can take the work of marketing out of your hands. That is one reason why I placed the *Personal* portion of this book at the beginning. It is the most important part of this job. You must be a people-person and love the people you work with as a personal trainer. Be genuine with your intentions to be an honest and hard-working trainer. By investing in your clients and truly caring about them as people, their word will benefit your business more than any other form of marketing out there.

When getting into the workforce, an eye-catching resume can attract attention from potential recruiters and businesses looking to hire. In the personal training field, your reputation amongst past and current clients is your resume. While a good resume tends to highlight your skills, experience, and qualifications to a future employer, as a personal trainer the way you treat and interact with those in your network holds more weight than fancy font, catchy adjectives, and a clean looking piece of paper. When used correctly, word of mouth is the most sustainable way to keep your current clients happy and satisfied, as well as the best way to drum up new leads.

One specific chain of events that occurred through this type of marketing took place early in my career. Before establishing the Seymour Health & Fitness brand, I worked in conjunction with another trainer, friend, and mentor. Together, we both helped prepare a shared client to step on stage for a bodybuilding show. Having already created a bond of trust and hit a personal goal of weight loss with the other trainer, this client was determined to do more. Her competitive spirit led her to bodybuilding, so she decided that would be her next mountain to climb. Being pulled into a successful, goal-oriented team was an honor for me as a new trainer. The three of us put our heads together to dial in her nutrition, workouts, and show preparation. As a result, she ended up receiving her Pro-Card and making quite the name for herself. After building a strong rapport with this bodybuilding dynamo, I began working with her son. His goal of strengthening his skills as a swimmer proved successful during our time together, as he went on to dominate his high school swim season and carried that over to collegiate swimming. After working together for a while, two of his teammates chose to partake in our workouts. All three put together some impressive resumes for themselves, as they each were State Champions. All of them went on to swim in college and one also chose to be a two-sport athlete, as he also ran track for his college. These three teammates connected me with their high school swim coach, who had built an empire in the area. This coach set me up with the youth swim program, which hired me as their Strength and Conditioning coach. These little connections allowed me to expand my clientele and experience a fun environment with a variety of individuals. This is an example that when you take care of your people, they will speak highly of you leading to more possibilities for you and your business.

Offer Free Time

As covered previously, another way to market business is to give away free time. By being willing to give away free time, people appreciate you not being overly pushy with sales and it shows you value their health first and the paycheck after. Giving away one free session to someone to either sit down and chat as an introduction, or getting others on the floor right away and showing them how you're capable of helping them without charging them is a great first impression. This shows you're there to help, first and foremost, but it usually catches people off-guard because they expect to have to pay for your time from the get go. Your time is very important and it should be honored, but if giving away a free hour to meet someone, get to know them, and give them a taste of your product is what opens the door and keeps them around, it is well worth it. Offering complimentary sessions takes away the pressure of trying to close; shows potential clients a bit of your training style; and eliminates the need for either party to get anxious over any obligatory conversation. Training costs a good amount of money. It can be a lot to ask for from our standpoint, and it can be a lot to consider from the client's perspective. Giving away free time is a great way to show others what they will be getting in return for their money. Never get too high on your horse where you lose sight of helping others as a top priority. We are good at what we do, but there are several benefits to making sure people know what they're getting themselves into before forcing them to financially commit to your services.

Social Media

Another very helpful form of marketing is social media. Social media can be your best friend, as it provides an opportunity to show off who you are, what you believe in, and allows you to reach a larger audience. Social media can also be the demise of you and your business, if you're not careful. The good thing about social media is it drives information rapidly to whoever whenever. The problem with that lies in the same: social media drives information rapidly to whoever, whenever. Being conscious of what is posted on your social media pages is a good step to prevent any negative cloud from following you and your business, whether it may be posted to your business or personal page. An even better step to avoid dealing with negativity or controversial issues revolving around you is to not put yourself in questionable situations. You don't always need to be in "work-mode," but understand that when you create a personal business, regardless of if you're at the gym or not, people will connect you to your business. That is as good or bad as you allow it. An easy way to avoid gossip and negativity surrounding your business is to respect others, be a decent human, and not involve yourself with situations that could end up reflecting poorly on you and those around you.

Creating a "fitness" account on social media is conducive to the way so many in today's world live on the internet. Utilize your business account to spread the message you would like to promote. Personally, I enjoy educating people and showing off the clients that work hard each and every day. The majority of my social media content revolves around the accomplishments my clients have made, educational subjects, and answering common questions we see frequently in the health and wellness fields. Social media is also a way to show your expertise and credibility. Posts can be simple and may not even have much of a caption. Let the picture or video tell the viewer the story being portrayed. Other posts can dive into specific topics, such as the importance of working the posterior chain, how unilateral exercises can help muscular imbalances, or how core stability and abdominal exercises may not always be the same thing. When delving into heavier topics, give a relatable description of the topic, while subtly dropping certain terminology or phrases that show your honesty and legitimacy. You want your information to be geared toward the population you are trying to market, not to prove you are smarter than everyone else.

If you scroll through my business Instagram (@seymour_healthandfitness), Collin's Instagram (@SHF_Performance), or our Facebook page (facebook.com/SeymourHealthAndFitness) you will notice that there aren't many photos of us exercising. We work out, but it rarely is in front of the camera. People don't want to have their timelines flooded with us working out every day. They would rather see an old friend squatting to a new depth, someone who resembles their body size working to deadlift some heavy weight, or a person who plays the same sport as their kid working on speed and agility to improve their sport performance. We try to show our people doing what they love. We also enjoy incorporating some sort of educational message with our posts, as it allows us another chance to help educate our followers, whether or not they are paying clients. Providing free knowledge boosts your credibility and is a great way to help others who may be interested in your content but not quite ready for training with you (yet). Being the page that is helping others, even when they aren't paying, is a good look. It will keep you constantly trying to improve your own knowledge base to provide accurate information to your followers.

Different posts, other than educational pieces, can be more celebratory of your clients. You can (and should) post when people exemplify perfect form or get personal records to emphasize growth and remind others that you also put importance on non-scale related victories. Posting before and after photos or videos are great ways to show how much the body can truly change or how form can improve so much with a little bit of effort. Showing bar path videos, breaking down and analyzing technique, and praising clients that listen to your advice by working on their weaknesses is also amazing content. The beauty of showing off your people is that it demonstrates how proud you are of them. Trainers don't always speak their minds, and we may not verbally tell someone how impressed we are with their progress. This is by no means a replacement for words or compliments, but it can be one way to celebrate those victories with you and your client. Posts you decide to put on social media will show potential future clients what you value the most. Scrolling through social media is a great way to truly see what workouts look like with certain trainers. Posts may not tell the whole story, but the content of a social media page can really show you what values are important to the account holder.

Another benefit to social media is you can influence and educate your followers, and you tag your clients in your photos. This is another way you will reach their friends and followers. Before ever posting any content, be sure to ask for permission from your clients, to make sure they feel comfortable with you putting their images or videos out there. For example, when people are tagged on Facebook, it is shared to their profile, which is then viewed by all of their friends. When their friends see that post, they may interact with it and sometimes that will then share the post to the person who interacted with its page. The amount of people who can see a post in which you tag others is amazing. This web of connections through sharing a photo or video of your clients exercising (with their permission, of course) is a way to get new referrals. If you have clients that would prefer to not be shown on social media, be respectful and don't push them to do it. You will have plenty of clients who will allow you to post about them and you shouldn't take "no" personally. Some people just like to ride under the radar, which should be an honored and respected choice.

The same situation goes for Instagram, Twitter, and other social media platforms, as there are ways for you to reach new depths of the internet by having your content revolve around other people. Have clients share Instagram posts on their stories. Retweets and likes on Twitter will pop up on other timelines. The list goes on and on. The social media platforms you choose though, should align with the audience you are trying to attract. TikTok and Facebook may reach people you train who are in different age ranges. Cater your social media presence toward the demographic you are trying to attract. If you want more high school athletes, use Instagram to post about your athletes, while asking them to share your post to their stories. Post them being explosive, changing direction, sprinting, doing sport specific drills, and then even add in photos of them in their sport, celebrating a state championship, or a picture of them with you at one of their events you attended. Those are all great ways to attract other people in similar situations as them, but also an important reassurance to possible future client's parents to show you are truly invested in their kids, in and out of the gym.

Should we, as trainers and coaches, post ourselves on social media? Yes, but very strategically. We want to highlight our clients, first and foremost. In building your business up the right way, people want to see successful stories and learn more about your training philosophy and business. They aren't following your page to see you flexing in a mirror and wearing barely any clothes. That being said, it is important you promote how you live the lifestyle. The last thing you would want is for people to consider you a hypocrite because you make your clients do workouts, but never hold up your end of the bargain by working out. Not every trainer needs to have washboard abs and bulging muscles, but every trainer should understand that if they are preaching the different habits that makeup a successful, well-rounded health and fitness program, then they should listen to their own advice.

When you do show yourself on your social media, remind yourself before posting that your content is seen by a lot of people. Be smart and conscious about your content, as it will elicit some type of reaction from your followers, whether that be good or bad. There will be a point in time that social media content will be seen by potential employers. You can determine a lot about a person based off of their social media pages. Create a page that in the future you won't regret.

Another facet of social media revolves around building a website. If technology isn't your strong suit, find or hire someone to help create a site that invites people to see what you are all about. Having a website identifying your brand and business is a great platform to bundle all of your content together. You can have a blog, store, photo gallery, prices, contact information, testimonials, and all sorts of other pieces that emphasize who you are and what you provide. The beauty of this journey is that it is all yours and in the end, you get to choose what to put on there and who you want to become. Again, be smart but be creative and think outside of the box. Show off what makes you unique. Showcase why people should train with you.

Local Outreach

One other form of marketing is connecting with local businesses and other professionals in your area to create and grow your network to expand your outreach. When I began Seymour Health & Fitness, marketing and creating connections were now weighing on my shoulders, as opposed to relying on the brand of my previous job to take care of that. After brainstorming, I figured out a handful of ideas that would lead me to grow my network, build my brand, and consequently, increase the amount of people in front of me. The more people you get in front of you, the better chance that you will mesh with one of them and create a connection that leads to training together.

One of those simple, yet effective ideas was reaching out to local businesses. Unless your business and your brand are spread through social media or word of mouth, it can be difficult to grow. Being proactive by doing some digging and emailing or calling local businesses that you could see yourself potentially partnering with is the first step. In doing that research, start by reaching out to fields that would attract similar clients to what you are looking to add to your book of business. For example, physical therapists, nutritionists, dieticians, athletic clothing stores, and health-conscious restaurants are all businesses that may attract a similar clientele and could be useful partners to contact. When reaching out to local businesses, you need to first get your foot in the door. Don't be too pushy and make sure you don't come off as arrogant. Be kind, yet confident, and be clear and concise in what you are asking. Go into that initial conversation with a plan and be direct with what you are looking for. There is no need to beat around the bush, because if you provide a service that the business, or their employees would benefit from, they will show interest. For example, as our brand focuses on improving people's overall health outlook, we reached out to a local healthy meal company. In doing so, we were able to advertise the benefits of their healthy meal kits and they posted flyers, shared our social media posts, and promoted us online and in their business. I also have connected with a self-employed registered dietician who has similar values and sees eye to eye with me in regards to health and fitness. She has been great about recommending us to her clients and when our clients are looking for some more guidance with their food I send them her information.

Reaching out via email and/or phone are great ways to get in initial contact with businesses, but if you can schedule an in-person meeting, it is a more likely opportunity. Do what you can to sit down with someone, even if you ask them for five minutes of their time. If they seem interested in a short meeting, they may be inclined to have interest in learning more about potential partnerships. Make the most out of your meetings by going into them with a plan and clear objectives.

Not every business you contact will get back to you, and even some of those that do will not necessarily have interest in utilizing your scope of practice. If you are rejected, respond respectfully and with integrity. Becoming angry and belittling the company you reached out to could tarnish that relationship for good and might severely hurt your brand's reputation. Not everybody will be interested in what we have to offer. Getting that through our head is important. Do not allow a "no" to affect the possibility of getting a "yes." Businesses that we reach out to are typically independent of one another so just because one turns you down, doesn't mean that the next one will say no. When we get denied, keep your composure, wish them well, and depart peacefully.

One thing that can be very underappreciated when it comes to meetings with other businesses, or even with potential clients, is never allowing them to leave empty handed. Every single time you sit down with somebody, whether they are a potential client or business partner, leave them something reminding them of you. This doesn't have to be a physical copy of some of your programming, although walking in with a physical plan of what you would like to bring to the table wouldn't be a bad thing, but you should always leave them with your knowledge, expertise, and business cards. Show them you aren't just an average Joe who stumbled into a gym and lucked into his/her personal training certification. Through your conversation, show them how insightful you are and connect your education with the values they deem important in their business. Similar to how you would research a mission statement of the company for which you are interviewing and using key terms from that vision in the answers of your interview, you should connect the dots from your business to theirs. Let them understand how your values both align together to let them better envision why your partnership would be a good fit.

Utilizing various methods to reach out to businesses in your community can open doors to unexpected opportunities. Signing a contract as an independent fitness instructor at a large retirement firm, complete with its own fitness center; receiving invitations to and partaking in local health fairs; having an article written about me in the local newspaper; and accepting a request to interact on a podcast were pathways which opened up for me by meeting with others in my community. Will you immediately feel your wallet overflowing with cash? Definitely not, but getting your name out there will lead to other great opportunities and even a handful of new clients along the way.

Seminars and Workshops

Another successful technique that will provide additional value to the services you offer, as well as boost your credibility, and expand your outreach is by hosting seminars or workshops. You can tackle this on your own, or you can do it in conjunction with other professionals in parallel fields. Finding a professional to pair with for seminars or workshops can broaden the depth of knowledge being shared with participants. Pinpointing a date and location; advertising using flyers, word of mouth, and through social media; and preparing unique and engaging content are the biggest tasks involved in preparing for talks such as these. Seminars or workshops can involve you sharing information on a wide range of topics, ideally catering toward your strengths. It is important to always choose categories that would be of interest to potential participants. For example, when hosting a squat seminar in conjunction with a local Physical Therapist, we dove into the importance of squatting, the muscles activated during squatting, how to perfect squat form for each individual, accessory movements that will help improve squats, the biomechanics of squats, and common injuries from poor form. Another seminar presented with the same Physical Therapist revolved around the shoulder joint, which as you know, entails many muscle groups and an assortment of very common injuries. After speaking and demonstrating certain movements, we opened up the workshop to a more interactive portion. People did certain movements and exercises as we led the participants through them and assisted them in correcting technique and focusing on form, rather than amount of weight, which we both highly stressed as a precursor to loading up too much additional weight to exercises. These workshops allowed us to demonstrate our knowledge, educate clients and non-clients, and gain experience speaking to larger groups that were made up of familiar and unfamiliar faces. These types of setups allow us to build rapport and trust amongst the audience, as well as actually help people work through issues with those topics and hopefully alleviate some pain during those movements.

Personal Contacts

To continue to grow your network, remain in contact with previous mentors. Being asked to speak at my alma mater by one of my favorite professors allowed me to gain practical experience in a classroom and share my career path with others. As this professor always went out of his way to ensure I was on the right track during my college years, it was an honor to give back to him and his students. Having someone you can look up to who also understands the impact they have on the career choices of their students is unique and life changing. Keeping former professors, mentors, and other formative role models in your life can enrich your career path experiences.

Newsletters

Educating others on a more personal level led the SHF team into writing bi-weekly newsletters that cover health, fitness, nutrition, and all other wellness related subjects. These free newsletters have become another branch of our marketing arm as they electronically reach hundreds of readers every other week. Diving into the importance of intaking adequate amounts of protein, mental health topics, interviews with athletes and other fitness professionals, the different energy systems, as well as other suggested topics are ways to inform and educate a larger audience on various subjects and further progress us all on improving our health and well-being. Positive feedback from these letters challenges the SHF team to continually dig into various areas of health and fitness to educate, appease, and grow our followers.

Apparel

On top of utilizing social media, connecting with local businesses, and creating partnerships with other fitness professionals in your area, there are still countless ways to get your name and brand out there to reach new clients. Apparel is a great way to have your supporters show off your material, all while quietly marketing to strangers whenever your friends and family wear your clothing items. When people you work with wear your apparel in the community, those around them may show interest or at least wonder what brand they are representing. Being someone trusted and positively known in the community takes time, but once your reputation is established and continually unkempt, apparel is a great, simple way to have your name out and about without pushing it too much. You can get your apparel to your clients by creating online stores with local apparel companies or handing out merchandise for certain events. Over the years, we've done both. Setting up online stores with various objects containing your logo can be as simple as contacting a local printing company and agreeing on terms for a store which can be linked to your company's social media pages. Starting out with t-shirts and sweatshirts, then expanding to hats, shorts, leggings, and other items all professionally stamped with your logo puts your name in the public eye. People who have access to online stores buy gear which is worn throughout the country. We have created stores for the people in our lives stemming from clients to friends to family to friends of friends to choose and purchase clothing items they like. We also make sure to gift our clients a select clothing item each year for Christmas as a small token of thanks for all they do for us. This select piece of apparel is something we only provide for clients investing in us. This shows our gratitude and appreciation for the constant support, trust, and belief in Collin and me, and it is another way for our logo to be shown on additional items worn by our clients. Creating and sharing apparel stamped with our brand logo is another strategy that has worked for us to show our thanks while continuing to market our business.

CHAPTER 64

Client Retention

Whether you are starting from scratch or branching off to create your own business, maintaining your original clients and obtaining new ones can be a real concern for trainers. What you will learn throughout your career is that the reason clients initially seek you out and the reasons for which they stick around may not be the same. If you create this desirable product that people recognize they can benefit from and then you provide exceptional service and an unmatched experience, you will set yourself up for not having to continually find new clients. Extending your business towards the lives of others in your community through the different styles of marketing is important for the growth of your business but if you already have an established book of business, first look at what is in front of you. The people you are currently working with are the ones already invested in what you provide. Taking care of and making your current clients happy should come first, as they have already proven their loyalty and appreciate what you offer. Retaining current clients is the best form of new lead generation. When you prove time and time again that you will take care of those in front of you, they will vouch for you, market for you, and remain loyal to you. You've already built up this level of mutual respect and trust with one another so asking current clients if they have any friends, family members, or loved ones who would be interested in working with you can be an easy way to send feelers out to at least open the door to that possibility. That route is much easier than cold-calling people who don't know the impact you've had on someone important in their lives.

For clients who do come with you, do what you can to make this transition as smooth as possible so they continue to feel prioritized, even in a new space with unfamiliar faces. That being said, when you make any transition you may notice not everyone will follow you. It may happen, but it will be okay. Some people don't like change. It can be intimidating and create anxiety for people to step out of their comfort zone. If this happens to you, take a deep breath and end things on a good note. Maybe this wasn't the right time for them. Maybe they don't feel comfortable yet, and you may have another opportunity down the road. Acting out and being visibly angry with any clients will only tarnish your name and start the brand of your new business off with a negative tone. More often than not, clients ending their tenure with you is not a personal decision. Typically, they either get frustrated with not seeing expected results, or they financially can't keep you in their budget. When either of these reasons come up, always assure your clients you will be there for them when they need you. Give them something when they leave. For example, a handful of at-home exercises or tips for nutrition are always great little pieces of advice that don't cost you much time and are a great gesture for those who had invested in you previously. Burning bridges, at any point along the timeline of your business, will come back to bite you later on.

Whether you are a veteran or a new trainer, attrition will happen. People cease training. It's just a simple fact. Because some clients do decide to terminate training with us at some point, upkeeping marketing techniques and maintaining an open mind to generate new leads are very important strategies to continue building your business. Although not every trainer and client are good fits with one another, we have the option to pass them along to someone that would be a better fit, or we can choose to adapt, learn, and adjust to what they need in order to become more well-rounded in our own practice. Whenever someone contacts you showing interest in training, they see something in you that they see beneficial to them. They sought you out for a reason. They understand you provide a service and recognize the product you sell is not free. Understand your value and know your worth. As for prospective clients, even if your schedule is booked full, you have the option to find a program that works for both of you. For me personally, I will not say no to a potential new client. The more the merrier. In our occupation, we often train when other people aren't at work. Although it is important to set boundaries for you to have time with yourself, your family, friends, and others, when you have the opportunity to take on an additional client, that is a choice that you have to make. At times, we are surprised with the ending of a training client, so having those additional clients, even if they are at unideal times throughout our week, can help as a cushion if/when we do lose a client or two. I believe that even on long days from 5 am until the evening, I have the power to help other people improve their quality of life and create new behaviors that can potentially flip their entire lifestyle around. That possibility overrides the fact that I may be a little tired when that day comes to an end. Those long days pay off (betterment of the lives of others, financially, and with continuing to grow the business), but there's no doubt they can take a toll on us. When you get to that point in business, maybe it is time to look into expanding your team or narrowing down your clientele to those who are willing to pay more so you can work less and balance your work with life outside of your job.

Just because a client decides to stop training with us, does not mean that is a permanent decision. I have worked with a handful of people on multiple occasions, even though we have stopped for an assortment of reasons for periodic times. As discussed earlier, do not burn those bridges. Those clients may always return or they may even send referrals your way, if they truly enjoyed their experience. If you treat your people well, they will rave about you. They will tell their family and friends and if you're good at your job, the results of your programming will speak for themselves. When clients thoroughly enjoy their time with you and get the desired results, people in their own lives will recognize the changes. Because of this connection and trust they may have together; this may be an easy "in" for you to help them out as well. People are hesitant to invest in something when they have no real connection. Your hard work and trusting relationship with your current clients can create a connection between you and potential other future clients. When you do take care of your people, it is okay to ask them for referrals, as well. When you provide life-altering advice and help people turn their lives around, it may seem like a big task but asking for their assistance in continuing to grow your business by vouching for you is a little request. Creating incentivized referral programs for your current clients will help push that objective a little more rapidly, but be wary about always asking for more sales. Take care of your people, show them that more money in your pocket isn't your only priority, and they may send family members or friends your way unprovoked. Let your results and relationships do the work for you.

As a small business, all new possible leads must come as a result of your own effort. At your previous location there may have been a constant, revolving door that would send prospective clients your direction. There are different ways to get new clients, depending on how you train. Many people could benefit from what we all have to offer but the timing, motivation levels, location, and price all have to be right for them to even think about pulling the trigger. With such a large amount of dependent factors and the high volume of other trainers in the area, why would people train with you? The first piece of advice is to let your work speak for itself. 'Work' is not only quantifiable results, but also how you treat your clients. People will remember how you made them feel, more than anything. Feeling good comes from movement, eating healthy, and placing uplifting people around you. Being able to provide all of those things as a personal trainer can really elevate others, especially those who put in the work and buy-in to what you are preaching to them.

Ultimately, from the business perspective, what works for you may be completely different than what works for others. This industry isn't one-size-fits-all. Your ability to find out what works best for you and your people so you can sustain and build the business you're looking to create is most important. Make connections, influence people, educate them, and grow your network. Spreading your name and brand around while showing you genuinely care, and proving your thorough training gets results, will gravitate people your way so you can build your business.

CHAPTER 65

Pricing and Rates

When discussing business in any industry, particularly one where a service is offered, numbers must be discussed. Regardless of why you got into your profession, you need to make a living, which people understand. Prospective clients understand your services cost a price. Deciding what your services should be valued at can be a difficult decision. When trying to figure out how much you should charge for your services, take into account the obvious time you spend working with one another. You also need to include the time it takes to prepare for each session; your education and previous experience; the growth and quality of product you now provide; comparable rates in your area; and how well you can justify your value through the services you provide. You are worth what you provide. If you merely provide a minimal service, don't offer exceptional customer service, and are winging workouts for your clients, it will be awfully difficult to retain higher-paying customers. On the other end, if you customize each and every workout down to the smallest detail, are always going above and beyond in the gym and outside, and you've done so for the time it takes to build up a quality reputation, you will be able to charge higher rates because clients realize they are getting a much better quality of product. The job performed by a personal trainer is similar to buying any product. Most people would rather pay more for a better item than less for something less reliable and may not last them.

To decide where to start with your rates, do your research. Look into comparable training services in your area. Decide what those businesses offer and what their pay structure looks like. Take that information, see how it compares to what services you offer as a personal trainer, and then decide where to place your cost. It's often hard to give yourself the credit you deserve in this occupation. Don't let self-doubt doesn't carry over into the prices of your services. Don't be afraid to proudly look yourself in the mirror and tell yourself that what you provide for others is more advantageous than the product of competitors. You are worth what you provide and if you provide exceptional services while making people feel better, your rate is going to be rightly justified. When deciding what to charge as your initial training rate, put together a price you think appropriately reflects what you do prior to each session to prepare, the hour of work, your follow ups, your experience, and the educational background you have in the material you are helping people with. For example, when training at a corporate gym, we were charging people $100-$130 per hour. This was in addition to the monthly rate they paid for being a member of the gym. Being fresh out of college, trying to find my groove as a trainer, and still in the learning stages, I was uncomfortable having clients pay that much for services.. When I branched off on my own, I felt that with all of those factors involved, I felt that my training service was worth $75 per hour at the time. This went over well for those who chose to continue training with me because they were saving a pretty penny and continued to get the same service just at a different location. For some, this price was out of the range they were willing to pay. My initial instinct was to give them a discount, but I had to respect myself and the work and time put into myself as a trainer and keep the rate consistent.

Once your business is up and running, you will sit down with prospective clients. In consultations with possible future clients, the conversation eventually leads to money. People come to us with interest knowing they will have to invest in us and our product if they decide to work with us. One mistake that a lot of us coaches and trainers make is during this point in the conversation. After you pitch the price you charge for your services, stop talking. You don't need to justify your rate. You know the quality and value of the service you provide. If a prospective client questions your fees, explain the different benefits this person will receive through working with you.

When deciding whether or not to raise prices, find a compromise. For new clients, you could increase your rate, if you feel the value of your product has improved. When Collin and I opened our own facility in 2022, we debated on raising prices for everyone to help cover the new costs, increased rent, and additional expenses, but we decided that the loyalty shown by our current clients outweighed the small price increase. Therefore, we kept our current clients in the same price range throughout our transition. I doubt any of them would have flinched if we told them we were raising their rates, but it was our way of honoring that relationship and the loyalty they've shown us throughout our business ventures. New clients had no problems paying our slightly increased rates, as we were in a new facility with brand new equipment, and they were receiving our high-quality services.

As it relates to payment methods, the options seem to be endless in today's day and age. When I first began, I had opened a business bank account and simply started by taking cash or checks. These were the simplest options and I didn't know enough about other card reading options to make a decision. As business expanded, so did payment options such as Venmo and PayPal. We decided to have a business Venmo account directly linked to our business bank account where we could offer that as a convenient option for clients to pay. When opening our own facility in 2022, we offered more group classes so we decided it was time to look further into other options to stick with the times. We found a local business (VizyPay) that helped us put a payment hyperlink on our website, provided us with handheld card readers, and made it a much easier process for a lot of our customers to pay for our services. To this day we still accept several forms of payment because we've found that people have different preferences. If we can make our business all about each client even down to that detail, they recognize they are our top priority. Whatever works best for them is what we try to do. Our various forms of payment options have proven to be appreciated by our clients and it hasn't negatively impacted us in any way. It's a win-win.

When it comes to prices for services you are providing, it is ultimately up to you to determine the structure of your pay scale. Some trainers offer larger packages that include discounted rates per session if they buy over a certain number of sessions. If you prefer to have each session remain the same regardless of how many people buy, that is absolutely fine too. I keep my rates the same whether clients purchase one or twenty sessions. My quality of service remains the same regardless of sessions so my rate remains the same, also. If you increase rates year over year, make sure you continue to improve the quality of your services to justify that increase.

Because people will purchase different packages and will use those in different timeframes, staying on top of tracking those sessions is important to ensure you don't over or undercharge your customers. This can be done in a variety of ways so ultimately, what works for you to keep track of sessions used can be done as long as you remain diligent that you don't miss or over track your clients. You don't want to find yourself in a situation where you ask them for a new payment when they don't actually owe you yet, nor do you want to work for free because you mistakenly tracked their sessions. I prefer good old pen and paper but there are applications that help tracking, scheduling, and payments so find what allows you to run your business the way you want.

With collecting payments, tracking sessions, and continuing to serve your clients, eventually you want to reap the financial benefits of your services. Whether you're self-employed or working for another fitness company, the way you get paid will vary depending on a number of factors. Some roles are paid strictly off commission and the more you work, the more you make. This is commonly seen in corporate gyms, where you charge your client an hourly rate, the gym takes their cut, and you get paid the remainder. This is also seen in self-employed personal trainers with the obvious reason being the money they bring goes towards their expenses and what they decide to do with the leftovers is ultimately up to their discretion. This is the route I started with when working for another company and because I was familiar with it, until recently, I stuck with a similar format. When I first began Seymour Health & Fitness, I didn't write myself a paycheck for a while. I brought in money but I had expenses that I had to handle to ensure I stayed on my feet. I had rent, an accountant, insurance, liability, and some new fees that came with beginning a small business that I prioritized over putting any money in my pocket. I made it a goal of mine to build up my business bank account to a certain amount before writing myself my first paycheck. Since I've been established for a while now and I've found more stability in revenue, I have sense shifted my payment to a salary, as I decided on an amount that I felt I was deserving of, that also took into account all of our business expenses, while still keeping our business bank account above a certain number. I write these paychecks every two weeks because that's when I pay other trainers.

For other trainers working for me, I pay them a very fair percentage of the amount of money they bring in. Collectively, we sat down and laid out our financials, expenses, and expected income, and agreed to an amount each month that covered their share of the expenses that I would then deduct from their paychecks. Once this amount was withdrawn, the remainder was profit for them so there was additional incentive for them to continue working to bring in more customers since they would benefit from that.

Another avenue that is possible in the personal training space is something I experienced from the opposing point of view but is an option for gym owners. Renting space as a personal trainer is very common and is how I began after leaving the corporate gym space. Now, as a gym owner, we have the option to rent out our space to other trainers to help provide them and their clients with a welcoming facility to workouts, as well as enjoy some supplemental income for me. If this is something you have the opportunity to do, I would recommend it as long as the trainer is reputable, agrees to the stipulations within your gym that you lay out, and they remain respectful of your clients, your space, and you. This is a helpful way for both the renter and gym owner to benefit in their business and surround themselves with another individual both parties can learn from and enjoy being around. There are several other ways to bring in additional money but my only piece of advice with some of those would be to stay within your scope of practice and be sure you are continuing to prioritize what you think is most important in your business so those supplemental income opportunities don't distract from your main focus.

CHAPTER 66

Payments (and When Not to Charge)

Your value deserves to be compensated but at times, you may benefit from giving away free time. The concept of giving away your time has been covered already, but it's important to emphasize giving people a taste of the value you provide so they can understand how beneficial you can be to them. Prove to people why it is worth it to invest in your services. Giving away your time is a great way to increase the number of people in front of you and also shows that your primary incentive is not money. Being money motivated is a good thing, but it can't be your only motivating factor. There is a negative insinuation toward those who claim to be money motivated. When done correctly, building a personal training business has a high-financial ceiling and making money for distributing quality, unmatched content should allow for you to bring in some good paychecks. Yet, if money is your sole motivation, this field isn't for you because that greed will lead to choosing money over your clients and their wellness which could turn into a disaster.

Giving away free time and providing complimentary sessions, especially for new prospective clients, acts as a form of persuasion to get people into the gym. If they take you up on this free offer, it signifies they have interest in something you are providing.

This offering doesn't always lead to a sale, and that is expected. Finding a trainer with a 100% closing rate would be extremely impressive. There is an honest message sent to your possible clients when you offer them the first meeting or session complimentarily. There are great trainers who may charge a pretty penny for a consultation, which may be a turnoff for potential clients. Our time is valuable, but so is our client's. You securing a long-term client after a freebie is well worth the one-time fee you would normally charge. Now, not every free session turns into a client but if that's the case, make sure that they at least learned something or received some takeaways so they can work on things on their own. In our field, we don't always get to eat the fruit the same day we plant the seed. Give everybody you come in contact with a positive experience, regardless of sales. If you provide them with a fun, educational, and helpful session, they will rave about you to their family and friends, will contact you down the road if they decide to eventually train, or even reach back out with questions. Not every person you help will be a paid client. If you go into each day with that mindset, it will allow you to set aside the sales portion, be yourself, and help others which oftentimes turns into sales, anyways.

Before I branched off on my own, sales had been the biggest struggle. I was fresh out of college, had never been in a sales role, nor did I really know that personal training had a major emphasis on sales. Being in the corporate personal training world is a learning experience. At the time, we were fed numbers, numbers, and more numbers. Numbers are important in business, but that emphasis has driven so many great trainers out of those doors. Many talented trainers have branched off on their own because of the corporate philosophies of sales being the number one priority. Rather than force feeding trainers to sell, sell, sell with endless pushing from management, branching off can allow you to let the quality of your services sell your products for you. Without showcasing your skills and getting to really know the prospective client first, it can be difficult to try to sell a personal training package. Some trainers thrive in selling situations and it shows through their sales numbers. However, I thoroughly believe in demonstrating your product, letting your potential buyer test drive it, and then getting to the sales conversation. People know there will be a fee involved if they decide to work with us. Showing what they are going to get instead of being overly pushy and sales-y on the first meeting has been a much more successful route for me. Everybody has their own way of promoting their product. I challenge you to create a routine that works for you. Just remember, being genuine, helpful, and listening to others is always a good way to show your top priorities and what you have to offer as a personal trainer.

As stated previously, people understand we cost money. Some people will try to take advantage of you. Giving away some of your time to showcase how you train is fine to an extent, but it is important to know your worth. This goes for every career path. Don't let people bulldoze you and push you around. You are good at what you do. You know your stuff. You provide a service that has the potential to help turn people's lives around. You are worth whatever someone is willing to pay you. After any initial free sessions, remain firm on receiving payments for further training experiences. Find a reasonable rate that you believe you are worth and stand your ground. Honor prior commitments regarding past cost expectations you may have made with loyal clients, but if you feel like you are worth a certain amount, stick with that. Show why you are worth each session fee and go above and beyond so people forget about the money.

Money can be a difficult talking point for anybody. Reminding yourself that you are worth the charging price and setting that standard from the get go will help make easier, more fluid conversations. Once you get past that initial selling point and your clients are on board with training, make sure you have a policy for payments. At most of the corporate gyms, it is normal to have recurring electronically funded transactions (EFT) where their payment runs automatically every so often, depending on how large of a package was purchased. This is in effort to eliminate conversations on late or missing payments from happening and help with retention. If this is the route you decide, find a system or app that allows you to set this up and it is no longer an issue. If you decide to take a different route, it could force you to have more monetary conversations, but does allow for flexibility with each individual client. As explored in Chapter 65: *Pricing and Rates*, you can allow the client to decide what method of payment works best for them. Some pay in packages of 5-20 sessions, depending on how often they train, while others simply pay each month based on how many sessions they will get in that upcoming month. The reasoning behind this route was because the EFT would often build a backup of sessions if that month didn't line up exactly as the previous month. Then this caused a large chunk of sessions to either go unused or unpaid, which could have proven to be confusing or frustrating for clients. With clients each purchasing different sized training packages, it does force you to be more diligent with keeping track of your sessions, but in doing so, you make sure everyone is on the same page and each session is accounted for. This can be done in a variety of ways and ultimately is determined by you, as the trainer, but programs and applications may take care of this or you may need to stay on top of keeping track of sessions if you do your books by pen and paper, spreadsheets, or any other way.

You may face many hurdles when dealing with money collection and being fairly paid, but try to stay calm and avoid escalating the situation. If circumstances arrive when a client is struggling financially, but they are excelling in the gym, you may have to have difficult, but realistic conversations about payment expectations. Trust your people, because they trust you. Be smart with your money, but remain understanding with each individual situation. When deciding how you want to structure your payment methods, figure out what is going to work best for you, for your people, and move forward. Most people can make a variety of methods work, so if you decide on one standard method of payment to make things simple and you find it works for your business, good for you. Don't overthink it because at the end of the day, people will be willing to pay for your services however you need them to if you are fulfilling your promise to help them in ways aligned with their expectations.

CHAPTER 67

Increase your Value

In order to create a desired product in your business, it all starts with the value you provide for others who may be searching out that service. If improving value is the optimal outcome, we must prioritize the daily habits which increase value. At the very base, this starts with the interactions we have with one another, whether those are in person, online, or other virtual outlets. Creating value and continuing to improve through repeated intentional interactions with others is a great place to start in pursuit of producing a more desired product within your business.

Through intentionally interacting with those seeking you out, you will notice improved relationships, better client retention, reassurance of mutual investment between your clients and you, and more people being referred your way because of the value you provide. When people recognize you are genuinely interested in helping them feel their best as a person through your business, they will rave about you to others. When people feel good about themselves, they like to spread word of their accomplishments and recognize those who helped them achieve any desired goals.

Some additional ways to increase the value of what your business provides are by being outgoing and relatable. When people feel a sense of belonging from somebody who goes out of their way to help others be part of that inner circle, they feel included. That inclusivity allows others to open up, connect deeper, and create bonds that otherwise wouldn't have been formed. Including others and helping them feel part of the community begins the moment they step in the door, or even right before they enter your facility. A simple greeting and asking how they are or saying how good it is to see them is a great way to start on the right foot. Prior to that, use your manners and open the door for them if you're not working with another client. Simple behaviors such as those are ways to make others feel welcome. A few other ways to create inclusivity in your gym include following through on your words and promises with the way you act. Don't just preach that your gym is inclusive to all, act upon that. Use your social skills to interact with and get to know everybody in your space. Introduce them to others. Invite them to group workouts and provide the opportunity for others to work hard together. On Saturday mornings, our gym holds a class workout that is usually completed with a partner. Anybody that wants to join, whether they are part of the classes, do personal or partner training, or are simply interested in trying out our gym is welcome. There's something about being together with a group when everybody is pushing and working hard as one unit. That brings everybody together.

Within those interactions, we can use our people skills to converse and connect with others so there can be a bond formed. As stated previously with the personal trainer to client relationship, finding ways to relate to clients might be discussing researched information with a client on how to address previous or current injuries or rehab; pinpointing specific exercises which would align with the client's goals to improve in specific areas of the body; remembering past conversations and recalling shared details about a client's life or story; showing excitement with their attained goals; or even associating commonalities between your lives outside of the gym.

When working to increase value, always follow up and deliver promises faster than expected. Respond to messages, call others back, check in on them, and if you promise to deliver something, be sure to honor that commitment and don't push it too far down your priority list. Even if they may seem small, following through on promises could be crucial for others. When you remember little things, and prioritize clients and their needs, they know you care. When you tell someone you will do something for them, do that and then some. Provide more value through your services by consistently outperforming your clients' expectations. This will take work, but that effort will be recognized. Your dedication and commitment to your clients may be reciprocated through their own personal efforts, achievements, and accomplishments, as well as their financial compensation.

Another way to create and expand the value of your product is by making sure what you provide is unique. The idea of supply and demand applies very well to this thought. Supply is an amount of goods or services that are available to consumers. Demand is the desire of those consumers to purchase said good or service. When the market of goods and services is saturated with numerous options that are all the same and may not be exactly what you are looking for, demand goes down. When there is a supply of goods or services which stand out and become desired by the consumers, the demand inflates. Working in this business, we know there are many other trainers out there. At the surface level, personal trainers all provide roughly the same service: exercise prescription and accountability with those workouts. Capitalizing on your strengths and what sets you apart from others and then promoting that to consumers can increase your demand. When you dig deeper and set yourself apart by exhibiting a different and better-quality product, the demand for your services skyrockets and your value increases. Trust that what sets you apart can be used as a step ladder to elevate you above your competition in this field.

Sometimes when seeking out products with high value, the simpler the better. Although we, as trainers and coaches, may need to learn the complexities of the science behind exercise and the body, it doesn't always mean our clients want to know that information. Although some may enjoy geeking out with you about the depths of those areas, most probably want you to take care of the behind the scenes work for them, give them a good workout, listen to and converse with them, and be their release from stressors in their life outside the gym. For a good number of clients, it is your job to give them a workout which fits their needs, wants, and goals. By the same token, other than explaining, teaching, and walking them through exercises, your clients may simply want the convenience of coming to you knowing that they don't have to think about what it is they are going to do for the next hour. The convenience of you taking care of them may be part of the service they are looking for, which adds value to what you provide. Keep things simple, check all the boxes each individual client is looking to receive from your services, and make sure you do what it is they are coming to you for so they don't feel the need to seek outside assistance. Your value is what your clients deem it. Prescribe workouts they are looking for, and keep it simple. If you adhere to their requests, your value to your clients will continue to remain high.

One last objective to help increase value ultimately is prioritizing customer service. "The customer is always right" is a common slogan. Is that true? Possibly, yet the point is to make sure you conform your services to fit the customers' needs. Understanding each individual's needs is the first step. This may be evident at your initial consultation or it may take a few sessions to figure out. It is always easier to fit your programming to the needs of your clients when you promote communication. Feedback and conversation about what they are looking for and what you provide is important. Not every client may be the best fit for you, but willingness to meet in the middle can be a resolution. If you realize your client's needs are not being met, use your web of trainers in the surrounding network to refer them on if you think they'd be a better fit working together. For clients who choose to retain your services, make their experience enjoyable, easy, and beneficial. Follow through with your promises, deliver results, be a light in their life, and make the most out of your time together. Make your gym a place to which people want to return. Be that steady rock in their lives where they know they get better, feel better, and come out a better person each and every time they interact with you or leave your facility. The value of your product and services can be determined by what you provide others. When you take time to reflect and really work to improve what affects your clients, you can elevate your business to new heights.

CHAPTER 68

Market Your Product as an Investment, Rather Than an Expense

Marketing the training product that we provide as an investment, rather than an added expense, allows people to resonate with buying into what we have to offer. Help prospective clients comprehend and understand the value of your product, as well as the incredible changes they can make, by speaking to them in ways relating to their particular circumstances. One comparison, used with a more mathematically-inclined potential client, would be to the stock market. People tend to participate in the stock market because generally when played correctly, they have a good chance of seeing their money grow at a faster rate than if it were sitting in a savings account. When we deposit money into the market, we are gambling to an extent, but if we are smart about it and have someone helping guide us through strategies, we can come out ahead down the road. Many of your clients may depend on the stock market for their retirement and that the end amount of money is the only number that matters. There will be ebbs and flows. There will be days where stocks are traded at lower costs. There will be bullish and bearish patterns that happen along the way. Regardless, if we stay patient and make moves when advised, we can come out on top when we decide to cash out in the long run.

Replace your money and the stock market with your health and fitness. Why do we invest our money so regularly, but are hesitant to invest in our well-being? We are in a society which prioritizes money over other important factors, such as relationships and physical and mental health. Help reassure potential clients that investing in their health and fitness through working with you leads them on the road to improving their long-term health.

Deciding to invest in our health is a long-term asset. We are dealt different hands and some of those cards may be outside of our control, but exercising, eating a balanced diet, surrounding ourselves with wholesome people, and creating healthy habits and thoughts will do so much to elevate our quality of life, now and as we get older. When investing in our health and wellness, we save money in the long run. By grabbing our physical and mental wellness by the horns, being proactive through positive changes, and creating healthy behaviors, we allow ourselves to improve the chances of living healthier and happier lives. More than likely, we will either spend money on improving our health and wellness now, or we will end up spending it on trying to fix illnesses when we are older.

Time, money, and effort are three of the limiting factors, or excuses, that cause people to drag their feet when it comes to exercise. When expanding on this concept to encourage prospective clients you, as the trainer, must emphasize the fact that to change physical, mental, or emotional wellbeing, it will take effort on the client's end. In order to change, one needs to invest time, money, and put in effort otherwise you will remain stagnant. Similar to investing in the market, in order to come out ahead, it may be advantageous to educate ourselves or ask a professional how to go about getting to where we want. Setting aside a certain amount of time to consistently repeat healthy habits, such as working out or cooking, should be one of your talking points when discussing your programming with possible clients. Share the idea that it is important to invest monetarily in health for the best chance of success. Open up options during initial discussions to help people see they can achieve healthier lives by working with a personal trainer, simply getting a gym membership, or being more conscious about the foods picked out at the grocery store. Letting potential clients know their health is a priority can confirm their choice to invest in you as their trainer.

Most people have the time, money, and choice within their budgets to get where they want in life. Finding ways to use time, money, and choice for the betterment of one's health is all about priorities. Guiding clients into analyzing their current ways can help them understand why allocating time and money in a health plan will lead to better, healthier choices in their lives. Think about how time is spent. How many hours of the day are consumed by watching Netflix or scrolling on a phone? Could that time be better spent out on a walk or in the gym? Reflect on daily expenses with clients. Being a regular at the local Starbucks, eating out for every meal, indulging in happy hours, or buying another pair of shoes might be patterns which could be shifted, thus allocating more money to invest in gym memberships or cover group class workout costs. If it is the effort clients are struggling with, understand that it won't be easy. Your job, as the personal trainer, will be to push clients, mentally and physically in ways they may not have done before. You have to help possible clients understand that instant gratification, when it comes to exercise, may not be in the form of immediate results. It may be shown in happiness of correctly performing an exercise through full range of motion, hitting a new PR, or even clearing your mind and using the gym as a mental release. Let clients know you will be there to support them along this journey. Building a full picture of how time, money, and choices can be restructured for clients to afford your personal training services can eliminate excuses and encourage positive change in their lives.

Change is scary. Investments can be scary. There is risk involved in both. You will not see results as quickly as you may want. You will go in spurts where you are progressing rapidly and then you plateau or even regress. The important thing when battling with these ups and downs, is not to compare your route to where it was yesterday, but to where it was at the beginning of your journey. Be honest with your clients about all of these aspects of personal training. When using the stock market analogy as compared to our business, propose a scenario such as this. If you dumped $5,000 into the stock market and after six months it was at $7,000, you won't get hung up on the fact that that wasn't necessarily an exactly linear path, but you will focus on the fact that your money trended upward from where you began. When enduring a fitness journey, some days will be better than others and not every day will be a step in the right direction, regardless of how hard you try. The important thing is to see where you've gotten after six months, one year, and five years of hard work. Those peaks and valleys become insignificant, even though they seemed detrimental at the time. The most important thing is to encourage clients to continue without quitting to witness progress over time.

This concept applies to weight loss, muscle hypertrophy, strength, relationships with others, the psychology and conversation going on with yourself between your ears, food intake, and all kinds of other health-related parts of our lives. Not every meal, thought, relationship, workout, or repetition will be the best. As long as we recognize those, learn from them, and work to better ourselves, we will continue to grow toward a goal. The investment in health takes time. This pertains to you, as a personal trainer, as well as your clients. You may not be where you want to be tomorrow or even next year. Don't be a day-trader when it comes to your health. Little daily habits do create behaviors that can help shape the outcome of our fitness journey, but we need to step back and look at the bigger picture. Focus on improving in one facet or another each and every day. If you proactively do so, you will progress and continue on the path toward an end goal. Don't beat yourself up about mistakes here or there because like the day-to-day shifts in the trend of the stock market, we shouldn't pull all of our money out as soon as things drop a bit. Ride it out and adjust as needed. Be patient and remind ourselves that it isn't easy. We must invest our time, money, and effort in order to reach new heights.

Realigning our values to prioritize health is something nobody will regret. Once a client decides this change is only going to benefit them and help in all aspects of their life, it can be such a refreshing choice. Investing in health teaches so much about patience, drive, mental fortitude, and allows for understanding on how much better life can be, on the outside and inside. Not everything happens overnight and good things take time. Learning to enjoy the process and ditch the concept of instant gratification will allow for each of you to understand how valuable it is to invest in yourself.

This stock market/health analogy has been a very effective comparison in potential clients committing to improving their lives. For the most part, people know what they need to do to get healthy, lose weight, or accomplish whatever health or fitness goals they may have, but they need a little push to get that ball rolling. Paying attention, learning about individuals, and finding ways for them to connect to the product you are pitching will help them understand how and why they should invest their time, money, and effort in you.

CHAPTER 69

Make Your Business Known for Prioritizing the Little Things

You already know about the importance of marketing your services as an all-inclusive product. But from the business perspective, when you design and market your services in that way, as opposed to simply a workout program, you need to follow through. Deliver more than just a program while prioritizing the little details. Anybody can write up a workout to sell to others, but the content provided between sets, after workouts, and even when clients are away from the gym will really set you apart from your competition. Little details such as providing individuals with more than just a workout in the fitness sense, by helping educate them, providing them with suggestions or resources to improve nutrition, assisting them in sleep recommendations, and creating a personal connection with each client, increases the value of your product. The personal training business is result oriented, but in order to accomplish those results, we need patience. As much as we all wish there were some magic pill to ingest and instantly receive the physical results you want with your health or physique, we all know that those quick-fixes are a big scam. Preach patience to your clients. Help them understand why it is so important to be patient, be disciplined enough to show up each day to put in the necessary work, and to continue pushing themselves. Guide clients into recognizing that the benefits are well worth the wait. In order to make the timeframe from your first session to the days when clients begin noticing the results, you have to continually provide them with an unmatched experience. Remember to prioritize small gestures such as having meaningful conversations, getting to know them, helping them feel more comfortable with you, building trust, and on a more day-to-day level, filling the space between your exercises. Don't overwhelm clients by only speaking science, exercise, and lifting terminology. Don't be a robot. Be human. People notice little things, so figure out what small actions you can do in and out of the gym to have your business stand out.

CHAPTER 70

Stick to the Plan But Learn How to Go Off-Script

You don't need to have it all figured out right now. Having goals and a plan to attain those goals is very important because it gives us a direction of where we want to go and how we want to get there. It's inevitable you will be put in situations you hadn't expected. You'll be thrown curveballs, lose clients, gain clients, and other twists and turns that will happen within your business. A business plan is important and using it as a framework is the best way to accept things as they come while still working toward a specific direction. Life is going to happen and that may even cause the direction of your path to change. Not everything will play out the way you expected. Having the versatility to adapt to changes will allow you to benefit even when things don't go according to plan. Roll with those punches and restructure your plan as you go along.

One main example that instantly pops into my mind was how our business attempted to stay afloat during the pandemic that began in 2020. If anyone reading this was training, coaching, or working in any field at the time our entire world was shutting down in early 2020 due to the COVID-19 virus, you understand how much we all had to take life as it came, adjust as best we could, and do whatever we could to stay above water until things settled down back to what we'd call "normal." Looking back at the day when I found out gyms and all businesses deemed as being "Nonessential" were to be closed, we were required to figure out our individual situations. Working in a profession where the main focus is helping others improve their health, fitness, and overall well-being, I knew I could continue to help, even without being face-to-face in a gym. With gyms being closed and most people quarantined to their homes, we really had to think outside the box. Obviously, those negatively impacted by the virus potentially dealt with some very trying physical difficulties. Being stuck at home, with fear of the unknown running rampant throughout the media outlets, and nobody truly knowing what laid ahead, I wanted to use my platform to provide people with a bit of continuity amongst all the changes happening. The physical benefits of exercise are well-known, but exercise also has many psychological and mental benefits. Equipped with this knowledge and the proven concept of exercise acting as a positive release people, I did what I knew to be one of my best abilities, prescribing exercise.

The afternoon we were forced to shut down gyms and temporarily lock our doors, everyone experienced such a wide variety of emotions. Even attempting to become better informed about the virus, to better address my clients' needs, was confusing as so many opinions and different news outlets projected uncertain information. This pandemic became so polarizing and started to divide our entire society, country, and world. However, most of my concerns were centrally focused. I was worried about business and whether or not I'd be able to last through this. I was worried about how my clients would handle things. I wanted them to remain on track with the goals we had been working on but at the moment, those seemed so unimportant. As it turned out, the desire and support of my clients to continue prioritizing their mental and physical wellness was what allowed me to continue with my business throughout and after the pandemic.

In all of the world's uncertainty at the start of the pandemic, I chose to lean on my skills to help others. I sat down the exact day when gyms closed and began working on a project to provide to anybody who wanted it. The project began as a few simple workouts, but when I posted a question on social media to see if anybody would be interested in some at-home workouts to tide them over for the time being, I received HUNDREDS of replies. People were used to working out, and just because they didn't have access to a gym didn't mean they planned on stopping. The response was overwhelming. Current clients, as well as those from my surrounding community; friends and family back home in Dubuque; and random people reached out to me. I knew I would be able to provide some silver-lining to those who wanted to continue working out, but didn't have the means or the knowledge to create those workouts. I brainstormed and got creative for them. Making the workouts with a variety of movements, at different difficulties and levels of intensity, which were all able to be accomplished with common household items became my goal. We did Bulgarian split squats with one back leg on the couch. We did passive shoulder external rotation with a broomstick instead of a PVC pipe. We did workouts based on playground equipment. Whatever I could think of to provide people with some fun variety to have in a workout once a day, I did it. I offered the workouts to anyone who wanted them and didn't charge anybody. I figured we were all dealing with enough and paying for the ability to workout at home in a time like that was unnecessary. Unexpectedly, in return people donated money. Those simple offerings brought tears to my eyes and made me further realize the importance of this job. Even though we don't always recognize this, we bring so much joy to others. We are a staple in their lives so when we are thrown curveballs, we need to understand how we can still help them. In times like this, we must get creative and think outside of the box to continue to provide others with the joy our profession brings.

CHAPTER 71

Your Schedule May Revolve Around Their Schedule

For the first handful of years in this business, there's a good chance your schedule will revolve around the hours where other people are not working. You're going to have early mornings and late nights, oftentimes with big gaps in the middle of the day. It doesn't always have to be structured like that, but to begin, it's highly suggested you remain open to training clients whenever their schedules allow. Your bills will get paid for by your clients, so biting the bullet at the beginning of your training career and scheduling at their convenience is a great way to initially build up a steady clientele base. Doing so proves to clients that you are willing to make sacrifices to help them pursue their goals. Most of the adults you will train work some sort of daytime job. This means that if they want to work out, it either has to be before or after work, over their lunch hour, or on the weekend. Fortunately, more hybrid model jobs have evolved into the workplace, which may give clients more flexibility when scheduling time with you. There are some professions that also allow flexibility to train during quieter, lower demand hours of the day, such as realtors, hair stylists, self-employed entrepreneurs, or even retired individuals.

If you can slide those people into hours that others don't necessarily want but work well for their lifestyle, it can be a great way to decongest those early and late hours, while filling the gaps during the middle of your days.

If you stick around in this business and work with people whose schedules allow some flexibility, there's a much better chance you can construct your schedule the way you want, to some degree. This may allow you to get away from working a split shift that includes waking up before the crack of dawn and not going to bed until after the sun goes down. Either way, it's important to be able to function well enough to provide your 5 am clients with the same quality of service as those 7 or 8 pm clients. However, you need to create a work-life balance that fits your own personal needs. The phrase "fill up your cup" refers to replenishing your mental, emotional, and physical energy. Refilling your cup could include catching up on sleep, preparing meals, programming for the week ahead, and spending quality time with loved ones. It's essential to pay attention to your own needs outside of the gym to continue to train during the scheduled hours needed to accommodate clients. In order for me to refill my cup each week, I prefer to keep my weekend activities to a minimum. I typically work a few hours Saturday and a few hours Sunday (at one point, there was a 74 day stretch I trained at least one client everyday), but other than that, my weekends are mainly set aside for me.

As you become more established in your personal training business, you can begin to set boundaries with scheduling. Setting parameters, once demand for your services increases, may mean having people commit to set days and times each week to ensure we can work together. Some clients prefer to commit to specific days and times and their life allows that to happen. Others have schedules which may not be the same week to week, therefore you may have to schedule weekly, based on your availability. Because of these various reasons, this career path may not present the most ideal work schedule. If you're willing to commit to your clients and have some flexibility to work with them, they will return the favor and you'll potentially be able to rework your schedule down the road. Keeping lines of communication open allows us to figure out what works best for all of us.

CHAPTER 72

Create a Network of Other Health Professionals

"Andrew and Collin are outstanding trainers and healthcare profession-als. They give their clients everything to help set them up for success. As a former physical therapist in the DSM area, they were a great referral source for when patients needed that next step for return to perfor-mance/sport. Would definitely recommend for all training styles."

One of the best decisions you'll make en route to having a long, successful career in this field is seeking out and making connections with other fitness and health professionals. Finding connections within different avenues of this field will broaden your outreach and will not only allow you to meet potential clients, but will grant you the opportunity to learn from others who share similar goals. Seek advice and conversations with other personal trainers, nutritionists, dieticians, chiropractors, physical and oc-cupational therapists, physicians and other medical doctors, as well as those in parallel fields within education, such as profes-sors and teachers. Find the people who are in their field to help others, not just make a quick paycheck. Find those who flourish in areas where you may have difficulties. Learn from them. Ask questions. Dig more into techniques they may be using in their practices. Observe and learn from different styles. Figure out why they are doing things certain ways, and decide if those are things you would like to adopt. Remind yourself to be open to other paths to success. Expand your toolbox and learn from others who may be in the same field, but have different experiences. Connections with other professionals can not only make you both better at your own specialties, but can create a two-way referral pipeline where you can send your clients to someone you trust and know has their best interest in mind.

Connecting with others in our field could initially seem threatening, as we are all vouching for virtually the same client base. If we can work together for the betterment of each other's client experience, a sense of community is created. The more we as business people grow together, the more we will be establishing positive names for our businesses. Going out of your way to network, finding fitness professionals whose values align with yours, and keeping a transparent conversation between them, your client, and yourself will help all parties. Taking care of clients is our first priority, and connecting with others in this field is a way to provide clients with what they are looking for. Secondarily, building trust and a caring reputation amongst other professionals in the industry will help those fitness professionals send people your direction when they are looking for someone to help with their clients. It all comes back to taking care of others. You take care of them, and they will take care of you.

CHAPTER 73

It Never Hurts to Have a Conversation

It never hurts to have a conversation. This can apply to all sorts of situations. For this instance, when a business opportunity presents itself, it never hurts to hear from others and at least have a conversation to see potential possibilities. I've had multiple opportunities to take different routes in business and you will too. Being offered ownership in a CrossFit gym; having random gym owners reach out to gauge our interest in purchasing their facilities; having professional baseball players reach out to contemplate becoming possible business partners; working with nutritionists; and even getting into sport coaching instead of strength and conditioning coaching are a few of the offers which may come your way. It is always nice to feel wanted. Being contacted by other professionals to have conversations about business opportunities can be exciting, but take time to really think before you make any rash decisions. Make sure any new business ventures align with what you are trying to build. Ask yourself pertinent questions relating to your business and ethical philosophy. Will you still be able to take care of the people who have devoted their time and effort to you? In adding any new branches to your business, will you be able to maintain the reputation you have and are working toward?

Personally, many endeavors have been put in my path as a result of professional relationships established in this field. The first opportunity that popped up was when the gym owner at the first location from which I rented space after leaving the corporate facility approached me with a business proposition. The owner rendered the opportunity for me to buy-in as an owner of the gym. Though being flattered and caught off guard, after hearing him out and taking time to reflect, I realized ultimately that the vision of our businesses' futures didn't necessarily align. Though I declined the offer, I really started thinking about growing my business outside of a one-man crew as a personal trainer.

Another opportunity to have a conversation was brought to our attention in 2021, when we were approached by a group wanting to piece together a team of individuals to fill a space in a nearby area. There was immediate excitement as we would be potentially working alongside an eight-year Major League Baseball veteran and a supporting cast of others. The connections he had, alongside the possibility of growth, made this conversation very intriguing. Meetings were scheduled, numbers were laid out, and dialogue was had. Our decision to decline this opportunity was due to disagreements on financials. No bridges were burned, but we decided to pass, as we felt we had other plans brewing.

During one of those meetings, we crossed paths with a familiar face, a local chiropractor. He was also someone this most recent group wanted to join forces with, rightfully so. He was highly-sought after as the best sports chiropractor in the metro area. After seeing him at these meetings, it got us thinking a bit. If he was entertaining those conversations, similar to how we were, there had to have been some interest in starting a new trek along his business path. This led to some conversations between him, Collin, and me, which ultimately entered into the territory of us possibly forging our own partnership. Pairing his sport chiropractic business with our personal training and strength and conditioning business could be a solid affiliation. Talks escalated and in February of 2022, we signed a lease and moved into our shared facility, with the front third of the space being built out as his chiropractic clinic and the back two-thirds being filled with turf, weights, and our gym. The partnership with Metro MVMNT has been a great ordeal for both of our businesses. Whenever a client or member of ours is dealing with some sort of nagging injury or have some questions or concerns, we know by referring them his way, they will be in good hands and well taken care of. He has also felt comfortable sending his patients our way, as it is a great way to bridge the gap between their rehabilitation work and getting them back to moving and feeling their best. We both have mutual respect for each other's space and time, and have similar work ethics, which confirms that making connections and having conversations can cement a strong business partnership.

Another surprise call came across one summer evening in 2022. The interested person, through social media, had kept an eye on how Collin structured his youth strength and conditioning classes. This was the same person with whom we had been in contact previously regarding baseball training. He noticed how much the kids enjoyed being in the weight room with us for those classes. That is exactly the structure this business person wanted to supplement athletes he had been training at his facility. Ultimately, he hired Collin as the Iowa Prospects Strength and Conditioning coach to help their athletes learn how to properly and safely strength train, build explosiveness and power, increase speed and agility, and establish a positive relationship with the weight room. Receiving that call goes to show the importance of not burning bridges. You never know who may cross paths with you again down the road and opportunities may come your way because of the way you carry yourself.

The most recent opportunity that presented itself was in the world of academia. Through some brief interactions with faculty and staff at Drake University, as well as aiding in an externship project for the Kinesiology Capstone class (as discussed in *Chapter*

85), I had made some quality connections within that department. In the fall of 2023, I received an email gauging my interest in creating the curriculum for and teaching a Plyometrics and Sprint Training course as an Adjunct Professor for Drake University. The idea of getting into the education world had always piqued my interest and when this department head contacted me, I was very intrigued. Although I was unfamiliar with what went into teaching a collegiate course, I was open and excited to take on the workload, research, structuring the curriculum, and educating the students on these specific subjects. Fast forward a few meetings, email threads, and other conversations and I was chosen to lead that class for the spring 2024 semester. Unfortunately, at the end of the day there were not enough students signed up for the class so they had to cancel it before we had the chance to start. Regardless, had I not reached out to surrounding colleges and universities a few years prior, the chance to dip my toe in these waters may have never arisen. Hopefully another opportunity arises down the road but either way, establishing those connections proves to pay off in a variety of ways, some being ways that nobody ever expected.

March 26, 2021 was a big day for the advancement of our kid's strength and conditioning branch of our company. Having had the pleasure of training two young, serious basketball athletes led to an opportunity which expanded the SHF brand as well as our clientele base.

The Program Director of the CY Select Wolves, a girls AAU Basketball program, approached me after having observed positive outcomes during our training sessions with her two basketball-focused daughters. This mom wanted to start doing some one-on-one personal training. She had always been an athlete, but with basketball season around the corner, she decided to set aside time for herself to prioritize her physical and mental health. She also hoped to show her daughters that becoming strong, lifting, and exercising for health are more important than chasing a certain body type or weight. During our sessions, we talked our way through and covered all kinds of subjects, one being the Wolves. One conversation led to another and I asked her if she ever would want to get the entire program into the gym to provide them with strength and conditioning to reduce the chances of injury, improve performance on the court, and to help them feel more confident with exercise and in the weight room. This was never my intent when we began training together, but thankfully this conversation arose.

As the conversations revolving around SHF partnering with the Wolves escalated, we all seemed to be on a parallel path toward where we wanted to take our businesses. The Wolves were started in 2005 with a roster of 11 boys. Over the years, the Wolves have transformed into an all-girls program that emphasizes development, empowerment, discipline, commitment, and heart. Since the conception of the program, it has not only grown into one of the most reputable programs in the state, but has created a community of great basketball players, and even better people. The philosophy of the Wolves was based on promoting strong, healthy athletes, therefore it aligned with our belief of putting the mental and physical health of our clients first. Collectively, we all agreed that finding long-term success in the gym and on the court truly stemmed from taking care of the person first and the athlete second. After much planning and many detailed conversations, we were finally able to pinpoint how we could all work together to smoothly implement this partnership into the services CY Select offered to the girls and families involved.

This partnership provides a service that no other AAU basketball program in the entire state of Iowa offered: an in-house strength and conditioning portion of the program. Having the leaders of the Wolves provide their athletes with this type of experience has been a huge staple in the growth of their program, but also a great opportunity for Collin and me to expand our outreach. It also let Collin work toward one of his lifelong goals of being in charge of a youth strength and conditioning program. This connection has led to us doing individualized training with some of the players, parents of the athletes, and the growth of our brand to hundreds of new eyes. Working together with the CY Select girls throughout the years has also resulted in productive and fun interactions with hard-working dedicated girls; opportunities for Collin and me to expand upon our knowledge of training athletes of various age ranges; great feedback from families involved in the CY program; and a fair and steady new flow of income. Finding such a special connection with another business that has aligned values and sees a similar vision is hard to come by, but if you ever get that opportunity to do something similar, I highly suggest it.

Other conversations we have agreed to have with businesses include doing some video production work with the Hy-Vee Kids Fit Club (affiliated with a Midwest-based grocery store chain), partnering with and educating students in the Waukee APEX program, and talking with local high school programs to work as their speed and agility coaches. Meeting with other business owners proves it never hurts to network, connect with new faces, and have a conversation. Anytime there is a situation that presents itself as an opportunity, agreeing to have a conversation and going into that with an open-mind can lead to future possibilities. It never hurts to have those exchanges and see what opportunities present themselves.

CHAPTER 74

Be There

B e there. In the personal training field, there are perks to finding sustained success, building a reputable name and business, and simply being there when opportunities come your way. When trainers get burnt out, decide to change professions, move away, or stop providing services for one reason or another, their clients will want to continue training and will be searching for a new person to keep them on their fitness path. If you have built a solid reputation of always being there for your clients and for putting them first, there's an increased chance that those people will gravitate your way. This has happened a few different times in the SHF business timeline.

The first instance took place when a former colleague was promoted and had to relocate for his new position. As he could no longer keep his current client base, he recommended me to one of his most loyal, regimented clients. After observing me from afar and liking what she saw while watching me train others, this client ultimately decided to hire me to help her continue on her fitness path. Having this client referred my way has led to a long-lasting, rewarding professional relationship.

Another circumstance of simply being there and available for other trainer's clients happened when a friend decided to leave the profession. Being one of the best at his craft and producing life-altering habits in the lives of his clients, losing this trainer left a huge hole in the lives of many. After shifting gears leading to a career in the medical device sales world, but still having the desire to look out for his people, he assisted the transition of some of his clients to work with me. Having had a previous connection and prior interactions with some of his clients, as well as the information needed to pick up right where they had left off, these new individuals didn't miss a beat when they joined our training program.

Several other situations, stemming from us simply being available, happened when a trainer at the gym we were renting from decided to leave the field to return to school, when another trainer in the area moved out of state, and the third simply fell into our laps out of nowhere. The first two instances led to acquiring new clients who wanted that push, craved accountability, and were very hard-working people looking for guidance from professional personal trainers. As for the third situation, a personal trainer who had a positive reputation in town, messaged me out of the blue asking if I would be interested in chatting about a business proposal. Having heard about how our business focused on working with and caring for our clients, he wanted to see if Collin and I had interest in taking on more clients because he and his wife were moving to another state. He wanted to find someone he could trust to take care of the people with whom he had established strong bonds as trainer and client. This mutual feeling of respect brought about during our conversation led to a transfer of a few new clients from his hands to ours. These are just a few situations we have experienced during our years in this business. You may experience similar situations as you build your business. The impact you have on others and the connections you've made can change the trajectory of your business. Simply being available and open to accepting new clients is such an underrated way to continue to grow and improve your clientele.

In relation to just being there for our clients, we can act as their reassurance when things aren't going their way and they become frustrated. Being there for your clients means you are the steady rock in their life that they can always rely on, in the good and bad. Just because your client isn't seeing the results they/you want doesn't mean they are lazy, cutting corners, or need to change up their routine. Genetics, lack of resources, life stressors, mental health, sleep, hormonal fluctuations, and even the people surrounding your clients can all play huge roles in the health and well-being of each of us. Be conscious of what you say because you may never truly know what someone is going through. Don't shame people as a form of motivation. Instead, look inward to find what else you can do to help them. If they're having difficulties and they see you working extra hard to help them, it can impact their moods to be sure they don't get overly discouraged. Be kind and understand that the lives of others may not be entirely what it may seem from the outside looking in. Do everything in your power to help make their path easier and when they are hitting some road bumps, be there for them. Sometimes that's all some-body needs, and we can do that for our people. They are there for us, so we can be there for them in those times.

CHAPTER 75

Keep the Main Thing the Main Thing

This profession can be hard. We work long hours with early mornings, late nights, while talking to people for hours on end. It can drain you. It can even influence you to think about ways to supplement your income or even add a side-gig if the money isn't what you expected. At the end of the day, take a step back and refocus on your long-term goals. Short-term opportunities may derail your main focus from your long-term goals. If you want personal training to be a temporary job, side hustles can be helpful at the moment. If you want personal training to become a career, learn to be patient and roll with the punches. When times are hard, focus on what you can and how to get out of that rut. When business and life are good, pat yourself on the back, remember what it was that allowed for times to be that way, and keep working. Appreciate where you are in the moment, but don't forget to keep working for the long-term goals.

This should be emphasized to your clients, as well. It can be easy to want something in the moment to make things easier or to curb a craving, but veering from the path to exert more effort elsewhere can be distracting to your larger goals. Finding the right balance between job and free time will allow clients to enjoy and reap the benefits of all of their hard work more frequently.

If a client chooses to adjust direction and maybe take a break from training, encourage them to enjoy that time away, and then hopefully get back to concentrating on the goals they have set for themselves. Keep the main thing the main thing. If you or your clients are questioning what your main thing actually is, ask if what you're craving now is what you will want in the end. Instant gratification can be a sneaky thing to work through. Although something may elicit results immediately, we need to be sure that our main focus and the ultimate goals we are working towards exceeds the temptation and urge to accept something lesser now that may not align with what we actually desire to achieve in the future.

CHAPTER 76

Who to Work With

When beginning your training career, having big aspirations to work with a certain demographic can be a great goal. Understand that with any goal, it doesn't happen overnight and you will be required to fulfill certain requirements to attain those goals. For example, with my strength and conditioning background and the ultimate goal to work with athletes, I didn't have my foot in any doors that allowed for me to strictly work with that niche of people right off the bat. Additionally, so many people come out of school solely wanting to work with athletes because more than likely, they were athletes themselves. Working with other athletes is something with which they can resonate, and most likely played a major factor in their lives up to that point. What can be a difficult hurdle to overcome, for many in this profession, is coming to grips with the fact that you may have to narrow your blinders to accept any clients, not solely athletes. You may have difficulties paying the bills and staying afloat, particularly from the beginning, which means you should take opportunities to work with as many different people as possible. That isn't to say it is impossible, but narrowing your clientele portfolio to just one group can force you to miss out on chances that would have otherwise presented themselves. Having a niche is fine, but start out by not being picky about who you get to train as clients.

If you get to the point down the road in your career in which you want to specialize a bit more, try it out. That would make more sense than turning away others as a beginning trainer. As with anything, there are exceptions to the rule. When you are approached by someone you are not qualified to work with or not interested in training for whatever reason, you have a few options on how to acceptably handle the situation. When faced with a new client who brings about unique circumstances, you have a choice on whether or not you want to pursue working with them. If you are intrigued and think you can be of assistance, learn about their situation, do your homework and research, and be honest with them about how this is new to you. If it is something beyond your scope of practice or area of expertise, be honest also. There is nothing wrong with turning someone away who you don't feel comfortable working with, if it is out of your scope of practice. Having to turn down certain individuals can be gut-wrenching and difficult. Trainers never want to feel like they are letting people down. Yet, if you are truly not the right fit for a potential client, whether it is because of medical history, lack of knowledge, or fear of putting anyone in a higher-risk position to get hurt, it is best for both you and the client to decline working together. In accepting a client who you are not qualified to train nor comfortable training, you might be doing that person an injustice, which is unfair to both parties. If you are faced with a situation like that, I would recommend being honest with yourself and with the other individual. It may be hard to have that conversation, but you should always do what is best for the client. If faced with turning down a possible client, do your best to help them find someone who may be able to provide them with the service they are seeking. What we provide others, as personal trainers, isn't a perfect fit for everybody and the services they are looking for may not always be what we can administer. Regardless, do your best to serve them in one way or another or be their connection to another useful resource.

Within a training career, there will be ample opportunities to connect with a wide variety of prospective clients. If you're lucky enough to turn your first personal training job into a long-lasting career, you ultimately will get to choose who you work with, to an extent. You may find that working with a variety of clients, not just athletes, which seems to be a very common interest within aspiring personal trainers, is a great way to become a better, more well-rounded trainer. By working with others who may be outside your initially ideal clientele demographic, you will be forced to use different modifications, cues, exercise variations, and speak to people of every age and knowledge background. This can be helpful in testing your adaptability as well as your ability to think outside of your previously intended target world. Taking your business model in the direction of working with people to help them live healthier lives and more easily enjoy their everyday activities is a different beast than helping an athlete become more explosive, perform better, and be able to quickly adjust their body to outside stimuli. There can be a crossover in material between athletes and nonathletes. In working with both, you can become a better trainer for each of them because of this need to adapt who you are to what they need in a trainer. Whether you decide to work with one group of people or a wide variety, do what makes you feel comfortable and use your strengths to your benefit in helping your clients reach the goals you set out to achieve together.

CHAPTER 77

Be Picky With Whom You Surround Yourself

Surround yourself with others that bring out the best in you. Return the favor and build up those around you. Good things come to those who genuinely care about and for others. You don't want to be that trainer who is known for attacking and bringing others down. That type of reputation will eventually catch up to you. Yes, we are competing with other fitness professionals for the same pool of clients, but not many people choose to consistently pay the trainer who is creating drama and pulling others down. Be a leader amongst other trainers in your community. See how you can help other personal trainers, and see what they can provide you to improve both businesses. In the end, we are all attempting to help people make better choices and improve their lives. Creating a culture where you work alongside other personal trainers, who can do their jobs while learning from one another, can be an empowering environment where everybody grows through one another.

I view the success of Seymour Health & Fitness is measured by providing as many others as we can with the best service possible so they are able to accomplish and exceed their health and fitness goals. When you find success in this field, you'll notice your training schedule filling up and although that means you're helping more people than ever, that also risks putting your own well-being on the backburner. Those additional hours allow us to help a lot of amazing people, but we can't work much more without compromising our work-life balance or burning ourselves out. If your clientele list is expanding and you find you are not able to keep up, you need to think about expanding your business and creating a succession plan. Filling your gym with like-minded trainers who view this career path as a means of helping others, who put others' needs at the forefront of the thought process that goes into exercise prescription, and who bring a positive energy to the gym community would be ideal. Finding those people can be tough. You will want to make sure any new hires will respect the space and time of you, your current clients, and their own people. This trainer should also be willing to contribute to certain tasks in the gym, including cleaning, and they must be responsible for the equipment their clients use during sessions. You have every right to be picky when inviting new trainers into your gym space, as you want your clients to continue to receive the quality experience you have always provided for them.

In order to create a platform that advances the health and wellbeing of people, we cannot view other trainers as competition. Rather, we must observe, listen, and pay attention to who really provides the best service to their clients and to those who don't even pay those individuals for their services. Anybody can be nice to someone who is paying them, but true character is revealed when there are no financial obligations. These are the trainers you want working with you. Surrounding ourselves with a group of trainers who share our enthusiasm for helping others, who are eager to continue learning (formally and through gaining more experience), and to continue taking care of the people who believe in and take care of us is the ultimate goal.

CHAPTER 78

Never Stop Learning to Sharpen Your Craft

A s a trainer, you need to have some type of education to get into this field. The most traditional routes include either getting a personal training certification or majoring in a kinesiology-related field, although you may run across trainers that have no formal certification nor educational background relating to our field. Memorizing and mimicking every little detail of other professionally-educated trainers doesn't mean you'll be successful in this field. If you don't have any formal base in education within this field, at the very minimum you should at least ensure you are well-versed on the reasoning of how the human body adapts to exercise, what anatomy is used in exercise, and the physiology behind movement. Staying up to date on the latest findings within our world and continuing to provide the best service to your clients by knowing which numerous variations work best for them are important after you've entered the personal training field. To do that, you must continue your education. Continuing education may look different for each of us. Some prefer obtaining certifications, while others want a graduate degree. Others want to simply do their own digging and research without any formal structure. Every trainer should find what works best for them, by understanding new material; attaining and ingesting new information; and figuring out the best ways to apply it to their clients. Learning new information is useless unless you utilize it. It all comes down to the idea of theory and application. Whether you continue your education through the classroom, certifications, or surrounding trainers, you must take that information and apply it to your client's situations as needed. If you choose not to apply the new information, it doesn't help anybody and defeats the purpose of attempting to acquire more information and build upon your education.

No matter your preferred method of continuing your education, a good rule of thumb is to diversify the way you go about learning and where you seek out that material. Learn in the classroom. Learn from other successful trainers. Take responsibility for learning things on your own. Surround yourself with people smarter than you or who have experience in fields that interest you or apply to your clientele. Learn from them. Ignore your ego, but also understand and be proud of what you have to offer to help others grow. Read books and research articles. Discover blogs and reputable sites that provide quality content. Share your knowledge and learning with others, in the gym, in newsletters, or in workshops or seminars. If by passing on your updated knowledge clients can take such information and apply it to their lives or learn something, consider your educational quest a victory.

As you continue to educate yourself, build more experience, and grow as a business professional, reflecting upon your career can be a helpful tool. If you're still training clients the exact same way you were two or three years ago, you're toeing the line of stagnation and running the risk of them not sticking around. This field is an ever-changing profession. It is your job, as the professional, to recognize this and adapt to it through research and testing things out on ourselves as the guinea pigs. We should pride ourselves in staying up to date with the latest findings, figuring out what we should implement into programming for our clients, and how we can continue to grow as trainers. Reflecting on what your career has consisted of and patting yourself on the back while also having enough self-awareness to realize when adjustments are needed can be things we lose sight of when we work in this field, especially when self-employed trainers don't really have a boss overseeing us. Education, self-awareness, and the willingness and desire to continue to sharpen your craft will be what sets your business apart from others.

CHAPTER 79

Cancellation Policy

When you get into the personal training field, your initial purpose probably stemmed from a desire to help others work toward and reach certain health or fitness goals. It's awfully difficult to help others do that if they are continually canceling their sessions. As the business owner, it is up to you to decide how to best handle those situations for your clients and your business. This brings up the concept of setting up a cancellation policy. In our waivers, we have a cancellation policy stating that we require at least a 24-hour notice if a client will be missing a session. Otherwise we have the right to charge them their training fee for that session. To some, this may seem harsh, but realistically from a business point of view it makes sense. The cancellation fee pays for lost time and the fact that we may have been able to fill that slot with another paying customer. This policy is one used relatively subjectively with clients. Life happens. If somebody is dealing with a sudden death in the family, an accident, or it simply slipped their mind and missing the session was completely out of their usual character, I'm pretty lenient. I trust my people to be honest with me. If they are thrown an unexpected curveball, I want them to know if they choose to take care of that over our sessions, I will allow that once or twice.

When there is a recurring pattern of a client missing sessions, and you know you could open their spot for others to fill, it is fair to address the cancellation fee with your client. There are a few options to take during such conversations. First, you can tell them if they want to remain in their usual spot, you will have to charge them the rate, even if they cancel at the last minute. Help them understand you are missing out on lost wages when they do not show up for sessions. Another option is to move their recurring time slot to another time that might work better for both parties. This kills two birds with one stone as you may be able to fill another gap in your schedule with a paid hour and you can slide in someone else who wants that current spot with a more consistently paying client.

As it relates to the cancellation conversation, first and foremost, communication and care for each other will squash any feuds over this subject before they begin. As a trainer and business owner, be open and honest from the get go. Being comfortable enough to bring up payment and cancellation fee conversations is something every business owner must work toward. When you are honest and direct with conversation, people are usually pretty understanding. Your clients know what your fees are, what your worth is, the value you provide, and how you stick your neck out for them. They will want to continue to support you. Secondly, you must honor yourself and your time. You are running a business that revolves around others and their schedules, but that doesn't mean your time is invaluable. Your time is just as important as anyone else's. If you feel like your time is being abused or taken advantage of, it may be time to have another conversation with your clients. Lastly, to solidify this policy from the start, walk through all of the details relating to canceling sessions when presenting the document to clients so all parties are on the same page. If you both understand the policy from the beginning and you both agree to what it states, it makes those conversations of revisiting the cancellation policy much easier down the road.

CHAPTER 80

Look Presentable

Personal trainers get the unique opportunity to work in shorts and a t-shirt, or some similar outfit based on your business's outlook. However, since you are running a business, it's still important to make sure your clothing choices look presentable for your clients on a regular basis. Though it would be easy to take advantage of the fact that our typical uniform is fairly casual, it's best to remember your clothing reflects the professional aspect of this job. Showing up for each session wearing quality clothes will make you look much more presentable, respectable, and will make your services more attractive if an unexpected visitor walks through your doors looking to train. Keep the torn, smelly, and dirty gym wear in your backpack or at home to use on your own personal time.

In the fitness industry, we are extremely lucky to be able to simply throw on workout clothes as our work attire, but creating a high standard for your brand early on in your business is a great way for people to recognize who you are and what you stand for. Making apparel with your logos on it, and wearing that while training 90% of the time, promotes your business as well as you. The other 10% could include wearing clothing from other small businesses you support (Metro MVMNT, for example) and shirts purchased to represent clients who have participated in athletic events or who may have even created their own brands. Treat each training session with a sense of pride in who you are and the brand you represent. As you will be wearing brand apparel often, contemplate investing in higher quality, comfortable, breathable materials which will last wash after wash. Partnering with a printing company, which provides a variety of materials for their apparel, will give you options once you choose to imprint clothing with your logo. Wearing a comfortable shirt that represents what your brand embodies is a daily reminder that this business is in your hands. Stamping your logo on and representing yourself through apparel is a great way to improve accountability for who you are and the empire you're trying to build.

Filling your schedule with clients from early morning until late evening means you may spend all day in the gym. Bring a change of clothes to work each day. Personal training is one of the few careers in which you may move and sweat in a similar type of clothes you work in. That doesn't mean you need to wear those same sweaty clothes all throughout your entire workday. Please take time to change outfits between clients if you notice the sweat or scent secreting from you could be offensive to others. As you should take responsibility in living the lifestyle and exercising on a regular basis, you must find time to get in your regular workouts. When you do, which may occur between scheduled clients, make sure you aren't the sweaty trainer who doesn't change out of their stinky clothes. This can be an easy, but gross, habit to get into when you time your workout out so it ends promptly at the top of the hour, precisely when your next training session is scheduled to begin. Workout when your schedule allows, but prioritizing your client's paid session over your workout should be important enough to cut your workout five minutes short. These few minutes could allow you to shower before your next client arrives or at least change out of your drenched clothes. Make sure you are presentable and ready for the next session. Take your hygiene seriously and clean yourself up before each session. You may want to keep a toothbrush, toothpaste, and deodorant in your bag or your office. Brush your teeth after lunch or coffee if you work in close contact with certain clients. Be cognizant of people's sensitivity to smell when contemplating whether or not to wear extra scents, such as cologne, perfume, or scented lotions during sessions. Your clients are paying for a professional, make sure you present yourself as such.

CHAPTER 81

Timing is Everything

In order for things to work in your favor for your business, starting with the client-trainer relationship, so many pieces of the puzzle need to fall into place. Most importantly, in order to get a new client started, they have to take the initiative of making the conscious choices to contact you and walk through the door of your facility. It is one thing for an individual to reach out and inquire about training. It is another to meet in person for coffee to discuss plans about working together. It is a whole different story for a person to actually show up on the first day of a scheduled workout and commit to investing in your program. In order for all of those aspects to align with one another, your client needs to be at a place in their lives where they feel motivated and compelled to take action; to switch things up; and rely on a credible source for guidance and advice.

That's where good timing comes in. When someone comes your way, in order for a partnership to seem appealing to the client and for that partnership to work extensively, your views and philosophies need to align with what they are looking for in that moment. Not every trainer is the same. Not every trainer approaches each session in the same manner. Not every trainer is the perfect fit for each client walking through their doors. When someone shows interest in training, the most important thing is to help them understand how you can be of service to them.

This not only includes the exercise portion, but if you cultivate your brand as a wider spectrum of services, you can show them how you can help improve all avenues of their life. Having a skill set which includes a multitude of talents, interests, and teaching tactics will help you connect with many more potential clients. Showing off those skills and relating them back to your client will show that you not only know your material, but you are intrigued by the opportunity to work with them in their pursuit of reshaping their health and wellness. If you are the trainer who meets their needs at this specific time in their lives, you are the lucky one.

If timelines don't sync up between the trainer and client at one moment in time, don't be discouraged. It is our duty to ensure that potential future clients receive a positive interaction and some information they can leave with to work on self-improvement. Whether someone buys any service from you or not, they should always walk out the door knowing they are better than when they walked in. Leave them with advice, an at home plan, or some tidbit that helps them on their way. Closing meetings on a positive note may not provide you with a sale in that space and time but could blossom into something in the future.

If somebody walks out after your first consultation or even after a few training sessions and decides not to come back, don't attack them or ignore them. You have the right to ask why they decided not to begin or continue. Receiving feedback can be difficult, but if you want to grow and continue to improve upon your skillset, hearing why people may opt out of training with you can be very eye-opening as a means of self-reflection and improvement. This allows you the opportunity to be better in your next interaction and to learn from what may have been possible mistakes. If there is nothing you did wrong, and they decide to cease training for timing or financial reasons, make it known that your services will be provided for a long duration and if or when your paths cross again. Maintaining a positive attitude and mindset as a trainer is crucial since not everybody is ready to dive right into training, even if they decide to meet with you for an initial consultation. Keeping those doors and arms wide open for paying and non-paying individuals will create an inviting environment. This strategy will allow for your business to be a place people want to be associated with, whether in the present or future.

Doing your homework and sharpening those skillsets early on in your training career will open doors to any and every client that comes your way. We will all learn more about our strengths and areas of improvement as we progress, but establishing those strong suits early on and using those to help display the unique product you offer to others will provide others with a depiction of what type of services you provide. The way that I train now is completely different than when I first entered this field. Some of the people I initially worked with to begin my career have stuck with me through the entirety of my growth. Because of furthering personal and professional development, my clients have reaped the benefits of better training, resulting in better overall results and more enjoyable sessions. When I first got into training, not every client and I clicked. You will experience situations throughout your career where personalities do not always align. In such cases, you must decide if your client/trainer relationship is contributing to or counteracting the desired health outcomes of the client. During these times, conversations should be held regarding future sessions. You will come to understand that not everybody looking for a trainer is looking for what you have to offer.

Not every match in the personal training field is made in Heaven. When you find yourself training someone who may be disagreeable, contrary, non-participatory, overly negative, unkind to others in the gym, or you two simply do not get along, you have a handful of responsibilities as a professional business person when addressing this client. Do your best to be patient and give them the education and information needed to see the success they want. Be sure to continue providing the best service you can. Try to find some type of commonality. Ask about family members, jobs, hobbies, favorite shows and movies, or vacations. Ask open-ended questions and as you lay that bait out, listen for certain subjects you can connect to and pounce at the opportunity when it is given to you. This job takes a certain level of social awareness and the ability to read others. When we are able to do this and connect with others on a deeper level, it may help our chances of improving our chemistry and ensure that partnership is a good fit at that particular time.

CHAPTER 82

Growth and Development

According to Jean Piaget (Nortje, 2021), there are four stages of cognitive development. During each phase, from ages 0 through adulthood, we are constantly evolving over time; adjusting responses to our environments, and updating our brains with "exposure to new information." Interestingly enough, these three statements parallel the job description of a personal trainer. We truly evolve our techniques over time; adjust to the environment and the people with whom we work; and are constantly searching for new knowledge.

Take pride in growing from your old training philosophies. If your programming tactics and ideology haven't grown or progressed from last year and the year before, think about the product you are selling. Consistency is important, and we must be patient, but if our clients aren't progressing and we aren't moving them onto bigger and better things, we are letting them down. We must take it upon ourselves to study, educate ourselves, dive into different viewpoints of kinesiology and to use that information on a practical level with our clients. They are paying us, but we cannot get complacent and we must always strive to improve and grow from year to year. We should always know more than we did last year. Take the responsibility and pride in owning and improving your business and the education behind your product.

Once we have established ourselves, it can be very easy to cave in to complacency. We get in a routine, train people day in and day out, and don't really set aside time to sharpen our craft. When that happens, clients can very easily notice things have gotten dry and their workouts seem repetitive. If you've never experienced this, feel free to skip this section. For those of you who can resonate with this concept, you're in the majority. This happens to the best of us. Although it isn't right and isn't fair to our clients, use this as an opportunity to not only progress your wealth of knowledge, but to also progress their quality of training. Obviously, you have some interest in bettering your product, otherwise you wouldn't be reading this. Now is the time to grow and better your service, if you haven't already.

Be your own critic and hold yourself to the highest of standards. Whether you are working for someone else, a corporation, or yourself, take responsibility and be accountable when it comes to your success. You are your brand, and your brand is the product people are buying. There are so many controlled variables you can take charge over to set yourself up for success in this field. We all have areas we can improve upon and if we get complacent, it can be very dangerous for our career growth. It isn't always easy to step back, evaluate, and figure out where you can do better and what you can improve upon to help your clients progress. Setting aside time on a semi-regular basis to reevaluate, reflect, and recognize areas for growth and change will grant you the opportunity to progress as a professional. In holding yourself to a high standard and being your own critic, you're also allowed to pat yourself on the back. It can be difficult to give yourself credit at times, so don't neglect that. Recognizing and focusing on your strengths is maybe even more important to growing in this field as working to improve your weaknesses. Finding positives and focusing on those strengths is a great way to continue to elevate your well-being and the product you provide.

From year to year, you should be able to look back, reflect upon your business, and recognize the evolution in your skills, abilities, and in all facets of your trade. We all have areas to improve upon, and we definitely have plenty of areas in which we aren't well informed. Use those areas of unknown as potential for improvement. It can be scary or hard to admit when we don't know something, but letting go of that ego, learning to use those unknown subjects as another opportunity to learn more, sharpen our mind, and provide more information to our clients can be a great spin-zone when we may otherwise not want to dive into a certain subject matter.

When you lose the desire to expand your proficiency in this field, you begin to let yourself and your clients down. We provide so many services and hold ourselves to such a high standard because of the drive we have to be successful business owners. We also feel responsible because of the reliance others have on us. Therefore, we have to keep up with the criteria we have set. Continue to elevate your service, knowledge, and communication to provide your clients with unmatched service so your competition can't keep up. When you reflect back at the trainer you used to be and the business you used to run, you should be proud of where you started and of how far you've come. Raise a glass to all of your successes, and get back after it. This field is ever changing and that requires us to adapt, learn, and grow with the times. If you become complacent and too comfortable, you may lose that drive and be swept away. Reminding yourself of your strengths and seeing your areas of growth as an opportunity, rather than weaknesses will help shift that mindset to a place where it will always be hungry for more information and knowledge to improve your product.

Be relentless with whatever you do in your daily effort to work on your business. Be relentless in your programming, your desire to continually educate yourself, your desire to help others, in practicing what you preach, leading by example, and teaching others to do the same. Show your clients how to keep putting one foot in front of the other regardless of what is thrown their way. This isn't meant to be a motivational speech, but just a little reminder of how, by continually putting forth your best effort with persistence and consistency, you can really accomplish unfathomable outcomes within your business. My dad always told us that no matter what we did in our lives, try to be the best at it. If we were flipping burgers at a restaurant, working at a desk, or helping out a neighbor, put your best foot forward and give your best effort. In being relentless with your actions and intentions for your business, the same idea applies. Be relentless in demonstrating the best version of yourself and with the necessary actions to accomplish what you want in your field of business. By doing that and applying that attitude to your everyday actions, you're going to notice a shift in your mindset because you may be happy with where you're at, but also hungry to continue to progress and grow. In a field such as personal training, you can be content, but never complacent. Through the relentless pursuit of being the best version of yourself, you can avoid complacency and will continue to provide maximal value with the services you offer to others. Maximizing the value of what you offer others is an easy way to stay ahead of the competition and draw interest from people who are looking at purchasing a higher quality of training service. Never stop developing, and don't be afraid to reassess who you are and where you want to take your career. This field is demanding. Recognizing your own growth, being able to be critically self-aware, yet proud, are traits that will allow you to find continued success.

CHAPTER 83

Self-doubt as a Business Owner

Self-doubt is normal. We all have negative thoughts. Don't overwhelm yourself with the thought that your product or service may not be up to par or inferior. Trust in yourself. Remind yourself that your work has gotten you to where you are and although you should always be open to more learning and growth, pushing doubt aside and being confident in your capabilities is a powerful feeling. Everybody gets in their own head at some point, especially business owners. Staying the course, following your own advice of trusting the process, and continuing to build on your wealth of knowledge will help eliminate those doubts from your mind to keep you evolving and adapting to the ever-changing world of health and fitness.

One trait you want to stay away from is pessimism. Negativity is something that can creep into any of our minds but learning to find ways to view the good in situations to avoid letting negative thoughts become too toxic will help you reduce doubt as a business owner. Your clients don't want to be surrounded by negative thoughts, words, or actions. They come to you for other reasons, not to spend time with someone who is constantly fixated on negative aspects of the world they're in. The thoughts we have, especially repeated over long periods of time, can influence our self-talk. The way we speak to ourselves impacts our outlook on how we view the outside world and that can dictate how we interact with others. Allowing that pessimism to evolve into a consistently negative energy that becomes part of who we are can deter others from wanting to work with you or associate with you for long periods of time. Don't feel you have to be overly cheery and overly positive because that can seem disingenuous and annoying in itself. Seeing life from the right side of the coin can give off such a better feeling for those around you. Keeping the energy positive in your gym helps create a welcoming, comfortable environment for your clients.

Anytime we have negative thoughts, we have the choice of what to do with those. We can listen, continue to dig a deeper hole of doubt and self-deprecation or we can shift our thoughts to more of a growth mindset. Carol Dweck (2016) is a big advocate of the growth mindset. Dweck suggests that a growth mindset can be viewed as a starting point for our personal development. When we have those self-doubting thoughts, we can choose to view those adverse situations as an opportunity for growth or a means to improve, rather than getting hung up on the negatives. This doesn't mean we ignore the negatives, pretend they don't exist, or forbid ourselves from having negative thoughts because those are inevitable. By consciously choosing to remain optimistic and viewing trials we face as a chance to grow, we can boost our self-confidence, perform at higher levels, and begin a snowball effect of carrying out that positivity from our thoughts to our actions. Just as negativity can be contagious, so can being optimistic and positive. Not everyone wants to be around someone who's overly positive and annoyingly optimistic, but there need to be more positive leaders in this field. By working to improve our own mindsets and conscious thoughts, we can have healthier thoughts, which will lead to a better chance of helping others find that same perspective on life.

With self-doubt, negative emotions, and pessimism as very common thoughts and feelings, leading by creating a positive environment for ourselves to shift away from those being the focal points of our self-talk, we can help others do the same. We need to take care of ourselves so we can better take care of others. Similar to how if we neglect our physical health, it makes it awfully difficult for our clients to buy into what we are preaching for their exercise selections, the same goes for mental health. We need to take our mental health, self-care, and the conversations in our head seriously. By beginning to focus on improving self-doubt and viewing negative feelings as an opportunity to grow and better ourselves, we will take the first step in the right direction to be the best version of ourselves for us and for our entire business.

CHAPTER 84

Overnight Success

It takes a long time to be an overnight success. That may sound contradictory, but that phrase is something people aspire to be even though it's essentially impossible. In order to be what others may perceive as an overnight success, you have to put in hours upon hours, years upon years of work and dedication to get to the point where you may eventually catch your break in the business world. Instead of trying to become an overnight success, get comfortable working on progressive overload. This term is very common in the fitness world, as it is a principle that states increasing weight or intensity in a strategic manner over time will allow our body to adapt, overcome, and build muscle and strength, as well as reduce the chances of injury and/or plateaus. The same applies to business. First make the conscious choice to start. Once you have begun, you should continue to grow. Work to build upon what you have already accomplished, provide a better and better product, avoid complacency, and be patient with the time it takes to grow into what you may envision for your business.

This combats the idea of being an overnight success. In today's world, the idea of instant gratification is highly sought after and everybody wants the easiest route to the end goal. This industry is a perfect example of how the easiest route may not be the best option. There are fad diets, pills, and programs claiming to be the best, but selling those to clients is just a way to make money, not actually help others. In fact, directing your clients down those routes can be detrimental to their long-term health. It can be tempting to take the easy route because it is less work which may seem more appealing. To accomplish lasting fitness goals we must put in the time, work, effort, and constant desire to continue progressing while not getting overly discouraged or down on ourselves. In doing so, we will be more satisfied with the results of the success we find, whether that is with our client's health or in our business because of how much more we put into it. Personal training truly is one of the most gratifying careers to be in. Along with helping others make life-altering changes by using health and well-being as the main tools, finding business success brings about feelings of pride, satisfaction, and happiness. Though this occupation isn't for everyone because of the enduring time, effort, and attitude it requires, you can find long-term success once you acknowledge it will not necessarily come to fruition overnight.

CHAPTER 85

Get Out of Your Comfort Zone

Get out of your comfort zone to allow yourself to create opportunities for you and your business, as well as to obtain unique experiences through the growth and courage required to go against your normal routine. The more you experience, the more you learn. The more you learn, the more knowledge you build up. The more knowledge you build up, the more you have to offer others. That's what our job is all about: providing services and education to others.

One prime example of getting out of my comfort zone was reaching out to local college professors to see if I could extend my reach to other students interested in beginning a career in a variety of exercise science fields. Some professors responded and of those that did, one awesome experience came from a professor at Drake University. After my initial outreach, the professor reached back out to me, inviting me to his office to get to know one another and discuss the possibility of future opportunities. After talking with him, we decided we could help each other through a mutually beneficial relationship. This professor in the kinesiology department saw me as an eager, young, fitness professional who could be a resource and connection for his students. From his view, I could provide his students with real-world knowledge on the health and fitness field, and an example of a possible path they could create upon entering the workforce. From my perspective, this was a chance to not only help fellow future fitness professionals, but to also create a positive relationship with a professor at a local school. There was no exchange financially, but the benefit of giving away free time invited a connection to establish a solid relationship with the Drake Kinesiology Department.

After further discussions, we scheduled some of the students in his Kinesiology Capstone class to partake in an externship with SHF. The professor was looking for his students to get insight into what the day-to-day structure was for a personal trainer, especially one who owned his own business. Since personal training involves more than programming workouts, this teacher thought it would be a unique chance for some of his students to observe trainers in action, so they didn't have skewed misconceptions of this career path upon graduation. The students were required to observe ten hours of relevant material. After becoming more familiar with these students, two shared they had their sights set on physical therapy programs after they wrapped up their undergraduate degrees. Since the professor left the externship formatting open to my discretion, the following is an outline of how I decided to structure the 10+ hour experience.

Kinesiology Capstone Externship

- Read through and fill out a New Hire Job Description and write 1 page of what career path you are planning to take with your Kinesiology degree and why. (30 min -1 hour)

- Schedule a face-to-face meeting (Zoom or in person) to discuss. (1 hour)

- Come up with a minimum of 5-10 questions that you have regarding this field prior to our meeting.

- Create a 3-month all-inclusive training program (workouts, food recommendations, sleep suggestions, activities of daily life, etc.) for provided, hypothetical virtual client. (2-3 hours)

- Adapt and adjust the program to whatever road bumps I create for your hypothetical client. (1-2 hours)

- Brainstorm 15 specific lead generation ideas. (30 min-1 hour)

- Brainstorm 15 ways to create culture that makes your clients want to stick around. (30 min-1 hour)

- Brainstorm 15 types of specific services that you would provide as a trainer to make your brand stand out amongst such a saturated field. (30 min-1 hour)

- Create 1-2 social media posts of subjects that are within your realm of expertise. Provide caption, appropriate information, and a photo/video for me to post on my Instagram and Facebook pages to highlight your work. (30 min-1 hour)

- Schedule face-to-face meeting (Zoom or in person) to wrap externship up and answer any additional questions. (1 hour)

The program was structured this way so each student experienced a unique opportunity catered directly toward their career path, while giving them some insight into a snippet of what is done in this job. The hypothetical client forced each student to not only program for that particular client, but to realize when thrown a curveball after creating specific programming, not everything always goes as expected. This aspect was important as the students needed to understand that road bumps come up all the time. This job consists of planning for what we think will happen. Preparing for any and all circumstances to turn out differently will demand we adjust and adapt to the situations thrown our way. Talking through each scenario with the students hopefully gave them some insight into the thought process taken when preparing for each individual client. Having them analyze all the possible factors which go into each session, made them understand training is more than just the workout. Throwing out questions allowed the students to process different scenarios and reasonings behind a hypothetical client's performance. What did they eat that day? How much sleep did they get the night before? What things are stressing them out at work or at home? Do they have aches and pains? How motivated are they that day? What unforeseen circumstances are they dealing with that may have thrown them for a loop? All of these questions can significantly alter the plans you made for that day of training. When these happen, we need to make changes in the spur of the moment and decide how to structure workouts based on information that was just thrown our way. For example, if a client didn't sleep well because work has been overwhelming and has them overly stressed, it wouldn't make sense to go ahead and continue with a high intensity workout planned for that day. Adding extra stress to the client's body may not be the right decision based on the emotional stress already experienced on that particular day. Maybe that day would be better spent doing some lower intensity strength training or even as a steady state cardio and mobility day. We need to make those choices with minimal knowledge in advance and sometimes it may seem like a step backwards. In reality, that impromptu choice can help alleviate some of those stressors and may be exactly what your client was looking for to ease their mind.

Having these students brainstorm different lead generation and culture-building ideas encouraged their minds to start churning around how this field entails so much more than just training on a daily basis. In this career path, we must stir up different ideas to generate prospective clients and increase our outreach to connect with more people, but also the right people through our doors. We must figure out different ways to improve the culture of our brand. We can then break those ideas down even further to recognize what we must do in our daily lives to build to those end goals. Having been granted these concepts, the students came up with insightful and unique ideas. Rather than seeing this as an easy 10 hours, it was very fun to see them get creative, use their own unique experiences, and tackle this externship head on.

Welcoming students into our gym for their externships was a win-win situation. Not only did they benefit from real-world experience, but I was able to learn from them. When we get into the daily flow of business, it can be easy to forget certain things and fixate on what is in front of us. To get outside perspectives and see things from a different point of view is always great to reevaluate and figure out what it is we need to work on. These students provided me with that refresher and reminded me there are things upon which I need to improve.

Getting out of my comfort zone and creating an externship opportunity for those students helped me in an assortment of ways. Again, it didn't put any extra money in my pocket, but some things are more valuable than money. We must always be hungry to learn and grow more in this field. The health and fitness fields are based on science. Science is ever evolving and we are constantly learning new material and more advanced information. Always be willing to grow and open your eyes to the changes happening around us. Inviting a new generation of learners into your gym can circulate fresh ideas and different approaches to situations. Do your best to get out of your comfort zone, however that looks for you, and be willing to learn from others.

The legendary Chinese military strategist Sun Tzu (1994) once said: "In the midst of chaos, there is also opportunity." You may find yourself unexpectedly thrown into uncomfortable situations outside of your comfort zone. Things will come your way which you would have never expected nor planned. You will be caught off guard. Find the positives in those situations and make the most out of the hand you're dealt. The pandemic was a prime example of chaos. Most people's lives were affected by the way we were all supposed to interact with each other differently. Though this was an extreme example, life was different for many individuals and they had to find the positives in unexpected times. Most often, we are thrown much smaller curve balls on a more regular basis. We have the choice on how we react to that adversity. Do we let unexpected changes or challenges us down as we let it linger and get hung up on it? Or, do we analyze the situation and figure out how we can work through it. We live in a world where there is so much negativity, drama, disrespect, and pessimism. What you can do to really stand out in this business is go against those societal norms and be optimistic. Be a light in other's lives. Stay out of drama, and have compassion because we really never know what others are dealing with. We all face adversity and run into difficult situations at times. By being a person who views life from a positive perspective and sees opportunities where others don't, your business and personal relationships will thrive and people will want to be part of what you are building. Allowing ourselves to recognize the opportunity in situations that may be uncomfortable is a trait that can greatly benefit you in this field and in life.

CHAPTER 86

Be a Critical Thinker

As a constantly evolving professional, it's important for you to be reading and researching often. Don't limit yourself to one side of the story. Seeing both sides of a story help you become better educated on that matter. Understand that not everything you've been taught turns out to be factual. Realize that what you read, whoever you talk to, and whatever other information you intake is stemming from one source or a group of sources. Take that information, comb through it, and determine whether you view that as gospel or just additional information to take into account. There may be other sides of the story and learning *how* to think is so much more important than learning *what* to think. Dig deeper, ask questions, and truly think before you adopt a firm position. Critically think about any newly acquired information. Recognizing how information applies to your situation. Dig deeper into details to see if opposing views are out there to piece together a well-rounded opinion based on facts. Keeping an open mind, being a bit skeptical, and thinking critically can help you become a more well-rounded, up-to-date trainer who understands the importance of evaluating gathered information.

CHAPTER 87

Keep It Simple

This one is short and sweet. Simplify things as much as possible. Take little, consistent steps in order to incrementally grow and you will be less overwhelmed. We all have large goals and big achievements we are working to accomplish, but we need to put one foot in front of the other. Check off little goals one at a time, and as we all well know, those little goals stacked on top of each other will add up and pay off. Keep things simple and keep chipping away.

CHAPTER 88

Collin Seymour - Put Good People in Your Corner

"Collin makes sure to explain the workouts in a way that we under-stand and asks for our input for future programming. He is mindful of our goals and is dedicated to getting us where we want to be. Collin is always willing to go the extra mile for his athletes and his passion for his work shows. I find it admirable how hard of a worker he is towards his personal goals as an athlete himself and now a business owner. He also finds time to make sure we are having fun and enjoying our time in the gym. Seymour Health & Fitness is the place to be and I cannot wait to see it grow."

O ne fellow trainer for whom I have the utmost respect happens to be my partner in crime, business partner, and brother, Collin. Seeing him go from a novice coach with zero personal training experience to being voted the Best Personal Trainer in the Des Moines area has been fun to watch. He exemplifies what it means to be a servant leader. He pushes his clients while being sure to take care of them. He knows how to pull the best out of the people he works with and does so by creating a hard-working, enjoyable, motivated community with those around him. He leads from the front and sets his own health goals. In 2022, he was asked by a few friends of his if he'd be interested in running a marathon later that same year. He accepted and immediately created a well thought out plan of how to peak on race day. He did his research, ran for hours upon hours, and made sure to prioritize nutrition and recovery so he didn't put himself in a compromised position to be hurt or sick. He basically took his own advice that he would give a client and researched, prepared, worked his tail off, and reaped the benefits of performing well on race day. Instilling the training philosophy of intelligently preparing, working hard, and accomplishing goals is similar to how he would coach one of his clients. From a client's point of view, seeing your coach set those goals, put in the necessary work, and sticking with it through the end can be reassuring that you are in good hands. Having a coach who is innovative and creative with programming, all while keeping the wants and needs of his clients at the forefront of his decision making, confirms the fact that working together with another trainer like Collin creates an ideal business situation.

Collin's presence is an asset to me, our business, his clients, our family and his friends. He makes those around him better. He doesn't tear anyone down, but rather continues improving on his own while trying to lift others up. That is the true definition of a strong individual; one who boosts others up while helping them improve, individually and as a community, instead of stepping on others to climb his way to the top. He has inspired me and helped me grow our business, as well as continuing to help me become a better business owner, trainer, brother, and friend.

I truly feel I have a lot to offer as a trainer but without other trainers, like Collin, I would not be the trainer I am today. Having another trainer around allows you to pick up on coaching cues, tactics, movements, and programming ideas. Together, you can learn what you do and don't want from other trainers. As trainers, we should not imitate others, but rather pick up on certain tendencies that would benefit you and create your own version and path with those strategies.

Find people who make you a better person and trainer, and keep them in your corner as a way to help yourself, them, and those investing in your business. Finding individuals who inspire and push you to be your best can be one of the best things you do to grow your network and team. Having that accountability and someone to bounce ideas off of, while working toward a common goal is a good way to continue progressing yourself and your business, especially when self-employed. A rising tide lifts all ships, and when we take that approach by wanting others around us to find success, the community you grow will be highly sought after.

CHAPTER 89

Two of the Most Impactful Comments I've Received in This Business Venture

"I don't want to sound like a mom but I'm so proud of what you and Collin have done with your business!"
-AK. July 14th, 2022.

This sentence from a client absolutely made my day. AK is someone I have worked with for what seems like forever because of how close we've gotten, but it's only been a few years. She is someone who was referred to me, we clicked early on, and we've grown very close. She epitomizes hard work, does absolutely whatever she can for her family, and has shown so much growth since we've met. She has become a good friend to me and someone I know would be there if I needed anything, in or out of business. To hear someone who means so much to you say something like that, it sticks. It creates a feeling of realization that what we do with our business reaches past the walls of our gym. The support we have and the love others show us is what keeps us going. Creating a successful business takes time. There will be ups and downs. Ride those out. Be patient. When in doubt, keep treating your clients with the respect they deserve and always give more than you take. With that type of service, along with being an expert in your field, people will place their trust in your business. Then you'll really be able to showcase your area of expertise to those who believe in you and give you a chance. Simple words or comments from clients or those around you can justify the reason for doing what we do each day as personal trainers.

"Andrew, three of my favorite hours each week are with you.
I appreciate you putting up with me."
-BP. October 12, 2022.

First off, there's nothing to "put up with" when working with clients, especially those who are genuinely kind people and role models for others. When being able to train people who you can look up to, time in the gym with them will be the highlight of your week. Hearing little comments like that can turn a bad day into a great one and stick with you longer than the person saying it may realize. When a client shares words that make your day, let them know it's a two-way street. Comments and compliments to others can change days, put smiles on faces, and shift moods. Don't forget that this is a people-focused business and simple statements can help others through their day.

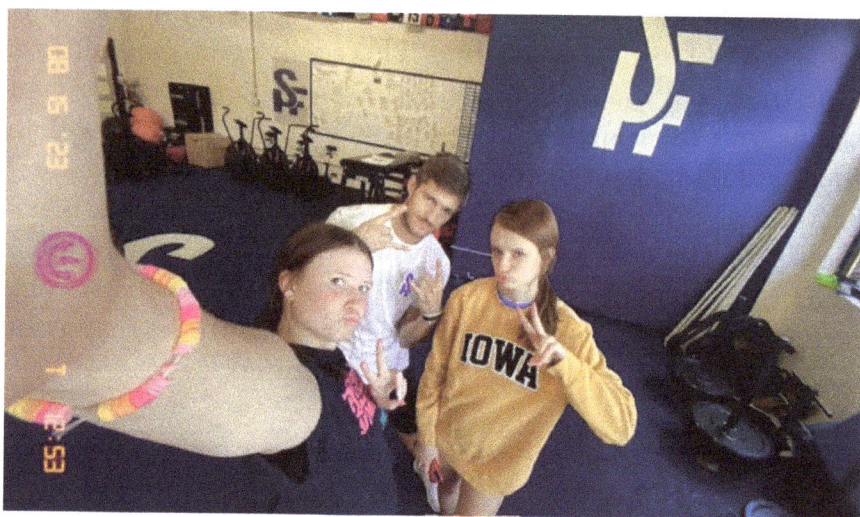

Gratitude is something we should all show more of. Expressing how grateful you are for someone never gets old or unappreciated. I probably don't thank my people enough but to make sure I do say thank you again, I wanted to include this portion below. These awesome humans have all played a major role in me having the best support staff I could ask for. From believing in me when I began Seymour Health & Fitness in 2017 to wrapping up this book, and to everything in between, I can't tell you each how thankful I am for you.

Vernesa-for being my better half, my person, my biggest supporter, my best friend, and for holding down the fort on some early mornings mixed with long nights and busy weekends. I can't do this without you and I wouldn't want to go through life with anybody else.

Growing up, I never really had a hard time connecting with others, as I felt confident with any group and I've always enjoyed being around others but connecting and truly communicating are two different things. You have helped me develop and improve my ability to communicate, which is such a necessary skill in a field that requires transparency, vocalizing thoughts and feelings, and reading others to see how their body reacts to different stimuli. As with any of us, we have things to work on and you helping me communicate more efficiently helped me build better business and personal relationships. When you learn to open up and build trust with others who mean so much to you, those relationships can grow immensely and the ability to communicate has such a positive impact on all of that. For that and for so much more, I can't thank you enough.

Collin-my business partner who constantly brings fresh life and hunger to build our brand together. You've always been the most athletic in the family and in some ways you've followed in my footsteps, but in reality you've sprinted past my footsteps and created your own path in this world. When you switched majors from environmental science to kinesiology, I instantly started brainstorming what we could accomplish together. What we've been able to create and where we are headed is beyond what I ever imagined. Watching the coach and leader you've grown into is fascinating and the lives you impact on a daily basis is inspiring. You spoke at my wedding about how you've looked up to me but you don't understand how much I look up to you. You're the best business partner I could ask for and seeing you grow as a fitness professional and into the adult that you've become is special. Keep being you. I'm so proud of who you are and the way you carry yourself.

Erin-the best sister I could ask for and such a beautiful soul with your constant desire to help others. Your open mindedness and care for others has helped me learn that differences don't have to separate people, but can be a breeding ground for a deeper connection through acceptance and educating one another on those differences. You've always been so accepting of everybody and you've wanted to help this world become a better place. Mission accomplished already.

Mom-teaching is something I have learned so much from you and Erin. The passion you have for your students and how you are always going above and beyond for them is admirable and has acted as a cornerstone of how I wanted to run this business. You put others first, always go the extra mile for those you love, and your motherly love resonates throughout our family as well as those who aren't relatives. I've always been a momma's boy and I can't express how much you've helped me in this business and throughout my life.

Additionally, for your countless hours of editing, brainstorming, formatting, suggestions, and passion that you put into this book, I cannot express how grateful I am. What you've done for me throughout the process of writing this is something I'll never be able to thank you enough for.

Dad-you taught me the mantra that I've based my life around: attitude and effort. The two things in life that you have control over, no matter the situation. That was one of countless life lessons you taught our family, with others being the importance of the work ethic to climb the ranks into a position of leadership and to see the good in people. Our relationship dynamic has shifted over the years into what I would consider the best type of friendship and I can't thank you for being my best friend throughout my entire life.

Brandyn-not only did you help me get my foot in the door directly out of college and introduced me to my first client, but you were one of the most helpful individuals in regards to my personal training development. You challenged me, helped me sharpen my craft, and introduced me to so many people and such great resources. I can't thank you enough for all that you did for me when I began my career and throughout the first few years. I'm still waiting to start Movement University so let me know when you're ready. To top off all that you've done for me, thank you for taking the time to read through, edit, and give a unique perspective to this book. You've always been someone I looked up to and for you to take the time out of your busy life to help with the final edit of this book, it really means the world.

Ashley-taking a chance on a small business owner who wanted to focus a portion of their training on working with prescribing strength and conditioning for athletes has been one of the most rejuvenating and enjoyable experiences since I began training. Thank you for trusting me, providing me with the opportunity to work with such a great program, and for your friendship. Introducing Collin and me to the Wolves provided us the chance to expand our business to new heights. That meant the world, but trusting me to work with your entire family meant so much more. Your passion for leading others, empowering young athletes, and prioritizing your mental and physical health are things that I aspire to do in my profession so thank you for being a model coach, leader, parent, and friend.

Ben-the resource that I trusted entirely to send my clients to when they needed rehabilitation assistance. You can squat higher amounts of weight than I can count to but more impressive is your care for others and the physical therapy service you provide. Your therapeutic efficacy is unmatched and your love for helping others is amazing to see.

Tanner-the man who has constantly believed in me and sent me his patients who needed to bridge the gap back into exercise. I can't thank you enough for putting your patients in my hands. The care for your patients and the referrals you've sent shows me how much faith you have in the services I provide. For those connections and that belief, I hope you know how much that means to me.

Lg-taught me the importance of showing up to support clients, in and out of the gym. This should be clear and obvious but it didn't really click until conversations with you and through watching you set aside time outside of the gym to go watch your athletes in their sport. You have had such a positive influence on me and I know I'm not the only person who thinks that. Your joy for working with your athletes is something every sport coach should learn from. You help others so much more than you may know and I hope this shows a small token of that appreciation. Also, when I grow up, I want my arms to look like yours.

To each person who trained with me, thank you. You each have shown so much support in more ways than you know. Collin and I are so fortunate to have gotten to work with hundreds of amazing people. To those who have remained ever loyal since the beginning of my career in 2016, to those we've met along the way, to those who worked with us and have since parted ways, and for those to come, thank you for not only taking a chance on us, but for supporting us in ways you may not even realize. We love doing what we do because of who we get to work with. We love all of you and truly could not do what we do at Seymour Health & Fitness without your help and belief. Thank you, all.

In conclusion, my hope is that this book provides you, the reader, with some sort of additional information to take in, digest, and apply to provide an improved service for those you work with. Although I've only been in this field a handful of times around the sun, there is still so much to learn, so much improvement to be made, and so many others to help find their ideal health and fitness routine. I hope to continue providing the best tools and resources necessary for those who trust and believe in me and Seymour Health & Fitness to better their lives. I genuinely believe that through breaking down your business into the three pillars of Personal, Training, and Business, you can focus on maximizing the value you provide for those interested in your services. Pride yourself on taking care of the person first, provide the expertise they are looking for out of a personal trainer second, and finally figure out how to best run the business you want to build.

This book has been a documentation of what has worked for me and our business but is by no means the sole way to progress forward in this profession. Create your own way of training, use your strengths to help others the best way you know how, utilize qualified resources to expand your knowledge, and please never hesitate to reach out if you need anything from me. I look forward to continuing to learn from others in the field, my amazing clients, family and friends, and through other avenues related to this field. Thank you again for the constant support, from near and far. Without the overwhelming support and belief from those around us, we would not be able to continue living out our dream job at Seymour Health & Fitness.

In health,
Andrew Seymour

REFERENCES

Anuar, N., Cumming, J., & Williams, S. E. (2016a). Effects of applying the PETTLEP model on vividness and ease of imaging movement. Journal of Applied Sport Psychology, 28, 185–198. doi:10.1 080/10413200.2015.1099122

Anuar, N., Cumming, J., & Williams, S. E. (2016b). Emotion regulation predicts imagery ability. Imagination, Cognition and Personality, 36, 254–269. doi:10.1177/0276236616662200

Dweck, C. S. (2016). *Mindset: The New Psychology of Success.* Ballantine.

Garza, D. L., & Feltz, D. L. (1998). Effects of selected mental practice techniques on performance ratings, self-efficacy, and competition confidence of competitive figure skaters. The Sport Psychologist, 12, 1-15.

Gordon, J. (2017). *The power of positive leadership: How and why positive leaders transform teams and organizations and change the world.* Hoboken, NJ: Wiley.

Lesson 5 Applicational Content: Focus and Concentration. (n.d.) [MODULE THREE APPLICATION PDF]. Retrieved from Canvas.

Lesson 8 Applicational Content: Imagery and Hypnosis in Sport (n.d.) [MODULE FIVE APPLICATION PDF]. Retrieved from Canvas.

Nortje, A. (2021, May 3). *Piaget's stages: 4 stages of Cognitive Development & Theory.* PositivePsychology.com. Retrieved March 16, 2023, from https://positivepsychology.com/piaget-stages-theory/

Post, P. G., & Wrisberg, C. A. (2012). A Phenomenological Investigation of Gymnasts' Lived Experience of Imagery. *The Sport Psychologist, 26*(1), 98-121. doi:https://doi.org/10.1123/tsp.26.1.98

Personal trainer demographics and statistics [2022]: Number of personal trainers in the US. Personal Trainer Demographics and Statistics [2022]: Number Of Personal Trainers In The US. (2022, September 9). Retrieved March 16, 2023, from https://www.zippia.com/personal-trainer-jobs/demographics/

Quinton, M. (2013, May 24). Imagery in sport: Elite athlete examples and the PETTLEP model BelievePerform - The UK's leading Sports Psychology Website. Retrieved November 18, 2020, from https://believeperform.com/imagery-in-sport-elite-athlete-examples-and- the-pettlep-model/

Smith, D., Wright, C., Allsopp, A., & Westhead, H. (2007). It's All in the Mind: PETTLEP-Based Imagery and Sports Performance. *Journal of Applied Sport Psychology, 19*(1), 80-92. doi:https://doi.org/10.1080/10413200600944132

Sullivan, G.S. (2019). Servant Leadership in Sport: Theory and Practice. New York, NY: Palgrave Macmillan.

Sullivan, G. S. (2020). Focus and Concentration. [PowerPoint presentation]. Retrieved from Canvas.

Sullivan, G. S. (2020). Imagery. [PowerPoint presentation]. Retrieved from Canvas.

Thelwell, R. C., & Maynard, I. W. (2002). A triangulation of findings of three studies investigating repeatable good performance in professional crickets. International Journal of Sport Psychology, 33, 247–268

Tzu, S., & Sawyer, R. D. (1994). *The art of war.* Westview Press.

White, A., & Hardy, L. (1998). An in-depth analysis of the uses of imagery by high-level slalom canoeists and artistic gymnasts. *The Sport Psychologist, 12*(4), 387–403.

White, J., Greene, G., Farewell, D., Dunstan, F., Rodgers, S., Lyons, R. A., Humphreys, I., John, A., Webster, C., Phillips, C. J., & Fone, D. (2017). Improving mental health through the regeneration of deprived neighborhoods: A natural experiment. *American Journal of Epidemiology, 186*(4), 473–480. https://doi.org/10.1093/aje/kwx086

www.ingramcontent.com/pod-product-compliance
Lightning Source LLC
Chambersburg PA
CBHW071012280326
41935CB00011B/1326